Economic Transitions to Neoliberalism in Middle-income Countries

While presenting a powerful analysis of the global structural transformations involved in the transition to neoliberalism, this volume avoids the trap of seeing this transformation as a primarily homogenising force. On the contrary global neoliberalism has reconstituted the economic and social institutions of capitalism differently in each country and region. It is precisely these differences that constitute one of the strengths of neoliberalism. This book is the definitive exploration of neoliberal transitions in a range of the most important middle-income countries.

(Terrence McDonough, Professor of Economics, National University of Ireland, Galway)

Neoliberalism is based on the systematic use of state power to impose, under the veil of 'non-intervention', a hegemonic project of recomposition of capitalist rule in most areas of social life. The tensions and displacements embedded within global neoliberalism are nowhere more evident than in the middle-income countries. At the domestic level, the neoliberal transitions have transformed significantly the material basis of social reproduction in these countries. These transformations include, but they are not limited to, shifts in economic and social policy. They also encompass the structure of property, the modality of insertion of the country into the international economy, and the domestic forms of exploitation and social domination. The political counterpart of these processes is the limitation of the domestic political sphere through the insulation of 'markets' and investors from social accountability and the imposition of a stronger imperative of labour control, allegedly in order to secure international competitiveness.

These economic and political shifts have reduced the scope for universal welfare provision and led to regressive distributive shifts and higher unemployment and job insecurity in most countries. They have also created an income-concentrating dynamics of accumulation that has proven immune to Keynesian and reformist interventions. This book examines these challenges and dilemmas analytically, and empirically in different national contexts.

This edited collection offers a theoretical critique of neoliberalism and a review of the contrasting experiences of eight middle-income countries (Brazil, China, India, Mexico, South Africa, South Korea, Turkey and Venezuela). The studies included are interdisciplinary, ranging across economics, sociology, anthropology, international relations, political science and related social sciences. The book focuses on a materialist understanding of the workings of neoliberalism as a modality of social and economic reproduction, and its everyday practices of dispossession and exploitation. It will therefore be of particular interest to scholars in industrial policy, neoliberalism and development strategy.

Alfredo Saad-Filho is Professor of Political Economy at SOAS, University of London.
Galip L. Yalman is Assistant Professor of Political Science and Chairman of the European Studies Graduate Programme at the Middle East Technical University, Ankara. He is currently the President of Turkish Social Sciences Association.

Routledge studies in development economics

Economic Transitions to Neoliberalism in Middle-income Countries

Policy dilemmas, economic crises, forms of resistance

Edited by Alfredo Saad-Filho and Galip L. Yalman

Routledge
Taylor & Francis Group

LONDON AND NEW YORK

First published 2010
by Routledge
2 Park Square, Milton Park, Abingdon, Oxon OX14 4RN

Simultaneously published in the USA and Canada
by Routledge
711 Third Ave, New York, NY 10017

Routledge is an imprint of the Taylor & Francis Group, an informa business

Typeset in Times by Wearset Ltd, Boldon, Tyne and Wear
First issued in paperback in 2013

British Library Cataloguing in Publication Data
A catalogue record for this book is available from the British Library

Library of Congress Cataloging in Publication Data
Economic transitions to neoliberalism in middle-income countries : policy
dilemmas, economic crises, forms of resistance / edited by Alfredo Saad-
Filho and Galip L. Yalman.
p. cm.
Includes bibliographical references and index.
1. Developing countries–Economic policy. 2. Globalization–Economic
aspects. 3. Neoliberalism. I. Saad-Filho, Alfredo, 1964– II. Yalman, Galip
L.
HC59.7.E3135 2009
330.9172′4–dc22

2009019795

ISBN13: 978-0-415-74622-9 (pbk)
ISBN13: 978-0-415-49253-9 (hbk)
ISBN13: 978-0-203-86591-0 (ebk)

Contents

Figures

Tables

Contributors

Alejandro Valle Baeza, Department of Economics, UNAM, Mexico.

Pınar Bedirhanoğlu, Department of International Relations, METU, Ankara, Turkey.

Henry Bernstein, Department of Development Studies, SOAS, University of London, UK.

Armando Boito, Department of Political Science, University of Campinas, Brazil.

Al Campbell, Department of Economics, University of Utah, USA.

Hasan Cömert, Department of Economics, University of Massachusetts, Amherst, USA.

Seyhan Erdoğdu, Faculty of Political Sciences, Ankara University, Turkey.

Ben Fine, Department of Economics, SOAS, University of London, UK.

Seongjin Jeong, Institute for Social Sciences, Gyeongsang National University, South Korea.

Bob Jessop, Department of Sociology and Director of the Institute of Advanced Studies, University of Lancaster, UK.

Dic Lo, Department of Economics, SOAS, University of London, UK, and School of Economics, Renmin University of China.

Alessandra Mezzadri, Department of Development Studies, SOAS, University of London, UK.

Alfredo Saad-Filho, Department of Development Studies, SOAS, University of London, UK.

Susanne Soederberg, Department of Global Development Studies and Canada Research Chair, Queens University, Kingston, Canada.

Hae-Yung Song, Department of Development Studies, SOAS, University of London, UK.

Ngai-Ling Sum, Department of Politics and International Relations, University of Lancaster, UK.

Aylin Topal, Department of Political Science and Public Administration, METU, Ankara, Turkey.

Galip L. Yalman, Department of Political Science and Public Administration, METU, Ankara, Turkey.

Ergin Yıldızoğlu, Centre for European Studies, METU, Ankara, Turkey.

Filiz Zabcı, Faculty of Political Sciences, Ankara University, Turkey.

Yu Zhang, School of Economics, Renmin University of China.

Introduction

Alfredo Saad-Filho and Galip L. Yalman

The chapters in this collection address three key issues for middle-income countries. First, how can neoliberalism be defined and distinguished from other phases, stages or configurations of capitalism. This includes the relationship between neoliberalism, markets, society and the state, neoliberalism and economic policy, and neoliberalism and globalisation. Second, how to interpret the transition to neoliberalism and the transformative processes that have ensued from it, as well as the resistance against it in eight middle-income countries (Brazil, China, India, Mexico, South Africa, South Korea, Turkey and Venezuela).[1] Third, what are the prospects for the neoliberal order and for resistance in these countries, given the ongoing crisis of global capitalism.

It would have been impossible to impose a narrow interpretative framework across all chapters included in this book because the transition to neoliberalism, the performance of the neoliberal regimes and the resistance against neoliberalism are context-specific. Nevertheless, the contributors to this volume depart from a set of common perspectives which facilitates cross-country comparisons. Neoliberalism is the contemporary form of capitalism, and it is based on the systematic use of state power to impose, under the veil of 'non-intervention', a hegemonic project of recomposition of the rule of capital in most areas of social life. This project emerged gradually after the partial disintegration of post-war Keynesianism and developmentalism in the 1970s and 1980s, and it has led to the reconstitution of economic and social relations of subordination in those countries where neoliberalism has been imposed. The tensions and displacements embedded within global neoliberalism are nowhere more evident than in the middle-income countries.

At the domestic level, the neoliberal transitions have transformed the material basis of social reproduction in these countries. These changes include shifts in economic and social policy, property rights, the country's insertion into the international economy, and the modalities of exploitation and social domination. The political counterpart of these processes is the incremental limitation of the domestic political sphere through the insulation of 'markets' and investors from democratic and social accountability, and the imposition of a stronger imperative of labour control allegedly to promote international competitiveness. These economic and political shifts have reduced the scope for universal welfare provision and led to regressive distributive shifts and higher unemployment and job insecurity in most countries. They have also created an income-concentrating dynamics of accumulation that is largely immune to (marginal) Keynesian and reformist interventions.

The inability of the neoliberal reforms to support higher levels of investment, growth and welfare provision for the majority of the population is well known. However, this is not sufficient to demonstrate the 'failure' of neoliberalism. For the primary purpose of the neoliberal reforms, although presented otherwise, is not to promote faster growth, reduce inflation or even to increase the portfolio choices of the financial institutions. It is to subordinate local working classes and domestic accumulation to international imperatives, promote the microeconomic integration between competing capitals, and expand the scope for financial system intermediation of the three key sources of capital in the economy: the state budget, the banking system and the balance of payments.

Resistance against neoliberalism has taken a plurality of forms, including mass revolt and the development and implementation of alternative institutions and frameworks for economic and social policy. This book examines these challenges both analytically and empirically in specific contexts. Correspondingly, the chapters are grouped into two parts, 'Neoliberalism and globalisation' and 'Country experiences'.

In the first chapter in Part I, 'Neoliberalism as financialisation', Ben Fine offers a broad-ranging review of neoliberalism and the current crisis. He argues that the current financial crisis has exposed the contradictions of neoliberalism, not simply as a dysfunctional economic system but equally as a hegemonic ideological project. Paradoxically, the state intervention to rescue finance appears both to conform and to break with neoliberalism in terms of its breach with the market, and the priority of support offered to the most parasitic forms of capital. This paradox is resolved through the prism of three separate perspectives. First, the scholarship, rhetoric and policies of neoliberalism are not necessarily consistent with one another and have a shifting relation to one another. Second, neoliberalism has gone through two phases, both actively promoting the 'market', but the later and current phase witnessing explicit calls upon the state to underpin the process and moderate its effects. Third, that the duration of neoliberalism across its two phases and its articulation of scholarship, rhetoric and policy are underpinned by the process of financialisation.

In Chapter 2, 'The continuing ecological dominance of neoliberalism in the crisis', Bob Jessop distinguishes four main forms of neoliberalism and relates them to the logic of capital accumulation and the territorial logic of imperialism within the world market and the interstate system. Although the high-point of neoliberalism occurred in 1985–97, neoliberalism continues to exercise 'ecological dominance' over the world market through its crisis-tendencies and path-dependent policy effects. This chapter defines ecological dominance, and shows how financial capital can be interpreted as ecologically dominant in this context. It also suggests how the logic of the neoliberal regime shift in the United States has been shaped by the ecological dominance of finance and how this, in turn, has the most significant impact on the unfolding crisis. The chapter concludes with remarks on the contradictions and limits of US domination.

Ergin Yıldızoğlu examines 'Globalisation as a crisis form' in Chapter 3. This chapter claims that globalisation is a manifestation of the recurring crises of the capitalist mode of production, and that neoliberal globalisation emerged, originally, as a mode of crisis management. It eventually exhausted itself after transferring enormous wealth and power to the top echelons of society. With the arrival of the current financial crisis, the credit crunch and the post-bubble depression economy, this era is ending, and a new period of uncertainty is unfolding.

In Chapter 4, Ngai-Ling Sum reviews the 'Cultural political economy of neoliberalism'. This chapter applies cultural political economy to the recent emergence of competitiveness as a transnational constellation of hegemonic discourses and practices. This approach takes a cultural-discursive turn analysing the processes and mechanisms whereby hegemony is constituted and negotiated in and across (trans-)national institutional orders and civil society. It then turns to the role of economic imaginaries about competitiveness in constituting objects of economic calculation, management, governance, and so on. The Harvard Business School variant of competitiveness analysis provides a case study. This has moved from a theoretical paradigm to a policy paradigm and, most recently, a knowledge brand with significant effects in the neoliberal (re-) making of social relations. The chapter explores how this knowledge brand has been extended globally via knowledge apparatuses and other technologies of power, especially in East Asia. It then describes how this hegemonic logic of competitiveness is being challenged and negotiated.

Susanne Soederberg analyses, in Chapter 5, 'Socially responsible investment and neoliberal discipline in emerging markets'. Since the early 1990s, private investment flows have dominated global development finance. Alongside foreign direct investment, equity finance has become an important source of capital for corporations in the middle-income countries. Western institutional investors, primarily US-based pension funds, dominate this new geography of equity financing. The US-based public pension fund, California Public Employees Retirement System (CalPERS) is one of the largest pension funds in the world, but also the first institutional investor to employ a benchmarking strategy based on both financial and non-financial (social) criteria. This chapter contextualises CalPERS' benchmarking strategy, or the 'Permissible Country Index' (PCI), within the official development agenda. It is argued that the PCI mirrors neoliberal-led discourses and policies. It aims not only to encourage a greater involvement of the private sector in development, but also to legitimate deepening forms of dependency on, and discipline of, foreign capital in emerging markets.

In the sixth chapter, 'Global unions and global capitalism', Seyhan Erdoğdu examines the international unionism as represented by the ICFTU/ICTU and the global union federations. In the early 1980s, these organisations tried to develop a global Keynesianism to confront the emerging neoliberal globalisation. This short-lived project was replaced by a liberal reformist approach in the 1990s,

which conceived globalisation as an irreversible challenge with potential benefits, and tried to reform its negative aspects by adding a social dimension without
altering its basic structure. Since the turn of the century, as it became increasingly evident that neoliberal globalisation generates unemployment, poverty and
social exclusion, changes have emerged in the discourse of the global union
movement. However, the practical implications of this social reformism remain
to be seen.

In the final chapter of Part I, Filiz Zabcı examines 'Neoliberalism and the politics of war'. This chapter argues that the occupation of Iraq offers a striking
example of the relationship between war and politics, because it demonstrates
that war has become a key mechanism for the expansion of neoliberal policies
and financialisation. US strategy aims not only to control energy sources but,
more broadly, to support the expansion of corporate capitalism to regions where
neoliberal policies have yet to be implemented. In the case of Iraq, the invasion
was an instrument of toppling Saddam Hussein's interventionist state and implementing neoliberal economic policies. The new economic agenda and new economic laws imposed in the country paved the way for the privatisation of Iraqi
oil, and opened the market for foreign oil companies.

In the first chapter in Part II, 'State, class and the discourse', Pınar Bedirhanoğlu
and Galip L. Yalman identify the processes and strategies that have put an end to
class-based politics in the neoliberal period in Turkey. They focus on the implications of the 1980 coup d'état, 1989 capital account liberalisation, the rise of ethnic,
religious and nationalist conflicts, and the anti-statist hegemonic discourse. This
chapter argues that the neoliberal authoritarian form which the state acquired in the
1980s has persisted through the powerful articulation of economic, political and
cultural processes. It is also claimed that the AKP promises to reproduce neoliberal
authoritarianism in Turkey in a liberal-Islamist-cum-conservative form, suggesting
that it represents continuity in terms of state–class relations whilst claiming to initiate radical changes in state–society relations.

In Chapter 9, Alessandra Mezzadri examines 'Neoliberalism, industrial
restructuring and labour'. The rise of globalisation has triggered a process of
economic restructuring which profoundly impacted the industrial trajectories of
the middle-income countries. The shift to export-oriented industrialisation, in
particular, meant that several countries became production nodes within global
manufacturing chains, mainly competing according to their comparative advantage in cheap labour. Examining the Delhi garment industry, this chapter shows
the complexities behind the provision of cheap labour for neoliberal global production. Indian exporters reproduce their comparative advantage through a wide
variety of social institutions and structural differences, ranging across mobility,
gender, age and geographical provenance. On the one hand, exporters' strategies
to minimise labour costs trigger a process of commodification of labour power
which exploits the social profile of the workers even before they enter the labour
market. On the other hand, in the context of such strategies, Indian social institutions and structures are transnationalised and acquire broader regulatory meanings in the context of neoliberal global production.

Hae-Yung Song, in Chapter 10, offers an innovative interpretation of 'The developmental state and the neoliberal transition in South Korea'. This chapter assesses the Korean developmental state and its post-1997 neoliberal transformation beyond statism, or the notion that the state is separate and independent from society and the economy. This chapter critically appraises the established literature on the Korean state, and highlights how pervasive statist assumptions are in this literature, and how the statist framework confines the way in which the transformation of the Korean state is understood in terms of a pendulum oscillating between the state and the market and between the state and the global economy. This chapter proposes an alternative framework based on the form analysis of the state, and offers a novel reading of the Korean developmental state and its neoliberal transformation. It is argued that the neoliberal transition of Korea can be understood as the rise of a new modality of social domination rather than a reversal of the domination of the 'state' over 'capital' (or 'the economy').

Subsequently, in Chapter 11, Seongjin Jeong examines the 'Korean left debates on alternatives to neoliberalism'. These debates have flourished because of the decade-long period of low growth and deepening social polarisation in the country since 1997. This chapter evaluates these left alternatives from a Marxist standpoint. First, it criticises the thesis that the neoliberalism has established a 'finance-led accumulation regime' in Korea. Instead, neoliberalism has deepened the low growth trajectory of the economy, increasing social inequalities and promoting denationalisation. This chapter also claims that the economic policy of the current Lee Myung-bak administration combines an outdated version of Park Chung-Hee's model of state capitalism with the neoliberal 'big bang'. Other progressive alternatives, including Ha-Joon Chang's 'Democratic Welfare State Model' and the Keynesian 'Strategy for Social Solidarity' are contrasting variants of national reformism, and they are far from being anti-capitalist. This chapter concludes by confirming the relevance of Marxian socialist alternatives in Korea.

Chapter 12, by Dic Lo and Yu Zhang, examines 'China and the quest for alternatives to neoliberalism'. China's sustained rapid economic growth during the last three decades has been achieved mainly through a process of 'governing the market' by a set of structural-institutional factors that are China-specific, but can be of general importance for late development worldwide. This chapter claims that the Chinese experience offers important lessons for the quest of alternative models of economic development deviating from neoliberalism.

In Chapter 13, Henry Bernstein examines 'Globalisation, neoliberalism, labour, with reference to South Africa'. This chapter first revisits Marx's concept of the reserve army of labour, and then seeks to elaborate its utility for understanding processes affecting the classes of labour today, with special reference to the informalisation of employment and internal fragmentations of classes of labour. Those fragmentations reflect how the contours of social difference like gender, ethnicity and caste intersect with those of class to structure specific divisions of labour and labour regimes, with implications for class politics and resistance. This is illustrated in relation to the fortunes of the classes of labour in South Africa since the end of apartheid in 1994.

Armando Boito, in Chapter 14, reviews 'Social class and politics in Brazil'. This chapter argues that the Lula administration represents a new political phase of neoliberal capitalism in Brazil. At the level of political power, national and transnational financial capital was constrained to share their hegemony with the domestic industrial bourgeoisie. Among the working class, the new unionist elite has established an alliance with the domestic bourgeoisie against financial capital, while the poor and unorganised workers are linked to the Lula administration as a passive base for '*lulismo*', a political phenomenon separate from the president's Workers Party (PT). '*Lulismo*' expresses a paradoxical alliance between the richest and the poorest, bringing together the two extremes of Brazilian society in such a way that the bourgeoisie ultimately wins.

Alejandro Valle Baeza offers a broader analysis of neoliberalism in Latin America in Chapter 15, 'Is there an acceptable future for workers in capitalism?'. This chapter suggests that there is no decent future in sight for the workers, especially in the poor and middle-income countries. This is largely because of the growth of unemployment and precarious employment relations, connected to the ongoing 'race to the bottom' by workers trying to keep their jobs. This process has been going on for several years, but it is likely to intensify further with the current crisis of global capitalism. Socialism or barbarism is the dilemma that we will have to face in the not-too-distant future.

In Chapter 16, Al Campbell and Hasan Cömert examine 'Progressive Third World Central Banking and the case of Venezuela'. While neoliberalism was broadly adopted by capitalism around the world during the 1980s, it did not clearly articulate its own Central Bank policy until the 1990s, when it was declared that inflation targeting was the optimal Central Bank policy. The social, political and economic reaction against neoliberalism has included the development of a progressive flexible alternative Central Bank policy. While the goal of the former is to promote the development and profits of financial capital, the goal of the latter is broad economic, social and human development. Having considered these two opposing approaches, this chapter turns to consider the Central Bank of Venezuela (BCV). Despite the anti-neoliberal revolution that began in Venezuela in 1999, the BCV rather surprisingly remained largely neoliberal until 2005. As documented by both its declarations and its actions, that year the BCV consciously switched to a progressive orientation. While its specific policies and practices are, and will remain, in a state of constant modification and augmentation, the BCV today provides an interesting and important case study of both possible successes and problems linked to implementing a progressive Central Bank policy in a capitalist economy.

Aylin Topal, in Chapter 17, reviews the 'Transition to neoliberalism and decentralisation policies in Mexico'. The main purpose of this chapter is to explain why decentralisation policies were implemented together with the neoliberal transition in Mexico. This chapter suggests that this was because of the development of inter- and intra-class relations in Mexico, in the context of the crisis of hegemony of the post-war model of development. This crisis involved a shift in the economic development policies, and an institutional restructuring which reformed the ties between classes and political parties. In Mexico, collective pressures and struggles placed decentralisation policies at the juncture of these processes. While certain fractions of capital demanded a reorganisation of the state to allow market forces to operate at the local level, the working classes stepped up their demand for more participatory and democratic local politics. When the debt crisis hit the country in 1982, the international financial institutions steered the government's policy reforms, which took the form of the decentralisation policies.

We are deeply indebted to the contributors for being always prepared to return to their chapters over and over again to satisfy our demands and those of the referees and the publishers. We would also wish to thank the Scientific and Technological Research Council of Turkey (TÜBİTAK), Middle East Technical University, Faculty of Economics and Administrative Sciences (METU-FEAS), the British Council, the International Sociological Association (ISA) and Friedrich Ebert Stiftung for their generous support to the conference, organised by the Turkish Social Sciences Association (TSSA) to commemorate its fortieth anniversary in Ankara, where most of the papers included in this volume were initially presented. Funda Hülagü, Susan Haji-Javad and Ali Riza Güngen provided considerable support towards the preparation of this book. Bethany Lewis and Thomas Sutton from Routledge and their colleagues were extremely supportive throughout the life of this project.

Note

1 In this book, the category 'middle-income country' is defined, selectively, in terms of both GDP per capita and absolute levels of GDP. This includes countries with relatively high GDP per capita, for example Mexico and South Korea, as well as large and dynamic economies with low GDP per capita, especially China and India.

Part I

Neoliberalism and globalisation

1   Neoliberalism as financialisation[1]

Ben Fine

Engaging neoliberalism

When it first emerged, neoliberalism seemed to be able to be defined relatively easily and uncontroversially. In the economic arena, the contrast could be made with Keynesianism and emphasis placed on perfectly working markets. A correspondingly distinctive stance could be made over the role of the state as corrupt, rent-seeking and inefficient as opposed to benevolent and progressive. Ideologically, the individual pursuit of self-interest as the means to freedom was offered in contrast to collectivism. And, politically, Reaganism and Thatcherism came to the fore. It is also significant that neoliberalism should emerge soon after the post-war boom came to an end, together with the collapse of the Bretton Woods system of fixed exchange rates.

This is all 30 or more years ago and, whilst neoliberalism has entered the scholarly if not popular lexicon, it is now debatable whether it is now or, indeed, ever was clearly defined. How does it fare alongside globalisation, the new world order, and the new imperialism, for example, as descriptors of contemporary capitalism. Does each of these refer to a similar understanding but with different terms and emphasis? And how do we situate neoliberalism in relation to Third Wayism, the social market, and so on, whose politicians, theorists and ideologues would pride themselves as departing from neoliberalism but who, in their politics and policies, seem at least in part to have been captured by it (and even vice versa in some instances)?

These conundrums in the understanding and nature of neoliberalism have been highlighted by James Ferguson (2007) who reveals how what would traditionally be termed progressive policies (a basic income grant for example) have been rationalised through neoliberal discourse. At the very least, he closes, 'We will also need a fresh analytic approach that is not trapped within the tired "neoliberalism versus welfare state" frame that has until now obscured many of the key issues from view'. The tensions within the notion of neoliberalism have also drawn the attention of human geographers, not least because of their sensitivity to how a general and abstract term should allow for differences in time and place (or context) even to the point of inconsistency and, thereby, undermining itself. In surveying the literature, Castree (2006: 6) concludes, 'neoliberalism' will remain a necessary illusion for those on the geographical left: something we know *does not exist* as such, but the idea of whose existence allows our 'local' research finding to connect to a much bigger and apparently important conversation (emphasis added).

Are we, then, alongside globalisation for example, to accept 'neoliberalism' for its investigative and polemical purchase despite knowing that it is conceptually flawed to the extent of not existing at all?

To the extent that they can be, I seek to resolve these conundrums through a two-pronged assault upon them. The first, in characterising neoliberalism, is to distinguish between its rhetoric (advocacy or ideology), its scholarship and its policy in practice. Each of these is shifting in content and emphasis (across time and place) and, whilst they have connections with one another, these too are shifting and by no means mutually consistent. In addition, there is a complex and shifting relationship between neoliberalism across these three elements and the reality that they purport both to represent and influence. I have, for example, emphasised these considerations in unpicking the putative shift from Washington to post Washington Consensus (Fine 2008) most recently. But, second, these considerations around the contradictions within the spirit of an age, neoliberalism or otherwise, can be grounded in what has been a defining feature of contemporary capitalism over the past 30 years, the extraordinary rise and spread of finance.

As argued in the final section, by way of conclusion, it is this material factor that underpins, constrains and, thereby, defines the current period as neoliberal and which also is a major factor in explaining its otherwise illusory character. I begin, though, in the next section by addressing the role of contemporary finance.

Financialisation[2]

From a Marxist perspective, as a system of accumulation, capitalism is heavily dependent upon finance in the form of interest-bearing capital, that is finance deployed for the exclusive purpose of expanding production for profit. But this specific role for finance is embedded, to coin a phrase, in other aspects of the circulation of commodities, money and credit.[3] What is uniquely characteristic of the current period of capitalism is the extraordinary extent to which such embedding has been both deepened and broadened. Such developments have been best captured within the literature by the notion of financialisation. This has been addressed from a number of perspectives, but not always explicitly and wittingly since however much recognised as such, its effects are inescapable. The explicit literature on financialisation is both limited and marginalised from mainstream thought. For Epstein (2005: 3), 'financialization means the increasing role of financial motives, financial markets, financial actors and financial institutions in the operation of the domestic and international economies'. Stockhammer (2004: 720) offers an overview of financialisation, acknowledging that it 'is a recent term, still ill-defined, which summarises a broad range of phenomena including the globalisation of financial markets, the shareholder value revolution and the rise of incomes from financial investment'. His own focus is upon 'changes in the internal power structure of the firm'.

Before turning to this literature directly, three further elements need to be added. The first is the role of the state as regulator of the monetary and financial systems, and itself as a major agent in the provision of financial instruments, not least through its own indebtedness, paper bonds as a form of fictitious capital.[4] Second is the nature and role of world money, how it is that the relations, properties and functions of money in general are realised on a global scale in light of the presence of numbers of national currencies. And third is historical specificity in relation to both of the previous two elements and their interaction, reflecting particular patterns of accumulation at a global level. In this respect, there are generally identifiable and agreed historical periods in which the role of nation-states and of world money are distinct, most recently the rise and fall of the Bretton Woods system (see Arrighi (2003) for a deeper and longer account), for example.

The current period is one in which finance has penetrated across all commercial relations to an unprecedented *direct* extent. I emphasise 'direct' here because the role of finance has long been extensive both in promoting capital accumulation and in intensifying its crises, most notably in the Great Crash of 1929 and the ensuing recession. For Krippner (2005: 199), in her overview of contemporary financialisation in the United States, it neither necessarily 'represents an entirely novel phase of capitalism ... [nor] do these data allow us to draw any conclusions regarding the *permanency* of the trends documented here'. But, these reservations aside, in qualitative terms, finance is different today because of the proliferation of both purely financial markets and instruments and the corresponding ranges of fictitious capitals that bridge these to real activities. Most obviously, and a major element in the financialisation literature, especially in the United States, is the drawing in of personal finance in general and of pension funds in particular. As Langley (2004: 539) has put it, citing Richard Minns,

> it is this commitment to 'the extension and growth of stock markets and "liberalised" financial markets' that has underpinned pension reform initiatives in Anglo-American state-societies over recent decades, also becoming central to the 'model' for reform favoured by the World Bank and the Organisation for Economic Co-operation and Development (OECD).[5]

Yet the breadth of financialisation goes much further than institutionalised investment funds, as finance has inserted itself into an ever-expanding range of activities, not least in managing personal revenues as emphasised by Lapavitsas (2009) and dos Santos (2009).

As already indicated this fundamental feature of contemporary capitalism, other than in a piecemeal fashion dealing in it bit by bit rather than as a systemic property, has best been broached by the financialisation literature, limited in both volume and influence, and practically non-existent for developing countries. The work around Epstein (2005) is the most prominent, although more important in some respects is the initiative on financialisation furnished by the ESRC Centre for Research on Socio-Cultural Change at the University of Manchester (see especially Froud *et al.* (2006)).

From this literature, a number of important elements can be teased out, not least from a labour movement contribution concerned with the impact of financialisation upon labour market conditions (Rossman and Greenfield 2006). First is the rise of institutional investors and the extent to which their interests have been channelled more generally into financial channels concerned with 'shareholder value', effectively the making of money out of ownership as such as opposed to the making of investments with real returns. In effect, this is to acknowledge the increasing importance of fictitious capital, with the presumption that, second, all financial institutions are embroiled in light of the rising significance of market analysts. Third, the result is to place financial restructuring and short-termism in a position of precedence over long-term investment plans and productive restructuring. Fourth, the impact on wages, employment and working conditions is inevitably undermined as a high investment, high productivity, high employment, high wage nexus is broken in favour of low investment, low productivity, low wage and casualised employment. As Froud and Williams (2007: 14) suggest, companies have increasingly become perceived as a bundle of assets to be traded, an exercise in value capture as opposed to value creation. The result is to create a new cadre of intermediaries, continuously financially restructuring enterprises (Folkman *et al.* 2006). As Perry and Nölke (2006: 566) put it: 'Financial analysts gain power and traders/fund managers pay more attention to them; enterprise managers lose power ... Most of the principals in the financial system – i.e. investors, savers, pensioners, future pensioners (workers) – are not in the picture'. From Keynes' euthanasia of the parasitic rentier, we are suddenly confronted with the heroic financial entrepreneur, who creates nothing but fictitious value (Erturk *et al.* 2006). But the highly publicised benefits that have accrued both to corporate management and to those working in finance are real enough. As Erturk *et al.* (2004: 707) observe, 'the explosive rise in CEO pay reflects the value skimming opportunities of bull market euphoria', although bear markets are not without their opportunities either. This has to be set in the wider context of financialisation itself with two elements. On the one hand, the proportion of corporate profits as a whole being derived from financial activity has been rising, so this is where major sources of rewards are to be found (Krippner 2005). On the other hand, a point taken to be crucial in arguing for the presence of financialisation itself, non-financial corporations have been accruing increasing proportions of their profits from financial activity. Stockhammer (2004: 720), in particular, defines financialisation as 'the increased activity of non-financial businesses on financial markets', and finds that, 'For France, financialisation explains the entire slowdown in accumulation, for the USA about one-third of the slowdown. Financialisation, therefore, can potentially explain an economically significant part of the slowdown in accumulation' (739).[6]

Stockhammer and most others explicitly connect such financialisation to the issue of who controls the modern corporation. This obtains both systemically and at the level of corporate governance itself, not least, in citing Lazonick and O'Sullivan (2000), as 'retain and invest' gives way to 'downsize and distribute' in pursuit of shareholder value (Stockhammer 2004: 721). Erturk *et al.* (2004) set such issues in the longer term perspective of managerialism, deriving from Berle and Means and the separation of ownership and control. Far from shareholder value signifying the triumphant return of the shareholder, it is apparent that financialisation has driven up the rewards for both financial corporations and for the management of non-financial corporations, with potential for fluidity between the two. In the era of financialisation, CEOs within non-financial corporations have conformed to its dictates and have been correspondingly rewarded. Ertuk *et al.* conclude that it is even less appropriate to look to them to drive a wedge between real and financial governance than it was previously to see managers as exercising control against the interests of owners. For what has changed is the relationship between finance and industry. As Rossman and Greenfield (2006: 2) put it, citing Stockhammer:[7]

> Of course, companies have always sought to maximize profit. What is new is the drive for profit through the elimination of productive capacity and employment. Transnational food processors, for example, now invest a significantly lower proportion of their profits in expanding productive capacity. Financial markets today directly reward companies for reducing payroll through closures, restructuring and outsourcing. This reflects the way in which financialization has driven the management of non-financial companies to 'act more like financial market players'.

Such considerations have understandably led to a preoccupation with the relations between private capital and financial and non-financial corporations, at the expense of the role of public finance and world money, although these are addressed in other literature, macroeconomics for the mainstream. Inevitably this literature is both vast and oblique in its approach to financialisation for, as Duménil and Lévy (2005: 17) put it, 'neoliberalism is the ideological expression of the reasserted power of finance'. Thus, financialisation is the subject of all of the literature on neoliberalism, globalisation and stabilisation, critical, unwitting or otherwise.

What is apparent empirically, irrespective of how it is situated analytically, is that the current world financial system has become even more dependent on the US dollar as world money even as the US economy itself has experienced relative decline at a global level with peculiarities of its own. In a couple of papers, Eichengreen (2004 and 2006) has addressed the nature and significance of this for the continuing stability of global financial markets. His main conclusion is that, to the limited extent that the current system can be interpreted as comparable to the Bretton Woods system of the post-war boom, it is liable to enjoy a much shorter lifespan with prospects for instability and systemic change on the horizon sooner rather than later.

Across his analyses, Eichengreen does not offer a well-defined theoretical position but that does not mean there is an absence of analytical content. He seems to accept, for example, that the current system might be sustained for as long as China is willing and able to exploit surplus labour to underpin a trade surplus with the United States and to accept dollar-denominated assets in return. There are a number of important issues here. One is the emphasis upon the capacity to sustain accumulation through particular financial relations, although there is no reason why this should be confined to the Chinese reserve army of labour. Indeed, as Eichengreen is at pains to point out, it is not just China that is exporting to the United States in return for its currency. This is one reason why he anticipates instability sooner rather than later for the portfolio of (Asian) countries to which the United States is indebted is perceived to be heterogeneous and, consequently, less able and willing to underpin a collective will in support of the US dollar. This is contrasted with the greater uniformity of purpose and stages of development across Western Europe and Japan for the Bretton Woods period.

For the current period, this indicates just the beginnings of a broader understanding of how sustaining accumulation across the world involves many more considerations than the extent of cheap Chinese labour, with different countries situated at different stages of development, sectoral compositions and dynamics, and with differing structures and processes of economic and social reproduction. These factors benefit from much less consideration than those concerned with how they are complemented by finance. For Eichengreen, these include the capacity of private flow of funds to respond very quickly following crises, greater mix and extent of foreign holdings and speculation in capital flows, lesser control over these private flows, and the extent to which this has all been driven by the new technologies associated with financial markets and its dealings.

As indicated, Eichengreen's account is motivated by scrutiny of the prospective stability of the current financial system. From this, though, implications for the pace of accumulation more generally can be teased out. First is the observation that the weakness of the US dollar has induced developing countries to hold dollars in line with export-led growth. This is in part a result of the increased potential instability that has accompanied both the weakening of the dollar and the liberalisation of national financial systems. Eichengreen (2006: 5) observes:

> The uses to which developing countries have put foreign funds are very different than in earlier years ... emerging countries ... put into international reserves every single dollar of private capital received in the last five years, on net, from the rest of the world.

By contrast, continuing the text:[8]

> Traditionally, a not entirely desirable side effect of capital inflows has been a spending binge by governments, firms and households which has driven

up the real exchange rate, undermined export competitiveness, and diminished national creditworthiness, often precipitating a crisis. Spending by credit-constrained governments and households has been procyclical and capital inflows, by relaxing that constraint, have amplified their response. In the first decade of the 21st century, in contrast, the story has been different. The entire private capital inflow – and more – has been set aside in the form of international reserves rather than being used to finance additional purchases of consumer durables by households, to underwrite a construction boom, to support inefficient corporate investment, and to finance government budget deficits.

Leaving aside the cynicism, warranted or otherwise, attached to how such reserves might otherwise have been spent, this is indicative of developing countries coming to own their own national debt or, more exactly, that of the United States. This is not simply a distributional support to the United States – the rich exchange paper for the products of the poor – it is also a system at the expense of the potentially developmental goals and provision – household consumption, construction, corporate investment and budget deficits, all handmaidens of capital accumulation.

Second, though, the impact of these financial arrangements runs deeper still. For their origins lie in the liberalisation of financial systems under the Washington Consensus. As observed, this has led paradoxically both to the need for higher and higher levels of reserves and to the corresponding funding of US indebtedness. And, as observed by Eichengreen in his own way, once opened up in this fashion, capital markets incorporate a momentum of their own:

> Policy makers in emerging markets thus see capital account liberalization as part of the larger process of economic and financial development. They appreciate how globalization reinforces the fundamental argument for liberalizing international transactions: as a country is more deeply integrated into the global economy, it has an incentive to specialize further in order to capitalize on its comparative advantage, in turn making financial diversification more valuable as a risk-sharing device.
>
> (Eichengreen 2006: 18)

Thus, the impact of neoliberalism in promoting capital account liberalisation offers some explanation for the rise of US indebtedness – higher saving in emerging markets in the form of dollar-denominated reserves, and the corresponding lower levels of investment in the public and private sectors.

Third, though, in the last decade, there has been something of a reaction against neoliberalism, with the Asian and other crises having prompted a more cautious approach:[9]

> But policy makers in emerging markets also absorbed the lesson of the 1990s that financial opening should proceed gradually and be carefully

sequenced with other policy reforms. A one-sentence summary of the lessons of the Asian crisis is that capital account liberalization in advance of measures to strengthen domestic financial markets, reform corporate governance and adapt the macroeconomic policy regime to the imperatives of open capital markets can be a recipe for disaster. Taking these lessons to heart, emerging markets have moved away from pegged exchange rates, adopted flexible inflation targeting as a framework for monetary policy, and strengthened their budgetary institutions. They have recapitalized their banking systems, strengthened supervision and regulation, and reformed corporate governance to pave the way to life with an open account. The question is whether these reforms have proceeded fast enough, given the growing exposure of their economies to international capital flows.

(Eichengreen 2006: 18–19)

But the learning of these lessons is not to have restored the status quo *ex ante*. On the one hand, the financial markets have now been liberalised and function in entirely different ways requiring different, possibly more extensive, intervention to prevent them from being destabilising. On the other hand, as only vaguely hinted at by Eichengreen in terms of alternative uses of resources and the developmental ideology of policy-makers, these changes represent the support of financial interests and activities against those of others. This does itself suggest that the study of the global and national financial systems in terms of a parsimonious account of the relations between nations is entirely inappropriate. We have witnessed the excesses of financialisation in liberalising financial markets, and we have seen the financial elite and its activities extended as a result. Renewal of intervention, regulation and control has to be seen in this light rather than as a belated, if more sensible and balanced, approach to achieving some sort of neutral target of stabilisation. As McMichael (2004: 19) puts it, 'the preservation of money value increasingly governs institutional politics in global and national arenas, generalizing a cycle of liberalization and crisis management through structural adjustment, at the expense of sustained social policies'.

Revisiting neoliberalism by way of conclusion

To a large extent, the preceding discussion has focused upon financialisation as a prism through which to view more mainstream accounts of macro- and industrial finance. But, as already emphasised, financialisation has extended finance beyond the traditional to the personal and broader elements of economic and social reproduction. For the latter, it is not simply that neoliberalism is associated with privatisation, commercialisation and commodification but, where these do prevail, financialisation will not be far behind and even in the lead. As dos Santos (2008: 2) dramatically puts it for the sub-prime mortgage crisis at the time of writing:

By many historical measures the current financial crisis is without precedent. It has arisen from neither an industrial crisis nor an equity market crash. It was precipitated by the simple fact that increasing numbers of largely black, Latino and working-class white families in the US have been defaulting on their mortgages.

But it is not merely a matter of the extent to which financialisation has thereby rendered contemporary capitalism subject to crises of potentially greater depth *and* breadth, of both origin and incidence. Financialisation is also complicit in the persistence of slowdown of accumulation since the end of the post-war boom. It has created a dynamic in which real accumulation is both tempered and, ultimately, choked off by fictitious accumulation (although this may be preceded by bubbles of excessive accumulation, fictitious or real); it has undermined the role of the state as an active agent of economic restructuring; and it has also undermined the role of the state as an agent in furnishing the more general economic and social conditions conducive to accumulation, in health, education and welfare, for example, that alongside industrial policies underpinned the post-war boom as opposed to Keynesianism as such.

In this light, it is possible to suggest in broad terms that neoliberalism has experienced two phases. The first, following upon the collapse of the post-war boom, was akin to a sort of shock therapy of greater applicability than to the transition economies at a later date. This phase is marked by the state intervening to promote private capital in general as far as possible and financial markets in particular. The second phase exhibits two aspects. One has been for the state to intervene to moderate the impact of this financialisation, most notable now in the support given to rescuing financial institutions themselves. But, as is thereby evident, the second aspect is for the state to be committed to sustain the process of supporting private capital in general and of financialisation in particular.

Where does this leave 'neoliberalism'? Here, the distinctions around rhetoric, policy, scholarship and realism are imperative if subject to subtle application. For, of course, opponents of neoliberalism but proponents of capitalism will claim that the second phase is a departure from neoliberalism. And, in a limited sense, they are correct for the rhetoric and the scholarship are not neoliberal even if swayed in that direction by comparison with Keynesianism/welfarism. Indeed, the new market and institutional micro-foundations (of macroeconomics) and the post Washington Consensus are ideal complements for the new phase of neoliberalism since they rationalise piecemeal, discretionary intervention in deference to moderating and promoting the market in general. And, making markets work in general increasingly means making financial markets work in particular.

For, the era of financialisation entrenches new modes of corporate governance and assessment of performance, privatisation and state support to it rather than public provision, lack of coherent and systematic industrial and agricultural policy, pressure for user charges for health, education and welfare, and priority to macroeconomic austerity to allow for liberalisation of financial capital. In this context, market imperfection economics is not only weaker than Keynesianism/welfarism it is so in a context where it needs to be much stronger to be effective. As a result, it is both misguided and fails to get to grips with the systemic advance of financialisation and might even be thought to promote it. For Langley (2004: 541),

> invigorating the concept of financialisation requires that we recognise that particular but related discourses of economy are central to constituting financialised capitalism. The cultural making of financialised capitalism is not only derived from mainstream academic (neoliberal) economics, but also includes the theory and practice of the likes of management, accounting, advertising, marketing and insurance.[10]

To this might be added the whole development studies and policy industry! And, for accounting in particular, for example, far from being a politically neutral instrument of efficient and effective policy-making, Perry and Nölke (2006: 568) find that recent shifts in international standards towards fair-value accounting increases efficiency only if, 'one defines efficiency purely in pecuniary terms ... [and] one measures such pecuniary efficiency exclusively from the perspective of the financial sector'. Thus, 'this reflects and reinforces changed relations of production in which the financial sector increasingly dominates the productive sector, nationally institutionalized economic systems are undermined, and new forms of economic appropriation are validated' (581).

This is not to suggest that neoliberalism will sweep homogeneously across a globalised world, nor fail to be reversed. Krippner (2005: 203), for example, acknowledges the ambiguity for outcomes, as 'increased openness generates demands from citizens for "protection" from the vicissitudes of international markets ... but too much openness may embolden business interests, constraining the ability of the states to respond to such demands'. Welfare programmes in South Korea, for example, were expanded in response to the financial crisis, and the globalisation literature is marked by pointing to the continuing salience of the nation-state and heterogeneity in interventions and outcomes, especially in the field of welfare provision (see Kasza (2006) for an overview). Financialisation has shifted the modes of interaction and balance of power across vested interests but it does not rigidly determine outcomes. These remain contingent, especially in the wake of the continuing weight of state intervention, upon struggles to sustain alternatives, not least in seeking insulation against the logic of finance. If neoliberalism is not a temporary illusion, it is only because it is inextricably linked both to the state and to financialisation.

Notes

1 A much reduced and revised version of Fine (2007).
2 The earlier paper laid out the basis for addressing financialisation by reference to Marx's political economy of finance.
3 By fictitious capital is meant paper claims to future returns whose pricing is distinct from the value of the real assets on which they ultimately depend (with fraud only an extreme case of absolute fiction).

4 See Erturk (2003) for the importance of public debt in Turkey for financialisation and its role in undermining entrepreneurship and investment.
5 See also Cutler and Waine (2001) for occupational welfare more generally. They do observe, however, that 'in 1997–8 half the British population had financial wealth (excluding housing, pensions and bank current accounts) of less than £750'.
6 See also Orhangazi (2006).
7 And see McMichael (2004: 18) for financialisation and global corporate food regimes more generally, 'such that corporate strategies intensify vertical integration (from seed to supermarket) with flexible horizontal mergers and alliances'.
8 Eichengreen qualifies this account in three ways,

> The full picture, inevitably, is more complex, since emerging markets have also used private foreign funds to finance their residents' net investments abroad and to repay obligations to international financial institutions and official bilateral creditors. But the bottom line remains the same.

He adds in a couple of footnotes that 'the picture is much the same if we consider all developing countries', and that the result is to 'have not contributed as much as otherwise to the growth of global demand' (2006: 6), indicating a dampening effect other than from the US trade deficit.
9 See 'the new, more nuanced view of the IMF' (Kose *et al.* 2006: 34–5), cited in Chang (2007): premature opening of the capital account without having in place well-developed and well-supervised financial sectors, good institutions, and sound macroeconomic policies can hurt a country by making the structure of the inflows unfavourable and by making the country vulnerable to sudden stops or reversals of flow. Substitute a few words and you have the World Bank's rethink on privatisation, and probably most other things as well (Bayliss and Fine 2007). See also Kane (1996) for the dialectic of bank regulation.
10 Langley goes on to cite the work of Callon who, however, is ultimately drawn both to the position that economics makes the economy (rather than vice versa) and that capitalism is an invention of the left purely for the purposes of critique. See Fine (2003) for a critique of the ANT (actor-network theory) approach that has been influential in the study of finance.

References

Arrighi, G. (2003) 'The Social and Political Economy of Global Turbulence', *New Left Review*, 20, pp. 5–71.
Bayliss, K. and Fine, B. (eds) (2007) *Whither the Privatisation Experiment? Electricity and Water Sector Reform in Sub-Saharan Africa*, Basingstoke: Palgrave Macmillan.
Castree, N. (2006) 'Commentary', *Environment and Planning A*, 38(1), pp. 1–6.
Chang, H.-J. (2007) *Bad Samaritans: Rich Nations, Poor Policies, and the Threat to the Developing World*, London: Random House.
Cutler, T. and Waine, B. (2001) 'Social Insecurity and the Retreat from Social Democracy: Occupational Welfare in the Long Boom and Financialization', *Review of International Political Economy*, 8(1), pp. 96–118.
dos Santos, P. (2009) 'On the Content of Banking in Contemporary Capitalism', SOAS, mimeo.
Duménil, G. and Lévy, D. (2005) 'Costs and Benefits of Neoliberalism: A Class Analysis', in G. Epstein (ed.), *Financialization and the World Economy*, Cheltenham: Edward Elgar.
Eichengreen, B. (2004) 'Global Imbalances and the Lessons of Bretton Woods', *NBER Working Paper*, no 10497. Online, available at: www.nber.org/papers/w10497.

Eichengreen, B. (2006) 'The Future of Global Financial Markets'. Online, available at: www.econ.berkeley.edu/~eichengr/research/future_global_5–06.pdf.

Epstein, G. (ed.) (2005) *Financialization and the World Economy*, Cheltenham: Edward Elgar.

Erturk, I. (2003) 'Governance or Financialisation: The Turkish Case', *Competition and Change*, 7(4), pp. 185–204.

Erturk, I., Froud, J., Johal, S. and Williams, K. (2004) 'Corporate Governance and Disappointment', *Review of International Political Economy*, 11(4), pp. 677–713.

Erturk, I., Froud, J., Johal, S., Leaver, A. and Williams, K. (2006) 'Agency, the Romance of Management Pay and an Alternative Explanation', Centre for Research on Socio-Cultural Change, *CRESC Working Paper*, no 23, University of Manchester.

Ferguson, J. (2007) 'Formalities of Poverty: Thinking about Social Assistance in Neoliberal South Africa', *African Studies Review*, 50(2), pp. 71–86.

Fine, B. (2003) 'Callonistics: A Disentanglement', *Economy and Society*, 32(3), pp. 496–502.

Fine, B. (2007) 'Financialisation, Poverty, and Marxist Political Economy', Poverty and Capital Conference, 2–4 July 2007, University of Manchester.

Fine, B. (2008) 'Social Capital and Health: The World Bank through the Looking Glass after Deaton'. Online, available at: www.soas.ac.uk/cdpr/seminars/43279.pdf.

Folkman, P., Froud, J., Johal, S. and Williams, K. (2006) 'Working for Themselves? Capital Market Intermediaries and Present Day Capitalism', Centre for Research on Socio-Cultural Change, *CRESC Working Paper*, no 25, University of Manchester.

Froud, J. and Williams, K. (2007) 'Private Equity and the Culture of Value Extraction', Centre for Research on Socio-Cultural Change, *CRESC Working Paper*, no 31, University of Manchester.

Froud, J., Johal, S., Leaver, A. and Williams, K. (2006) *Financialisation and Strategy: Narrative and Numbers*, London: Routledge.

Kane, E. (1996) 'De Jure Interstate Banking: Why Only Now?', *Journal of Money, Credit and Banking*, 28(2), pp. 141–61.

Kasza, G. (2006) *One World of Welfare: Japan in Comparative Perspective*, Ithaca: Cornell University Press.

Kose, E. *et al.* (2006) 'Financial Globalisation: A Reappraisal', *IMF Working Paper*, WP/06/189, Washington, DC.

Krippner, G. (2005) 'The Financialization of the American Economy', *Socio-Economic Review*, 3(2), pp. 173–208.

Langley, P. (2004) ' "In the Eye of the 'Perfect Storm"': The Final Salary Pensions Crisis and Financialisation of Anglo-American Capitalism', *New Political Economy*, 9(4), pp. 539–58.

Lapavitsas, C. (2009) 'Financialised Capitalism: Direct Exploitation and Periodic Bubbles', SOAS, mimeo.

Lazonick, W. and O'Sullivan, M. (2000) 'Maximizing Shareholder Value: A New Ideology of Corporate Governance', *Economy and Society*, 29(1), pp. 13–35.

McMichael, P. (2004) 'Global Development and the Corporate Food Regime', presented at the Symposium on New Directions in the Sociology of Global Development, XI World Congress of Rural Sociology, Trondheim. Online, available at: www.agribusinessaccountability.org/pdfs/297_Global%20Development%20and%20the%20Corporate%20Food%20Regime.pdf.

Orhangazi, Ö. (2006) *Financialization of the US Economy and Its Effects on Capital*

Accumulation: A Theoretical and Empirical Investigation, PhD Thesis, University of Massachusetts, Amherst.

Perry, J. and Nölke, A. (2006) 'The Political Economy of International Accounting Standards', *Review of International Political Economy*, 13(4), pp. 559–86.

Rossman, P. and Greenfield, G. (2006) 'Financialization: New Routes to Profit, New Challenges for Trade Unions', *Labour Education, Quarterly Review of the ILO Bureau for Workers' Activities*, no 142. Online, available at: www.iufdocuments.org/www/documents/Financialization-e.pdf.

Stockhammer, E. (2004) 'Financialisation and the Slowdown of Accumulation', *Cambridge Journal of Economics*, 28(5), pp. 719–41.

2 The continuing ecological dominance of neoliberalism in the crisis

Bob Jessop

This chapter relates four main forms of neoliberalism and their development to the interaction of capital's economic logic and the territorial logic of imperialism in the world market and interstate system. An important, but by no means exclusive, role is played by US transnational capital and imperial interests. For, despite the loss of American economic hegemony and multiple challenges to its domination from the 1980s onwards, the ideational and structural capacity of US economic and political power to shape the world remains preponderant on a global scale. This is related to the active and/or reactive integration of key features of US economic paradigms into strategies pursued by many of the key economic and political forces in other economies and to the formation of transnational blocs organised under US hegemony (or, at least, dominance) that promote policies on scales ranging from the global to the local that tend to favour the interests of an imperial United States and its major economic and political allies. This reflects and tends to reproduce the continuing 'ecological dominance' (see below, pp. 28–32) of forms of financial innovation that have been promoted by the US federal government, related international economic apparatuses, and transnational financial capital.

This ecological dominance still holds after the financial crisis that emerged in mid-2007, rippled out through the world market in 2008 in the form of an increasingly deep recession, and is likely to become a global depression in 2009–10. In addressing these issues, this chapter comments on different forms of neoliberalism, identifies the highpoint of neoliberalism in 1985–97, discusses the nature of economic determination, argues that the logic of US neoliberalism is ecologically dominant in the world market, and concludes with remarks on the contradictions and limits of US domination.

The world market and neoliberalism

Marx argued that the world market is the most developed mode of existence of the integration of abstract labour with the value form. Here production is posited as a complex totality but, at the same time, all contradictions come into play (Marx 1973: 227). In contrast to crude versions of world system theory, this does not entail a single logic operating on a global scale with singular directionality.

Instead we find a *variegated* world market with an emergent logic based on interaction among different 'varieties of capitalism' and other forms of economic organisation as mediated through shifts in the balance of forces. As the world market has operated ever more as an integrated system in real time under the ecological dominance of neoliberalism, Marx's analysis becomes ever more relevant. Just as Marx once remarked that the classical political economists who theorised and advocated the market economy 'know more about the future than about the present', the same could be said about his critique of classical political economy and the logic of capital accumulation (Marx 1976: 289). Marx's comments on the world market do not exclude continuing uneven development. On the contrary, the latter is an important mechanism in driving neoliberal globalisation forward and intensifying the contradictions on a world scale. The real barriers to capitalist production are rooted in the capital relation itself (Marx 1972: 250) and, one might add, in its increasing destruction of nature. They do not reside in particular short-term fluctuations, medium-term cycles and crises, and long-term waves of accumulation but in the social relations that produce these phenomena. The pursuit of neoliberalism has brought these limits ever closer.

Four main forms of neoliberalism emerged in the last three decades of the twentieth century (for a useful survey of the social construction of neoliberalism as an intellectual-professional project, a repertoire of policies and a form of politics, see Mudge 2008). None involves a simple return to the nineteenth-century liberalism analysed so well by Polanyi (1944), even if some of the crisis symptoms associated with the treatment of land, labour-power and money as if they were real commodities appear very similar today to those in the period that Polanyi studied. Rather these forms emerged in reaction to the crisis of post-war models of capitalist development, including Atlantic Fordism in advanced capitalist economies, import-substitution industrialisation in Latin America and sub-Saharan Africa, export-oriented growth in East Asia and, in a different context, state socialism in the Soviet Bloc. The four main forms are presented as points on a continuum rather than in terms of chronological succession and we should note that they overlap at the margins.

The most radical form of neoliberalism was *neoliberal system transformation* in the national states that emerged from the former Soviet Bloc with Russia and Poland providing the two best-known examples from many. This involved a tabula rasa approach in which the 'creative destruction' of inherited state socialist institutions was expected to lead somehow to the spontaneous emergence of a fully functioning liberal market economy and society and a more gradual development of liberal democracy. Next in the continuum comes *neoliberal regime shifts* such as that from post-war settlements in Atlantic Fordism, which were based on an institutionalised compromise between capital and labour, towards economic policies that promote liberalisation, deregulation, privatisation, market proxies in the public sector, internationalisation and reduced direct taxation. These policies were intended to modify the balance of forces in favour of capital and have largely, if ultimately disastrously, succeeded in this regard (cf. Howard and King 2008).

The blowback from this success is now working its way through many regions of world society. Well-known cases are Thatcherism and Reaganism but similar shifts occurred in advanced capitalist economies such as Australia, Canada, New Zealand and, most recently, Iceland. While typically introduced by parties on the right of the political spectrum, neoliberal regime shifts have also been supported by centre-left parties, often under a 'Third Way' label. Moreover, with a little help from Northern friends and/or military dictatorships, many Latin American economies undertook such shifts (albeit in a context of crises, especially when they involve high levels of debt and high inflation, in the previously dominant ISI growth model rather than in reaction to the crisis-tendencies of the Atlantic Fordist model) from the 1970s through to the 1990s (for a discussion of the intellectual, professional and imperial roots of neoliberal regime shifts in North *and* South, see Delazay and Garth 2002). Indeed, the first major neoliberal experiment was tried by 'los Chicago Boys' in Chile under General Pinochet following his US-backed military coup d'état in 1973.

Whereas the second form largely emerges from domestic politics, whether in liberal democratic or authoritarian regimes, the third form comprises economic restructuring processes and regime shifts that were primarily imposed from outside by the leading capitalist powers and transnational economic institutions and organisations. This typically involves adopting the neoliberal policies in line with the 'Washington Consensus' as part of the price to be paid for financial and other assistance to crisis-ridden capitalist economies in parts of Africa, Asia, Eastern and Central Europe, and Latin America (e.g. Gowan 1996; Gwynne and Kay 2000; Robinson 2008; Saad-Filho and Johnson 2005; Sader 2008; Veltmeyer *et al.* 1997). Whether neoliberalism originates mainly in domestic or external political processes and its associated policies are pursued through democratic or authoritarian political devices and measures, there is often some overlap between the policies adopted in the second and third forms of neoliberalism when they occur outside advanced capitalist economies.

Fourth, there are more pragmatic and potentially reversible neoliberal policy adjustments. These comprise modest changes deemed necessary to maintain alternative economic and social models in the face of internationalisation and a global shift in the balance of forces. The Nordic social democracies and Rhenish capitalism provide some examples (cf. Becker 2007; Cox 2001; Lavelle 2007; Lindblom and Rothstein 2005; Streeck 2009).

The highpoint of neoliberalism occurred during the 1990s,[1] when there was a largely contingent combination of neoliberal system transformation, a stepwise shift from 'roll-back' to 'roll-forward' policies in neoliberal regimes, a temporary ascendance of cyclical neoliberal policy adjustments, and continuing efforts to impose neoliberal structural adjustment at almost every opportunity and in almost every country. This conjuncture enabled neoliberal triumphalists and neoconservative cheerleaders to proclaim that the whole world had become neoliberal or would soon do so. By the mid-1990s, however, there were signs that neoliberalism was failing on all fronts. Neoliberal system transformation had failed as a 'grand project', neoliberal regime shifts required flanking and supplementing by 'Third Way' policies, networks and public–private partner-ships, neoliberal policy adjustments rarely led to lasting neoliberal regime shifts even where that is a long-term aspiration, and the quack cure of neoliberal struc-tural adjustment can aggravate the underlying disease, leading, in Latin America, to the revival of populist politics more or less committed to distancing govern-ments from the worst excesses of neoliberalism.

Do these tendencies towards neoliberal failure justify ignoring neoliberalism or treating it as just one complex trend among many? No. We must also consider:

1   the geo-economic and geo-political effects of the failed neoliberal system transformation;
2   externally imposed structural adjustments;
3   the continuing efforts as late as 2008 to roll forward neoliberalism (Peck and Tickell 2002) and to introduce flanking and supporting mechanisms and policies to maintain the momentum of neoliberal regime shifts in the face of mounting resistance and/or growing signs of failure;
4   the alternation of policy adjustments where a neoliberal regime shift did not occur; and
5   the path-dependent legacies of the neoliberal highpoint taken as a whole, not only in narrowly economic but also in broader political and ideological terms.

It also matters whether neoliberalism occurs through 'normal' domestic politics in advanced capitalist economies or results from the 'exceptional' imposition of neoliberal policies and politics (sometimes in 'emergency conditions' and/or under military rule) in the struggle among rival capitalist and state interests for markets and domination in dependent (and often crisis-ridden) capitalist econo-mies. Neoliberal policies also shape the forms, timing and dynamics of economic crises (broadly understood) in regions where neoliberalism is still largely absent. For the global pursuit of neoliberalism tends to disrupt the structured coherence of modes of regulation and/or governance that are concerned to manage medium-to long-term material interdependencies rather maximise short-term financial returns.

Neoliberalism and economic determination

To establish why neoliberalisms have been and, despite their various crisis-tendencies and the current crisis, continue to be so influential on a world scale, it is useful to consider four forms of economic determinism, each of which is rooted in agential as well as structural causes.

•   Economic determination in the first instance. This can be expressed in the cliché that wealth must first be produced before it can be distributed or, in terms more relevant to capitalist social formations, value must be produced before it can be realised, redistributed and reallocated. This form of determination entails the primacy of productive capital and highlights the problems of the growing disjunction under neoliberalism between the real economy and the pseudo-validation of financial speculation in asset bubbles and artificial liquidity (on the latter, see Nesvetailova 2007). The scope for economic determination in this prosaic sense increases insofar as profit-oriented, market-mediated exchange extends into areas where other principles of social organisation once prevailed.

- Economic domination is rooted in control over strategic resources in a given supply or production chain or the wider economy, e.g. oil in the industrial Fordist economy (and, indeed, post-Fordism) or, more recently, patents in the contemporary knowledge-based economy, access to liquid capital in a systemic liquidity crunch, or, in the near future, water in many areas that will suffer from drought due to climate change. By analogy, economic domination also includes the relative 'strike' or 'blackmail power' of economic forces vis-à-vis non-economic agents, organisations, and institutional orders that depend on access to specific economic inputs.
- Economic hegemony derives from the capacity, linked in part to 'soft power' as well as material factors, to secure the primacy of a given techno-economic paradigm, business model or accumulation strategy, thereby leading other economic and extra-economic forces to internalise the hegemonic approach or, at least, to adapt their strategies to it.
- Ecological dominance is grounded in the capacity of the profit-oriented, market-mediated capitalist economic order taken as a whole – including its extra-economic supports – to shape other ensembles of social action more than they affect it. This includes the impact of both positive and negative externalities. Ecological dominance does not involve an automatic, one-sided *relation of domination* in which the prevailing form and dynamic of the economy always and everywhere unilaterally imposes its logic on other systems. For, as Morin (1980: 44) notes, there is no 'last instance' in relations of ecological dominance. Instead it should be regarded as always differential, relational, contingent and reversible. As we shall see below, analogous forms of ecological dominance can also characterise the relations among different fractions or forms of capital and different varieties of capitalism in the world market.

While these four forms of economic determination are materially and ideationally related to class domination, they are nonetheless analytically distinct from the latter. Economic class domination occurs in and through the struggle for dominance in the wage relation, the structuring and regularising of the circuits of capital and, more generally, the articulation of forms of labour and modes of growth in the world market. In turn, political class domination involves struggles over state formation and restructuring and state policies within and beyond the state insofar as these bear on the capacity to secure the expanded reproduction of capital within the world market. Ideological class domination involves struggles over means of mental production, ideological forms and specific imaginaries to bring people into conformity with the particular requirements of expanded repro-duction (cf. Gramsci 1971). All three modes of class domination affect the forms of economic determination but, depending on the prevailing balance of forces, may reinforce or undermine them (cf. Jessop 2002).

Factors favouring the ecological dominance of the capital relation

Neoliberalism privileges the exchange-value over the use-value aspect of all forms of the capital relation and tends to judge all economic activities in terms of the prevailing global average rate of profit. For it is capital in its exchange-value aspect that is most easily disembedded from broader socio-spatial-tempo-ral contexts and thereby freed to 'flow' relatively smoothly through space-time. Unsurprisingly, then, the pursuit of neoliberalism tends to privilege hypermobile financial capital at the expense of capitals that are embedded in broader sets of social relations and/or that must be valorised in particular times and places. It also encourages the extension of profit-oriented, market-mediated accumulation into spaces where it was previously absent. Moreover, even after the neoliberal highpoint had passed in the late 1990s, the dominant neoliberal economic, polit-ical and ideological forces still attempted to use multi- and bi-lateral domination to impose neoliberal measures on those responsible for managing economies that had not yet embarked on a neoliberal path. This sometimes occurred with the complicity of fractions of national capital or the interior bourgeoisie[2] and/or of compliant state managers.

Within the overall societal (or global) division of institutional labour, the capacity of a specific institutional order (such as the market economy, the legal system, political authority, the military-police order, education, science and so on)[3] to become ecologically dominant over others can be related to seven aspects of the social world (see Table 2.1). All seven aspects can characterise various social orders but they are closely associated, as we shall see, with the logic of capitalism, especially when the capital relation is generalised to a world scale in line with neoliberal principles.

First, as the capitalist market economy becomes increasingly disembedded from other institutional orders, direct external pressures on the market economy tend to diminish. Instead, internal competition tends to become the most power-ful driver of accumulation insofar as external pressures are mediated through the competition among individual capitals to profit from such pressures and/or to move capital elsewhere (including in liquid assets) to escape them. Furthermore, as financial capital tends to control the most liquid, abstract and generalised expression of capital, it is better placed to respond to short-term profit opportun-ities and threats (Bryan and Rafferty 2006).

Second, the anarchy of market forces and the dual role of the price mechan-ism in re-allocating capital and enabling learning and reflexivity on the part of economic actors mean that the profit-oriented, market-mediated economy tends, other things being equal, to have superior (but by no means infinite) capacities to tolerate exogenous disturbances. In particular, it has more internal complexity (multiplicity and heterogeneity of elements), looser coupling among these elements, and a higher degree of self-reflexivity thanks to the workings of the price mechanism. It is mainly through these flexible forms of competition and the resulting scope for local variation that capital as a social relation adapts to external perturbations (on the plurality of local neoliberalisms, neglect of which leads to the underestimation of the survival power of neoliberalism, see Peck and Tickell 2002).

Third, and relatedly, because money can dissociate economic transactions in time and place, capital can extend its operations in time and space (time-space

Table 2.1 Factors relevant to ecological dominance in the relations among societal systems

Internal	• Scope for continuous self-transformation because internal competitive pressures are more important than external adaptive pressures in the dynamic of a given system. • Extent of internal structural and operational complexity and the resulting scope for spontaneous self-adaptation in the face of perturbation or disruption (regardless of the external or internal origin of adaptive pressures). • Capacity to distantiate and/or compress its operations in time and space (i.e. to engage in time-space distantiation and/or time-space compression) to exploit the widest possible range of opportunities for self-reproduction.
Transversal	• Capacity to displace its internal contradictions, paradoxes and dilemmas onto other systems, into the environment, or defer them into the future. • Capacity to redesign other systems and shape their evolution by context-steering (especially through organisations that have a primary functional orientation and also offer a meeting space for other functional systems)a and/or constitutional (re)design.
External	• Extent to which other actors accept its operations as central to societal reproduction and orient their operations in this light (e.g. integrating its needs into their own decision-making premises and programmes as naturalised constraints). Organisations also have a key role here through their ability to react to the irritations and expectations of several functional systems. • Extent to which a given system is the main source of external adaptive pressure on other systems (e.g. through the impact of recurrent system failures, worsening social exclusion and positive feedback effects)b and/ or is more important than their respective internal pressures for system development.

Source: modified version of Jessop (2007).

Notes
a Luhmann notes that the structural coupling of function systems is especially promoted by organi-sations whose multi-functionality is the most likely to be disturbed by artificial distinctions among systems (1997, 2000).
b Luhmann (2002: 55), as cited by Wagner (2006: 5).

distantiation) and/or compress them in these regards (time-space compression). The mutual reinforcement of these processes facilitates real-time integration in and across the world market and gives capital greater flexibility to reorganise its activities.

Fourth, through these and other mechanisms, the expanded reproduction of capital tends to weaken the structural constraints associated with other institutional orders or societal systems and/or to resist their agents' efforts to control the economy. Capital can do this through its internal operations in time (discounting, insurance, risk management, futures, derivatives, hedge funds etc.) or space (capital flight, relocation, outsourcing abroad, claims to extra-territoriality etc.) as well as by extending the logic of exchange value into other systems, the public sphere and everyday life. This increases the 'indifference' of the profit-oriented, market-mediated economy to its environment (Lohmann 1991). Such indifference is very typical of international finance, which is more tightly integrated – for better or worse – on a global scale than other forms of capital. Nonetheless finance capital (let alone capital in general) cannot escape its long-term material dependence on the principle of economic determination in the first instance or its functional dependence on other institutional orders; and it always remains the prisoner of its own crisis-tendencies. Thus the massively disproportionate over-accumulation of financial capital enabled by its dissociation from, and indifference to, other moments of the capital relation eventually led to the bursting of financial bubbles around the world. More generally, as the world market grows in the shadow of the ecological dominance of neoliberalism, all its contradictions are generalised and come into play.

Fifth, compared to natural evolution, social agents attempt to redesign their environment, their evolutionary potential, and even to change modes of social evolution (Willke 1997). In addition to the immense innovative capacities within the market economy, with all its implications for social evolution, we should also note scope for redesigning the rules that govern the market economy and the ways in which it is embedded in the wider social formations. Neoliberal system transformation, neoliberal regime shifts and neoliberal structural adjustment all involve in their different ways efforts to redesign the framework within which class struggle, competition and accumulation occur, modifying thereby the capacity for exchange-value to become ecologically dominant. The strategic selectivities of the state and the changing balance of forces are both crucial here. This leads us to the sixth point.

Sixth, the primacy of accumulation over other principles of societalisation (e.g. national security, 'racial' supremacy, religious fundamentalism, adherence to the rule of law, social solidarity) is related to the power of their respective self-descriptions and social values, especially as articulated and represented in the public sphere and, above all, the mass media in the course of struggles for political, intellectual and moral leadership. The influence of such self-descriptions and values in everyday language and the mass media is seen in the role of economic considerations in choosing among alternatives in a non-economic institutional or organisational context, e.g. in designing school curricula, choosing research topics or deciding what is newsworthy. Struggles over the hegemony of diverse principles of societal organisation will be easier where the relevant institutional order is internally organised, like the world economy, on the basis of centre–periphery relations and/or stratification rather than in a segmented fashion with essentially similar units, such as sovereign territorial states (Luhmann 1996).[4] Hegemonic struggle is also easier where social forces that cross-cut functional systems seek to coordinate their respective operations via positive or negative coordination. A power bloc organised through parallel power networks provides an important mechanism of system and social integration in this regard (Poulantzas 1978; Baecker 2001).

Seventh, as a correlate of the first factor, and expressing the point in systems-theoretical terms, an ecologically dominant system is the primary source of external adaptive pressure on other systems. Translated into the current terminology, as the world market grows more complex, the environment of other institutional orders, institutions, organisations and networks becomes more complex too, forcing them to increase their internal complexity to remain operationally autonomous. Moreover, as Wagner (2006) notes, where the failures of one system (or order) have a disproportionate impact on other systems (or orders), this also reinforces its ecological dominance. This holds not only for the impact of market failures on resources and revenues required by other systems but also for the more general social repercussions of economic crises in an integrated world market. This is very clear in the dynamics of the current world recession (or, perhaps, imminent depression) insofar as it is the failures of neoliberalism more than its previous limited successes that are forcing the most significant adaptations elsewhere within social formations up to and including world society.

While these seven factors tend to promote the ecological dominance of the profit-oriented, market-mediated economy (as much, if not more, through its negative as through its positive externalities), other institutional orders (or, in systems-theoretical terms, societal subsystems) may gain short-term primacy in response to non-economic crises. No single institutional order represents, or can substitute for, the whole. Even an ecologically dominant system depends on the socially adequate performance of other systems and a normally subordinate system may become dominant in exceptional circumstances. This would occur, for example, where a non-economic crisis must be solved to reproduce the entire social formation – including the market economy. For example, during major wars or preparations for them, states may try to plan or guide the economy in the light of perceived military-political needs. After genuine or spurious states of emergency have ended, however, the primacy of accumulation is likely to be re-asserted even if there are path-dependent traces of such exceptional conditions in the normally dominant system.

How neoliberal globalisation favoured capital's ecological dominance

The *always tendential* ecological dominance of capitalism is closely related to how far its internal competition, internal complexity and loose coupling, scope for self-reorganisation, ability to engage in time-space distantiation and compression, displacement and deferral of problems, and hegemonic capacities are freed from confinement within limited 'ecological' spaces established by another societal system (such as the Westphalian interstate system with its mutually exclusive sovereign territorial states). This is where globalisation, especially in its neoliberal form, promotes the relative ecological dominance of the world market by expanding the scope for expanded capitalist reproduction to escape such political constraints. Neoliberalism promotes the opening of the world market and reduces the frictions introduced by national 'power containers'. It reinforces the dominance of exchange-value within economic organisation and frees money capital (the most abstract expression of the capital relation) to move at will in search of profit worldwide (Jessop 2002).

Liberalisation, de-regulation, privatisation, administrative commodification, internationalisation and the lowering of direct taxes all boost the scope for internal variation and selection in the profit-oriented, market-mediated economy. Along with commitment to shareholder value, this benefits hypermobile financial capital, reinforcing its competitiveness and ratcheting up its ability to displace and defer problems onto other economic actors and interests, other systems and the natural environment. Yet this also enhances the scope for the contradictions and dilemmas of a relatively unfettered (or disembedded) capitalism to shape the performance of other systems, undermining crucial extra-economic conditions for accumulation.

Even after the global neoliberal highpoint has passed and all the contradictions of neoliberalism have come into play, neoliberal logic still dominates world society through the path-dependent effects of policies, strategies and structural shifts that occurred during the highpoint and the continuing attempts to impose that logic. This is particularly (but by no means exclusively) associated with the global ecological dominance (using the term somewhat differently here) of the US economy in the world market and, as noted above, the ecological dominance of the world market within world society as a whole. This remains the case even in the current crisis for two major reasons: first, the weight of the US economy in financial and material terms in the world market, in spite (and, indeed, because) of the many disproportions with which it is associated on a world scale; and, second, the continued attraction of the dollar as a world currency in the unfolding crisis. In a crisis-ridden global economy significantly reshaped by various forms of neoliberalism, the failures of neoliberalism are causing more problems for other forms of economic organisation at different scales than other economic regimes had previously engendered for neoliberalism. Likewise the dynamics of a world market working in the shadow of neoliberalism cause more problems for the rest of world society than other systems can cause in the long-term for the economy.

Recognising the significance of neoliberalism in these respects indicates the need for a change in perspective on the place of the United States in the world market and world society. Often discussed as an economic superpower and/or as a hemispheric or global hegemon, the United States no longer enjoys the

economic domination and multiple hegemonies that it exercised in the immediate post-war economic order. At that time the United States enjoyed the
benefits of economic dominance through its technological supremacy, control
over oil reserves and other strategic commodities, gold and foreign currency
reserves, possession of the master currency, and 'soft' power exercised through
the cultural industries and ideological state apparatuses. Its rulers were willing to
sacrifice immediate economic interests for long-term global advantage by enabling economic rivals to join, directly or indirectly, an expanding international
economy. In the last two decades the United States has been losing this dominance, including in relation to Brazil, Russia, India and China as well as an
expanding European Union and Japan. The US neoliberal regime shift was a
response to this crisis in political hegemony and economic dominance but failed
to reverse the loss of US political hegemony (despite its appeal in post-socialist
economies) or the overall decline of US economic dominance (witness the continuing fiscal, budgetary and trade deficits in the US economy). As we have seen
especially clearly in the last two years, however, the United States still retains
the (destructive) power of ecological dominance. This still causes more problems for other economies than they seem able to cause for the moment for the
US economy. Indeed, neoliberalism was the US response to previous challenges
from these quarters.

The threats posed by deteriorating extra-economic conditions necessary for
continued accumulation and growing international trade and financial imbalances with other economic players (especially Japan and, more recently, China)
have long threatened the stability of the world market and, a fortiori, world
society. But the capacity to displace and defer the contradictions of neoliberalism onto other spaces and times has reached its limits as 'blowback' (using
Chalmers Johnson's term (2000)) has brought them back home, showing that
neoliberalism also has massive potential to damage the growth dynamic of the
US economy too. The coupling of the US and Chinese economies proved especially damaging, aiding the unsustainable growth of production in China and
consumption in the United States. The current global recession (and anticipated
depression) may forcibly re-impose the necessary proportionalities in the global
circuit of capital that have proved impossible to resolve politically. In addition to
the dramatic bursting of asset bubbles, we are likely to see an intensification of
financial mercantilism, 'competitive austerity' policies, trade wars and deepening imperialist rivalries.

These positive feedback effects are especially significant in the current period
because of the specific neoliberal and neoconservative policies pursued under
the exceptional political regime presided over by George W. Bush and its domination by a distinctive set of particular capitalist interests that are far from
general even among US capitalists. In contrast with the normal form of the capitalist type of state, a bourgeois democratic republic, in which class power is
largely structural and rendered invisible through the normal functioning of free
markets and political democracy, government under Bush more and more
assumed the form of an exceptional regime captured by special interests, seeking

to neutralise or dismantle democratic institutions and the normal play of democracy, and rendering class power in the United States ever more visible. In this regard the war on terrorism and promotion of self-help through 'faith communities' became 'exceptional' flanking mechanisms of an increasingly irrational pursuit of neoliberalism and neoconservatism. This contrasts with the earlier turn in neoliberal regimes to 'Third Way' rhetoric and policy solutions to facilitate the transition from roll-back to roll-forward neoliberalism (for example, under Clinton and Blair). In this sense, the ecological dominance of neoliberalism was crucially mediated (and made less accountable than normal) through the exceptional nature of its primary political protagonist.

Indeed, it is arguable that the 'war on terrorism' introduces a temporary rise in the primacy of security and the territorial logic of the state at the expense of accumulation – which is reflected in the US economy in problems in securing skilled knowledge workers from abroad and in the intensification of federal government deficits. But this does not mean that the close of the Bush regime will remove instantly the economic and political legacies of neoliberalism's ecological dominance. At most it will end this particular political mediation of neoliberalism without stopping the rearguard action of neoliberal political forces or the continuing contestation of neoliberal think tanks and other intellectual forces. The legacies of neoliberal financial capital within the circuit of capital and the impact of shareholder value as the supreme value in corporate governance will continue to shape the prospects for economic recovery for many years.

The ecological dominance of finance over other capital fractions

It is tempting now that the financial bubble has burst to focus on the long-term future of capitalism and ignore the irrationality of unregulated finance-led accumulation. The logic of financialisation (wherever it occurs, i.e. not just in the operations of US financial capital, if, indeed, this can be said to comprise a distinct fraction of capital outside the wider global financial system) undermines or restricts the operation of economic determination in the first instance (i.e. the primacy of productive capital) within overall dynamics of accumulation. In contrast with the structured coherence of Fordism and the post-Fordist knowledge-based economy, a neoliberal financial regime tends to undermine the structured coherence of accumulation regimes and their regulation. In particular, it weakens the spatio-temporal fixes with which regimes based on the primacy of productive capital manage the contradictions between fixity and motion in order to produce zones of relative stability by deferring and displacing their effects.

This can be seen in the impact of financialisation not only in Atlantic Fordism but also in the export-oriented economies of East Asia and the viability of import-substitution industrialisation strategies in Latin America and Africa. The destructive impact of financialisation in this regard is reinforced through the neoliberal approach to accumulation through dispossession (especially the politically-licensed plundering of public assets and the intellectual commons) and the dynamic of uneven development (enabling financial capital to move on when the disastrous effects of financialisation weaken those productive capitals that have to be valorised in particular times and places). It is also supported by the growing markets opened for the 'symbionts and parasites' of ecologically dominant capital fractions in their heartlands – which have their own forms of uneven development on regional, national and global scales. This is reflected in the growing antagonism between the globalising knowledge-based economy as the material and ideological expression of productive capital and the logic of a finance-led, shareholder-value oriented process of capital accumulation. We can note here that the crisis of neoliberal finance-led accumulation is stimulating calls for re-industrialisation in economies that had pursued the former path.

Conclusions

This chapter has argued that the logic of roll-back neoliberalism remains ecologically dominant in the world market despite the accelerating movement away from the neoliberal highpoint more than a decade ago. Given the nature of ecological dominance, it will be far harder to roll back the legacies of 'roll-back' neoliberalism on a world scale and/or to tame it through the recently tried flanking and supporting mechanisms of roll-forward neoliberalism on the same scale than it proved in national states where mechanisms of political accountability through normal forms of bourgeois politics were able to operate. Whether or not the new Obama administration signifies more than a rhetorical break with a failed neoliberal regime shift remains to be seen – the signs at the time of writing (late January 2009) remain uncertain. This apart, it is now a major concern that the ecological dominance of neoliberalism may be ended by the ecological dominance of the natural environment in a period of growing environmental crisis. As yet, however, there is no unified struggle against neoliberalism or the logic of accumulation on a world scale; and there is no common global space for a unified struggle.

Notes

1 These dates reflect:

   1   the development of neoliberal system transformation following the dissolution of the Soviet Bloc from 1989–91, which added the fourth form of neoliberalism to the others; and
   2   the rise of the Third Way in the UK and United States during the mid-1990s and its subsequent spread to other countries, the growing popular rejection of neoliberalism in Latin America and the rise of communist successor parties in Eastern and Central Europe committed to alternative policies.

   The 'Asian Crisis' in the late 1990s nonetheless gave a temporary fillip to imposed neoliberal structural adjustment policies.

2 This is the term introduced by Poulantzas to describe nationally-based fractions of transnational capital (1975).

3 For the idea of the division of labour in this context and its relation to specific logics of social organization, see, *inter alia*, Marx and Engels on *The German Ideology* and Engels' letters on historical materialism (especially to Conrad Schmidt in Berlin).

4 Centre–periphery relations refer to differentiation in terms of geographical cores and peripheries (e.g. the economic hegemony and domination of US capitalism in Atlantic Fordism and of the industrial and financial heartlands of the quasi-continental US economy in relation to their respective hinterlands); and stratification refers to the hierarchical organisation of social relations, with an upper class organised on national, macro-regional (e.g. European or transatlantic), or even transnational lines (e.g. the World Economic Forum).

References

Baecker, D. (2001) 'Managing Corporations in Networks'. *Thesis Eleven* 66, pp. 80–98.

Becker, U. (2007) 'The Scandinavian Model: Still an Example for Europe?'. *Internationale Politik und Gesellschaft* 4, pp. 41–57.

Bryan, D. and Rafferty, M. (2006) *Capitalism with Derivatives: a Political Economy of Financial Derivatives, Capital and Class.* Basingstoke: Palgrave.

Cox, R.H. (2001) 'The Social Construction of an Imperative: why Welfare Reform happened in Denmark and the Netherlands but not in Germany'. *World Politics* 53, pp. 463–98.

Delazay, Y. and Garth, B.G. (2002) *The Internationalization of Palace Wars: Lawyers, Economists, and the Contest to Transform Latin American States.* Chicago: University of Chicago Press.

Gowan, P. (1996) 'Eastern Europe, Western Power and Neo-Liberalism'. *New Left Review* I/216, pp. 129–40.

Gramsci, A. (1971) *Selections from the Prison Notebooks.* London: Lawrence & Wishart.

Gwynne, R.N. and Kay, C. (2000) 'Views from the Periphery: Futures of Neoliberalism in Latin America'. *Third World Quarterly* 21 (1), pp. 141–56.

Howard, M. and King, J. (2008) *The Rise of Neoliberalism in Advanced Capitalist Economies: a Materialist Analysis.* Basingstoke: Palgrave.

Jessop, B. (2002) *The Future of the Capitalist State.* Cambridge: Polity.

Jessop, B. (2007) 'What follows Neo-Liberalism? The Deepening Contradictions of US Domination and the Struggle for a New Global Order'. In R. Albritton, R. Jessop, and R. Westra (eds) *Political Economy and Global Capitalism: The 21st Century, Present and Futures.* London: Anthem, pp. 67–88.

Johnson, C.J. (2000) *Blowback: the Costs and Consequences of American Empire.* London: Little, Brown.

Lavelle, A.D. (2007) 'Social Democracy or Neo-Liberalism? The Cases of Germany and Sweden'. In G. Curran and E. Van Acker (eds) *Globalising Government Business Relations.* Frenchs Forest: Pearson Education Australia.

Lindblom, A. and Rothstein, B. (2005) 'The Mysterious Survival of the Swedish Welfare State'. Paper presented at Conference of the American Political Science Association, 2–5 September, Chicago.

Lohmann, G. (1991) *Indifferenz und Gesellschaft. Eine kritische Auseinandersetzung mit Marx.* Frankfurt: Suhrkamp.

Luhmann, N. (1996) 'Politics and Economics'. *Thesis Eleven* 53, pp. 1–9.

Luhmann, N. (1997) *Die Gesellschaft der Gesellschaft.* Frankfurt: Suhrkamp.

Luhmann, N. (2000) *Organisation und Entscheidung.* Opladen: Westdeutscher Verlag.

Luhmann, N. (2002) *Einführung in die Systemtheorie.* Heidelberg: Carl Auer.

Marx, K. (1972) *Capital, Volume III.* London: Lawrence & Wishart.

Marx, K. (1973) Introduction. In K. Marx, *Grundrisse.* Harmondsworth: Penguin, pp. 81–111.

Marx, K. (1976) Speech of Dr Marx on Protection, Free Trade, and the Working Classes. In *Marx-Engels Collected Works*, vol. 6. London: Lawrence & Wishart, pp. 287–90.

Morin, E. (1980) *La méthode: volume 2. La vie de la vie*. Paris: Seuil.

Mudge, S.L. (2008) 'What is Neo-Liberalism?'. *Socio-Economic Review* 6 (4), pp. 703–31.

Nesvetailova, A. (2007) *Fragile Finance: Debt, Speculation and Crisis in the Age of Global Credit*. Basingstoke: Palgrave.

Polanyi, K. (1944) *The Great Transformation: the Political and Economic Origins of Our Time*. New York: Rinehart & Company.

Poulantzas, N. (1975) *Classes in Contemporary Capitalism*. London: New Left Books.

Poulantzas, N. (1978) *State, Power, Socialism*. London: New Left Books.

Peck, J. and A. Tickell (2002) 'Neoliberalizing Space'. *Antipode* 34 (3), pp. 380–404.

Robinson, W.I. (2008) *Latin America and Global Capitalism: a Critical Globalization Perspective*. Baltimore: Johns Hopkins University Press.

Saad-Filho, A. and Johnson, D. (eds) (2005) *Neo-Liberalism: A Critical Reader*. London: Pluto.

Sader, E. (2008) 'The Weakest Link: Neoliberalism in Latin America'. *New Left Review* II/52, pp. 5–32.

Streeck, W. (2009) *Re-Forming Capitalism: Institutional Change in the German Political Economy*. Oxford: Oxford University Press.

Veltmeyer, H., Petras, J. and Vieux, S. (eds) (1997) *Neoliberalism and Class Conflict in Latin America: a Comparative Perspective on the Political Economy of Structural Adjustment*. Basingstoke: Palgrave.

Wagner, T. (2006) 'Funktionale Differenzierung und ein ökonomischer Primat?'. Online, available at www.sozialarbeit.ch/dokumente/oeknomischer_primat.pdf (last accessed 29 January 2009).

Willke, H. (1997) *Die Supervision des Staates*. Frankfurt: Suhrkamp.

3   Globalisation as a crisis form

Ergin Yıldızoğlu

We are going through an exceptionally interesting period in the history of the capitalist mode of production. The financial crisis, which started in early 2007, ushered in a new zeitgeist affecting the way the economy and society are generally understood among the politicians, managers of the economy and universities, as well as among the people at large during the past 25–30 years.

Then, the present and the future were all about neoliberalism and globalisation. Now these key concepts – almost 'master signifiers' giving meaning to many other economic and political phenomena – are progressively coming under scrutiny even in the pages of some of the truly global and globalist publications such as the *Financial Times*. With their high-power columnists, these publications had spearheaded the attempts to popularise the idea that there were no alternatives to neoliberalism and that it was futile to resist globalisation which was irreversible and truly global. Today they are no longer certain that globalisation indeed has a future, because as even Martin Wolf accepts, it is a human product and could easily be reversed.[1]

What a reversal of fortune for the globalisers! During the previous financial turbulences of 1997–2001, it was all about more neoliberalism and further globalisation. Insufficient liberalisation and a stubborn resistance to neoliberal reforms and globalisation were then judged to be the main causes of those severe turbulences. It is true that since the Asian crisis globalisation has been in tatters. There were complaints about the unfair distribution of its fruits or about the perils of 'military globalisation'; there was the collapse of World Trade Organisation's Doha Round of negotiations and the emerging resistance of the developing countries within the newly formed G20 group which made it easier for them to resist the pressures of the highly developed and rich block of G8 countries. There was of course the brief episode of a global uprising against globalisation, between the World Trade Organisation meeting in Seattle in November 1999 and the US invasion of Iraq in 2003. Still, the arguments of the globalists had generally prevailed, their place in 'the dictionary of the acquired ideas' seemed forever secured.

These days, due to the increasingly common observations amongst the opinion-makers of the media and popular economists on the 'state-led globalisation', and the ominous warnings about the dangers of a Great Depression harking back to the 1930s – or even the possibility of a systemic collapse – the globalist ideas seems to be irreversibly in retreat. A new zeitgeist is now taking shape and it is all about the 'end of an era', the turning of a page or leaving something behind. It is not about a new beginning. The new zeitgeist is only about an ending. Simply because we do not know what awaits us at the end of this period of transition (or collapse for the pessimistic). What is happening? Or more aptly what has happened? How should one understand 'now' and start thinking about 'tomorrow'? This chapter argues that, if globalisation is considered to be a form belonging to the recurring crises of the capitalist mode of production, and neoliberalism is thought as a mode of a crisis management that eventually exhausted itself after serving its purpose, it may be easier to think about the period we are leaving behind than the new period of uncertainty unfolding in front of us.

Did you say globalisation?

The concepts of globalisation and globalism have played an important role in the introduction, acceptance and implementation of neoliberalism in the developing countries (the 'peripheries'). Although globalisation was famously referred to by Valéry Giscard D'Estaing in the 1970s, in the context of the so-called 'irresistible global forces', and by Ronald Reagan as a project and as part of his fight against the 'evil empire', globalisation emerged as a buzzword at the beginning of the 1990s. In other words, the concept of globalisation entered our academic lexicon and our popular discourse at the same time that, first, the recession following the 1987 stock-market crash hit the centres of the world economy; second, a new economic space opened up to the valorisation of capital after the collapse of the Berlin Wall, presenting new opportunities for the 'spatial and temporal fixes' in capitalism, as discussed by David Harvey; third, financialisation was accelerating on the back of the transition to neoliberalism in the 'emerging markets', and US economic and cultural leadership was in decline: in Henry Kissinger's words, a foreign policy paradigm crisis emerged just as the Cold War had ended.

Globalisation as a new concept entered into conventional discourses almost as a metaphysical phenomenon: it was an unavoidable, unstoppable and irreversible process. It was everywhere and it did not have a subject (agency). It rapidly became the expression of the international economic and cultural leadership of the United States, and triggered a heated debate around the question of 'what is globalisation', almost creating a new industry in itself.[2]

However, ten years later, when David Held and Anthony McGrew collected the key arguments in the globalisation debate in a major book (Held and McGrew 2000), they concluded that there was still no agreement on what globalisation meant and no commonly accepted definition of globalisation. Still, they were convinced that the globalisation debate had produced two discernible trends: globalists argued that globalisation was an entirely new epoch in human history, while sceptics maintained that it was just an ideological construct, a myth. At the early stages of this debate, it seemed that the concept of globalisation pushed the notion of imperialism outside the debate in international relations; however, over time both sides of the argument have become more clearly articulated.

First, globalisation seemed to have certain features distinguishing it from the preceding period, and it developed a particular internal dynamic. On this basis, it could be seen as a new era or episode in the history of capitalism. But, when it came to defining this new era or episode, there seemed to be, as Justin Rosenberg (2001) rightly pointed out, a significant confusion at the centre of the debates about globalisation. Neither the observations on the increasing pace and density of the newly established social and economic links on the global scale, nor the arguments on de-territorialisation, could remove this confusion. Second, globalisation evidently displays certain secular features, including the acceleration in the movement of financial capital, commodities and people, a discernible increase in the fluidity of the social relations, an opening up of new territories to the valorisation of capital, the compression of time and space, and the emergence of related sensibilities. Therefore, it must be much more than a myth. However none of these secular trends are entirely new. It is possible to observe very similar trends in the period extending from the last quarter of the nineteenth century to the first quarter of the twentieth. In sum, although it is not entirely accurate to label globalisation as a myth, it is also possible to recognise it as an ideological construct representing and legitimising a series of material and secular developments corresponding to certain class interests in the global social formation.

A matter of perspective

Clearly, neither the globalist nor the sceptic approach opens up completely satisfactory avenues allowing the study of the phenomena included in the concept of globalisation. Neither is it possible to synthesise the best elements within these approaches. Therefore, the solution requires a change of perspective. For instance, one could start with the question of 'why' rather than 'what is globalisation?', and examine the reasons for the acceleration in the circulation of capital, commodities and people. Here, however, there is first a need to clarify *what type* of globalisation is at issue, because there may be more than one form of globalisation.

If globalisation is examined with reference to the verb 'to globalise', it could mean to transform something (the world economy) into a globe: a continuous surface that is not infinite, but that has no boundaries. Evidently, humans are symbolising animals and their civilisation has been globalising the world by continuously establishing symbolic (social, political, economic, religious and linguistic) as well as material (roads, markets) networks. Furthermore, because every technological shift and every new mode of production imprints this evolving process of globalisation, it is possible to identify one process which started in Europe around the fifteenth century. It was within this process that the rest of the world began to be globalised, and its surface has been restructured according to the dominant characteristics and the needs of the 'life world' of the (white, male and Christian) Europeans who initiated it, and made its resources accessible for themselves on a continuous space without limiting boundaries. It was this process that eventually established, to borrow Bob Jessop's term (see Jessop 2007 and Chapter 2 in this volume), the ecological domination of the capitalist mode of production on a world scale. So there emerged globalisation as a form of civilisation which continued its historic journey under the capitalist mode of production and according to the needs of the life-world of the Europeans. The latter has become known as modernisation, Westernisation, internationalisation, colonisation, imperialism and so on.

Therefore, one can in fact refer to two globalisation processes: one is the historical civilisational process, and the other is capitalist globalisation as a subspecies of the former. As Fernand Braudel and Giovanni Arrighi observed, there are recurring periods of expansion and acceleration of finance and trade within this ongoing process of capitalist globalisation. These expansions seemed to be closely (and causally) linked to, and supported by, certain politically and economically hegemonic relations. Furthermore, these expansions did eventually lead to the intensification of economic contractions and collapses, in parallel with the decline of established hegemonic centres and their replacement with new ones ushering new eras of expansion. It appears that these cycles so far have been repeated at least three times (Arrighi 1994, 2004). It is not the long historical globalisation as a form of civilisation, nor the capitalist globalisation in general that has been discussed since the early 1990s as globalisation, it is this acceleration, its nature and novelty. Once this is identified, it becomes easier to see the coincidence between these accelerations, especially the last one since the 1980s, with the so-called structural and recurrent crises of capitalism.

Crisis, financialisation and globalisation

The current crisis is a very controversial subject, perhaps even more controversial than globalisation. However, the following observations can be made relatively safely: profit rates begin to decline in the centres of the world economy in the late 1960s and early 1970s; the process of capital accumulation slowed down, and a phenomenon of overproduction and weakening effective demand emerged at that time (see Armstrong et al. 1987; Brenner 1998; Li et al. 2007 and Mandel 1982). In short, whether the declining rates of profit or the overaccumulation of capital and weakening demand are the main cause of the crisis, it is generally agreed that since the early 1970s world economic conditions changed. A period of slow growth, global turbulence and – more precisely – a structural crisis has set in.

In this context, the process of financialisation, one of the salient features of globalisation, can be linked with overproduction and weak effective demand. The demand for credit, as well as the magnitude of international credit markets, began to expand in the 1980s but especially rapidly in the 1990s, during the so-called globalisation era, in order to counteract the slowdown in capital accumulation.[3] Parallel to this process, consumer and housing credit started to expand strongly in order to counteract the weakening effective demand.

Another tendency for capital was to move progressively away from the sectors of production where profit rates had begun to decline and towards the sphere of circulation. Here it is possible observe an increase in speculative activities and the emergence of financial innovations dicing and slicing the accumulated but shrinking mass of surplus value, and making it possible for accumulation to continue in the sphere of fictitious capital. This process of financialisation inevitably empowered the fraction of the capitalist class nesting on this sector, and increased their capacity to impose their own economic and political interests onto governments. The empowerment of the capitalist class fraction nesting on financial capital played a determining role in the emergence of a new mode of crisis management, aiming to remove all impediments to the activities of capitalist enterprises, but first and foremost of financial capital. This class fraction also directly or indirectly mobilised parties, universities and the media in order to win the support of public opinion for this mode of crisis management which would become known as neoliberalism (see Chait 2007; George 1997 and Harvey 2005).

The political outcome of this process was the emergence of a hegemonic bloc led by financial capital in close alliance with internationalising industrial capital, and supported by large sections of the population especially in the centres of the world economy. During the period when neoliberalism had been the main mode of crisis management, a series of dramatic developments took place. First, there has been a noticeable transfer of wealth from the population in general to the hegemonic strata of the capitalist class (see Duménil and Lévy 2004 and Harvey 2005). Second, the cultural atmosphere has changed in parallel with a series of working-class defeats in the centre as well as in the periphery of the world economy. The direct assaults of the Reagan and Thatcher governments on the labour movement and on labour rights were mimicked in the other countries implementing neoliberal policies, in some cases with the help of military regimes, initiating a process of deformation of the working class at a global scale. This class deformation intensified due to the political decline of the left, especially after the fall of Berlin Wall in 1989. This has also contributed to the formation of, and was accelerated by, a new zeitgeist which articulated the interests of the hegemonic fractions of the capital with the concept of freedom and with the predominant ethical and the aesthetic values in society. As a result, almost all the structural and totalising criticisms targeting the hegemonic programme of financial capital, including neoliberal policies, IMF programmes and so on, were almost completely silenced by the media and in the artistic and academic institutions. This process paved the way to a cultural environment supporting a greatly accelerated consumerism and the financialisation which supported it (see Frank 1998, 2000; Heath and Potter 2006 and Migone 2007).

Other salient features of globalisation have been the accelerating innovations in information technology, data processing and telecommunications, which also led to the extravagant claims about the 'weightless' or 'new' economy being the novel characteristics of the capitalist mode of production. In fact, these technological developments and the so-called 'information revolution' can easily be linked to the processes which supported the acceleration in consumerism (data-mining for marketing, digital image-creating for advertising etc.), as well as in financialisation (electronic trading, digital transfer of funds, modelling and churning our complex equations to help risk calculations) during the era of globalisation. In short, it is possible to establish causal links between the two important features (financialisation and the information revolution) of globalisation and the crisis of capitalism.

Globalisation and the law of the tendency of the rate of profit to fall and its counter-tendencies

Important transformations can be observed in the economic structures, cultures and political regimes in the middle-income countries hit by the acceleration and expansion of the circulation of capital through the activities of industrial and financial transnational companies during era of globalisation. It is possible to establish a connection between the crisis of capitalism and the effects of globalisation on the economies, cultures and even the political regimes of these countries. In order to do this, it is necessary to return to Karl Marx's *Capital*, Vol. 3, Part 3, on the law of the tendency of the rate of profit to fall. There is no need to dwell here, on the law itself, which is considered to be the – or one of the – dynamic(s) at the roots of the recurring crises in the capitalist mode of production. A quick glance at the list of the counter-tendencies will be sufficient for the present purposes. These could easily be summarised (and interpreted) as follows:

1   Improvement of the labour productivity by the progressive mechanisation of the labour process.
2   Intensification of the labour process by minimising the periods where labour remains idle.
3   Acceleration of the circulation time of the capital by reducing the idle time during which the capital remains outside production.
4   Exporting commodities which do not have a profitable market in those economies where they were produced.
5   Exporting capital which cannot be profitably invested where it emerges.
6   Creating new credit to support consumption.
7   Creating new sectors of production in order to reduce the organic composition of capital.
8   Mergers and acquisitions or foreign direct investment to get access to raw materials to reduce production costs and enhance profitability.

These counter-tendencies tell us about the dynamics behind the sudden acceleration in the technological innovations, exports of commodities and capital, new organisational forms of capital, and the structural changes emerging in the world economy and, therefore, the dynamics of the so-called process of globalisation. They even inform us about the neoliberal reforms and IMF programmes. When commodities or capital are exported into new economic geographies, they must find condition suitable for their valorisation and the appropriation of profits. The corollary is that the host economies as well as cultures must be restructured in order to meet the needs of incoming capital. New infrastructures, including tele-communications and transport systems, must be constructed, new laws intro-duced, new consumption patterns and receptive subjectivities should evolve into what David Harvey has called 'the structured coherence' and 'the structure of sensibilities' (see Harvey 2001, 2003). As a result, alongside these more recep-tive subjectivities, new class alliances with their organic intellectuals inevitably emerge to support, maintain and reproduce the restructuring process promoted by by international organisations such as the IMF and the World Bank, and by the local state for the benefit of the incoming capital.

In sum, when the links between overproduction and technological innova-tions, on the one hand, and financialisation, on the other hand, are considered, along with the counter-tendencies to the law of the tendency of the rate of profit to fall, it is found that they constitute almost all the economic financial, technical and cultural patterns underpinning the process of globalisation. When one looks further back at previous epochs, when the circulation and expansion of capital, financialisation and technological innovations were simultaneously accelerated, the following conclusion can be reached. The process of globalisation which encompasses these accelerations is a recurring phenomenon which emerges during crises of the capitalist mode of production, as a synthesis of various forms of crisis management (that is, capital's attempts to deal with its own crisis ten-dencies through the mobilisation of the counter-tendencies, and the surrounding state policies).

Returning to the point of departure of this chapter, globalisation includes secular trends and developments linked to the crises of capitalism. However, the concept of globalisation – especially when it is loaded with such claims as 'unstoppable', 'irreversible' and 'entirely new epoch' – plays a key role of a 'supporting fantasy' within the symbolic universe of capitalism, supporting an ideological construct which suppresses the discussions around the least desirable aspects of international relations under capitalism, i.e. imperialism.

The emerging dissatisfaction with the key assumptions of the neoliberal model appearing in the *Financial Times* and even at the Davos World Economic Forum (2009) reflect its exhaustion as a mode of crisis management. The emerg-ing uncertainty about the future of globalisation is linked to this exhaustion, and it is reflected in the search for a new mode of crisis management which makes state intervention, regulation, economic nationalism and even financial and trade protection likely,[4] and perhaps even inevitable (Williamson 2006).

Notes

1 See *Financial Times*, 11 March 2009.
2 A book search with the words 'globalisation' and 'globalization' in Amazon returns with 80,213 entries; a similar query in Google finds 5.7 million pages (March 2009).
3 As the realisation of profits slowed down, demand for credit by firms and consumers increased, which would help to alleviate the pressures due to excess capacity in indus-try and services.

4 For instance:

> Much of the new money the Bank of England has 'printed' to stimulate the UK
> economy is ending up abroad where it will be of no benefit to UK households and
> businesses, according to an analysis of the Bank's 'quantitative easing' programme.
>
> (O'Grady 2009)

References

Armstrong, P., Glyn, A. and Harrison, J. (1987) *Capitalism since World War II*. London:
Fontana.

Arrighi, G. (2004) 'Spatial and other Fixes of Historical Capitalism', *Journal of World
Systems Research* 10 (2).

Brenner, R. (1998) 'The Economics of Global Turbulence: A Special Report on the
World Economy, 1950–98', *NLR* 229.

Chait, Jonathan (2007) 'How a Cult Hijacked American Politics', *The New Republic*, 9
October.

Duménil, G. and Lévy, D. (2004) 'The Neoliberal (Counter-)revolution', in A. Saad-Filho
and D. Johnston (eds) *Neoliberalism: a Critical Reader*. London: Pluto Press.

Frank, T. (1998) *Conquest of Cool: Business Culture, Counterculture and the Rise of Hip
Consumerism*. Chicago: Chicago University Press.

Frank, T. (2000) *One Market under God, Extreme Capitalism, Market Populism and the
End of Economic Democracy*. New York: Doubleday.

George, Susan (1997) 'How to Win the War of Ideas: Lessons from the Gramscian
Right', *Dissent* 44 (3).

Harvey, David (2001) *Spaces of Capital – Towards a Critical Geography*. New York:
Routledge.

Harvey, David (2003) *The New Imperialism*. Oxford: Oxford University Press.

Harvey, David (2005) *A Brief History of Neoliberalism*. Oxford: Oxford University Press.

Heath, J. and Potter, A. (2006) *The Rebel Sell: How the Counter Culture became Consumer Culture*. London: Capstone.

Held, D. and McGrew, A. (2000) *Global Transformations Reader – An Introduction to
Globalisation Debates*. Cambridge: Polity Press.

Jessop, B. (2007) 'What Follows Neoliberalism? The Deepening Contradictions of US
Domination and the Struggle for a New Global Order', in *Political Economy and
Global Capitalism: The 21st Century, Present and Futures*. London: Anthem Press.

Li, M., Xiao, F. and Zhu, A. (2007) 'Long Waves, Institutional Changes, and Historical
Trends: A Study of the Long-term Movements of the Profit Rates in the Capitalist
World-economy', *Journal of World-Systems Research* XIII (1), pp. 33–54.

Mandel, E. (1982) *La crise 1974–82 Les Faits, Leur interpretations Marxist*. Paris: Flam-
marion.

Migone, Andrea (2007) 'Hedonistic Consumerism: Patterns of Consumption in Contemporary Capitalism', *Review of Radical Political Economics* 39, p. 173.

O'Grady, Sean (2009) 'The Bailout Money is Flowing Abroad', *The Independent*, 14
March.

Rosenberg, J. (2001) *Follies of Globalisation Theory*. London: Verso.

Williamson, Jeffrey G. (2006) 'Globalisation then and now: Late 19th and late 20th Centuries Compared', National Bureau of Economic Research, working paper 5491,
March.

4 Cultural political economy of neoliberalism

The production and negotiation of 'competitiveness' as hegemonic logic(s)

Ngai-Ling Sum

This chapter adopts a 'cultural political economy' (hereafter CPE) approach (Sum 2004; Jessop and Sum 2006; Sum and Jessop forthcoming) to the emergence, from the mid-1990s, of 'competitiveness' as a transnational constellation of hegemonic discourses and practices. It has four sections. First, theoretically, CPE takes a 'cultural-discursive' turn by creatively combining Gramscian and Foucauldian analyses whilst recognizing the tensions between them (Sum 2009b). This approach explores the diverse processes and mechanisms through which hegemony (intellectual, moral and self-leadership) is constituted/negotiated in and across (trans-)national institutional orders and civil society. Concentrating on the discursive moments of the remaking of social relations, CPE focuses on the role of 'economic imaginaries' in defining objects of economic calculation, management, governance etc. 'Competitiveness' is one such imagined object and this chapter focuses on its Harvard Business School variant. Since the early 1990s, this variant has become a knowledge brand with a key role in shaping the making and remaking of neoliberal social relations. The second section focuses on how this knowledge brand has been rolled out on a global scale via knowledge apparatuses (e.g. indexes) and related technologies of power and, in particular, how it is being recontextualized in the East Asian region by (sub-)hegemonic actors. The third section discusses briefly how this hegemonic logic of competitiveness is being challenged and negotiated in a conjuncture marked by the financial crisis that first became evident in mid-2007 and has since deepened and broadened. The fourth section offers some conclusions on the contributions of a CPE approach our understanding of the remaking of neoliberal capitalism.

Production of hegemony: 'competitiveness' as a knowledge brand

The CPE approach focuses on the production of hegemony in the (re-)making of capitalism. This process-oriented perspective illuminates the strategic-discursive moments in the (re-)fashioning of neoliberal hegemony. It asks not only 'how' subjectivities and identities are constituted but also 'who' and 'what' are involved? Its starting point is that the production of hegemony is mediated through the selection of particular 'economic imaginaries' by networks of actors unequally embedded in the various socio-material terrains. Through meaning-making processes that are interactively constructed, contested and negotiated, these actors define the 'economy' as an object of calculation, management and governance. 'Competitiveness' is an important aspect of the economy in this regard and has a key role in neoliberal attempts to restructure global capitalism.

Competitiveness is a complex object of economic intervention that can best be understood by drawing on two recent theoretical currents. The first is the neo-Foucauldian school (e.g. Miller and Rose 1990; Dean 1999), which addresses the 'how' question of object/subject construction and the micro-physics of power involved in subjectification. The other is the neo-Gramscian approach to the pro-duction of hegemony, which explores the discursive-material moments of the 'who' and 'what' questions (see also Sum 2004; Sum and Jessop forthcoming). Combining these approaches facilitates answers to questions such as:

1   who gets involved in the discursive networks that construct objects of eco-nomic governance;
2   what ideas (or knowledge brands) are selected and drawn upon to recontex-tualize the referents of these objects;
3   how do these objects enter policy discourses and everyday practices;
4   how do they remake power relations, their logics, and dynamics in and across diverse social fields;
5   what identities get constructed in the production of hegemony;
6   how do these modes of thought discipline and governmentalize diverse subjects;
7   how do they integrate both intellectuals and laypersons;
8   how do they marginalize potentially antagonistic meanings;
9   what agencies and informal networks are able to enter hegemonic negotia-tions and/or power bloc formation; and
10 how does all this affect power reconfigurations, hegemonic struggles and alternatives?

In this chapter I answer some critical who, what, when and how questions for the construction of 'competitiveness' as an object of economic governance (for responses to other questions in this regard, see Sum 2004).

Discourses about 'competitiveness' have a long history and have been linked to different economic imaginaries. Most recently it has become central to the evolution and institutionalization of objects of neoliberal economic governance and their inscription in policies and everyday life. In this context, it has evolved through three overlapping stages since the 1960s, namely, from theoretical to policy paradigm and then to knowledge brand (for details, see Sum 2009a). The theoretical paradigm that underpins the neoliberal competitiveness imaginary draws in part on a Schumpeterian body of knowledge that emphasizes the crea-tive-destructive nature of innovation and the virtues of entrepreneurial competi-tion as well as the neoliberal emphasis on the role of market forces as the key driver in competition. This paradigm entered policy circles (e.g. the Reagan Administration and the OECD) in the 1980s and was subsequently translated into management/consultancy recommendations in the 1990s. Experts like business-school professors, consultancy firms, think tanks, chambers of commerce etc., have key roles in this regard. Competitiveness thereby acquired brand status and become a central motif in transnational knowledge circuits as part of 'saleable' meaning-making models bundled with claims to problem-solving competencies for economic/business restructuring.

This chapter concentrates on stage three through a case study of how a body of knowledge initially coming from Harvard Business School (HBS) and its associates acquired the status of a knowledge brand. A key figure in this regard is a prominent HBS professor-consultant, Michael E. Porter, who has a background in competitiveness analysis of firms, industries, nations and regions (Porter 1980, 1985 and 1990). His work won early attention in the policy field (e.g. Porter was a member of Reagan's Commission on Industrial Competitiveness) based on the 'diamond model' (see Figure 4.1). The latter is based on four factors: demand conditions, factor conditions, firm strategy, structure and rivalry, and related and supporting industries, whose interaction is also shaped by the nature of 'government' and its interventions as well as by 'chance'. These 'micro-foundations of prosperity' are strongest when they form 'clusters', a metaphor denoting 'a geographic concentration of competing and cooperating companies, suppliers, service providers, and associated institutions' (Porter 1990).[1]

This model is not immune from criticism or debate.[2] Indeed Krugman (1994) claimed that competitiveness had become a 'dangerous obsession'. For, while nations, unlike corporations, cannot go bankrupt, acting as if they could leads to trade conflicts and protectionism, thereby harming growth prospects. Similarly, Martin and Sunley (2003) attacked Porter's 'cluster' notion as chaotic, loose and imprecise, making it hard to deploy for concrete public intervention. Yet this approach is still obsessively pursued in policy circles. This can partly be explained by:

1   the long history of commercialization of research and knowledge by the HBS and associated institutes from the early twentieth century;

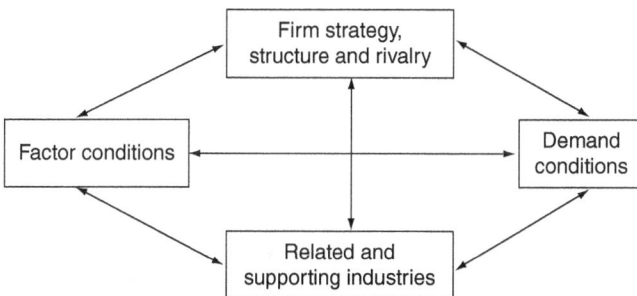

Figure 4.1 Porter's diamond model of national advantage (source: Porter 1990: 127).

2   the flexibility of the 'cluster' metaphor, which allows diverse interpreta-
    tions, frequent renewal, and building of possible alliances among actors
    involved in economic strategies;
3   the promotion and circulation of this body of knowledge across the interna-
    tional, regional, national and local scales;
4   the accumulation of credibility as it echoes within and across idea-policy
    networks – especially when backed by 'celebrity' guru-academics (e.g.
    Porter) and high-profile conferences and business media; and
5   the offer of ready-made policy advice (e.g. cluster building) as national/
    regional reengineering solutions in the face of growing pressures from (a
    naturalized, allegedly irreversible) globalization.

HBS has reinforced this commercialization of research and knowledge through
its recent involvement in selling the Porter model under its own banner. Riding
on its experience, cliché and quality guarantee, Porterian re-engineering solutions are marketed by related Harvard institutions (e.g. Institute for Competitiveness and Institute for Competitiveness and Strategy) and associated strategy
firms (e.g. Monitor Group and ontheFRONTIER Group). Through their joint
claims to expertise and efforts, Porter's cluster-based competitiveness concept is
flexible enough to apply to quite different countries (e.g. Canada, Denmark, New
Zealand, Portugal, Sweden and Switzerland) and regions/cities (e.g. Atlanta,
CENTROPE-Vienna Region, Singapore and Hong Kong/PRD). Strategy firms
like ontheFRONTIER Group have also adapted it to so-called 'emerging
markets' (e.g. Mexico and Rwanda).

Discourses of competitiveness – albeit not always purely Porterian in content
– have also been adopted/adapted on different scales by international organizations (e.g. World Economic Forum and UNIDO), regional banks (e.g. Asian
Development Bank), national agencies (e.g. United States Agency for International Development or USAID) and city governments/alliances (see Table 4.1).
Complementary sites in these knowledge networks include other business
schools, consultancy firms, chambers of commerce, think tanks, research institutes, business and mass media, town hall meetings, luncheon gatherings and
public performances (e.g. conferences and speeches). The enrolment of celebrity
consultant-gurus magnifies the impact of such media and events. In turn this
body of management knowledge circulates widely and resonates strongly in
policy networks in developed and developing countries, gaining credibility from
its promotion by idea entrepreneurs, strategists and consultants, opinion-forming
journalists and leading policy-makers who recontextualize, package and market
related discourses. Key apparatuses here include competitiveness indexes, strategic policy recommendations, development outlook, cluster strategies/best practices, training courses etc. These institutions, agencies and actors have quite
heterogeneous motives and their actions may have contrary or contradictory substantive effects even though 'competitiveness' discourses/practices are sutured
across different sites and scales as part of the hegemonic common sense (see
also pp. 52–6).[3]

Table 4.1 Examples of institutions and discourses related to competitiveness at different scales

Scales	Examples of institutions involved	Examples of competitiveness discourses/ instruments
Global/inter- national	World Economic Forum Institute for Management Development The Competitiveness Institute United Nations Industrial Development Organization (UNIDO)	• *Global Competitiveness Index* • *World Competitiveness Scoreboard* • *The Cluster Initiative Database* • *The Cluster Initiative Greenbook 2003* • *Clusters and Networks Development Programme 2005*
Regional	Asian Development Bank African Union Inter-American Development Bank	• *Asian Development Outlook 2003: III Competitiveness in Developing Countries* • *Pan African Competitiveness Forum 2008* • *Competitiveness of Small Enterprises: Cluster and Local Development 2007*
National	United States Agency for International Development (USAID) Japan International Coopera- tion Agency (JICA)	• *African Global Competitiveness Initiative 2006* • *Strategic Investment Action Plan (Competitiveness/SME) 2005*
Local/city	Numerous (inter-)city com- petitiveness projects and plans	• *The Hong Kong Advantage 1997* • *OECD's International Conference on City Competitiveness 2005* • *Remaking Singapore 2008*

Source: author's own compilation.

Given their pervasiveness across different scales and sites, Porterian ideas about competitiveness gradually acquired brand status in policy-consultancy circuits. Like commercial brands (Arvidsson 2005), knowledge brands address the rational and irrational aspects of human nature. Cognitively, a brand like Porter's competitiveness 'diamond'/'cluster' model is rationalized and legitimated by its association with HBS, its circulation among policy elites, its distinctive policy advice and re-engineering solutions. Individual careers also benefit. Emotionally, it addresses pride, anxieties, threats and social tensions linked to growth or decline, development and the pressures of economic restructuring in global capitalism. These rational and irrational effects shape struggles to make a brand hegemonic. In this context, a knowledge brand can be defined as a would-be hegemonic meaning-making device promoted by 'world-class' guru-academic-consultants who claim unique knowledge of the economic world and pragmatically translate this into transnational policy recipes and tool kits that address social tensions, contradictions and dilemmas and also appeal to pride, threats and anxieties about socio-economic restructuring. Circulating transnationally, such brands offer flexible templates that can be developed and recontextualized to global, regional, national and local conditions/conjunctures (Bernstein 1990).

Developing and recontextualizing the knowledge brand: indexes, clusters and chains

The development and recontextualization of knowledge brands is related, as we have seen, to an ensemble of different institutions, ideas, practices and agents that contribute towards the production of competitiveness as part of the neoliberal hegemonic logic. I now provide one global and one regional example of how one brand, namely the Harvard variant, has been developed and recontextualized via two knowledge apparatuses and related technologies of power that shape the making of competitiveness common sense. The first is the construction of competitiveness indexes and numbers on the global scale, and the second is the use of the metaphors of 'clusters and chains' that are found in economic outlooks/commissioned reports on a regional scale in Asia (see Table 4.2).

On a global scale: disciplining and visibilizing by indexes and numbers

The story of competitiveness is linked to the development of indexes. Globally, the two best known indexes are the World Economic Forum (WEF) Global Competitiveness Index, which is connected to HBS, and the World Competitiveness Scoreboard, which is produced by the Institute for Management Development in Lausanne (Switzerland). The WEF constructed the Global Competitiveness Report and the Global Competitiveness Index in 1979 and updates it annually. Despite increasing sophistication in index construction, this knowledge apparatus still relies on assigning numbers to countries by ranking and scoring them in terms of a business-school approach to performance and growth (see Tables 4.3 and 4.4). Despite its short history, this index is becoming part of the world's statistical furniture. It is frequently used by government officials, think tanks and journalists to communicate needs, desires and even panics

Table 4.2 Two knowledge apparatuses and knowledging technologies in the construction of 'competitiveness'

Knowledge apparatuses/instruments	Knowledging technologies in meaning-making	Major institutional sites/actors
Indexes and numbers constructed in: *Global Competitiveness Report and Global Competitiveness Index*	Technologies of performance and judgement Technology of visibility	World Economic Forum
Cluster-and-chain metaphors constructed in: *Asian Development Outlook 2003: III Competitiveness in Developing Countries* Other reports (see Table 4.5)	Technologies of agency (see Table 4.6)	Asian Development Bank Other institutions (see Table 4.5)

Source: author's own compilation.

of economic restructuring. For example, some actors narrate a fall within this index order as threatening and/or a sign of being 'hollowed out'.

This knowledge apparatus operates as a disciplinary tool (or paper panopticon) with surveillance capacities and implications for government policy and population. It encloses (more and more) countries in a number order and countries are compared in terms of economic performance to each other and/or over time (see Table 4.5). It deploys apparatuses such as indexes, numbers and tables to rank countries. Annual revisions create a cyclical disciplinary art of country surveillance that institutionalizes a continuous gaze through numbers that depicts and benchmarks countries' performance via changing rank and score orders. Its power operates through the hierarchization of countries and their division into high/rising and low/falling economies in the competitive race.

As Table 4.1 shows, such performance and judgement technologies subject countries to the treadmill of competitiveness and make them vulnerable to pressures to change economic and social policies in line with specific recommendations and best practices. Countries with a low or slipping position in the rank order are visibilized, targeted and/or encouraged to take steps to become more competitive through building clusters, enhancing FDI, promoting SMEs/education/sustainable development etc. This involves pressures on governments, firms, communities and, indeed, individuals to refashion themselves to become competitive subjects and economic categories (e.g. entrepreneurs and catch-up economies) in the race to aspire to world-class rankings or, at least, do better than their immediate comparators.

On regional-local scales: framed by cluster-and-chain metaphors

On the regional scale, there have been increased efforts to promote competitiveness discourses and practices since the early 2000s. Notable examples include the USAID's African Global Competitiveness Initiative, the Inter-American

Table 4.3 Main elements of the World Economic Forum's Global Competitiveness Index

Background	The WEF's annual Global Competitiveness Report started since 1979 drawing on the Porterian model on 'competitive advantage' and using data complied by Michael Porter and others
Approach	Business school approach in measuring performance of countries
Number of variables	Over 90
Weighting system	Different aggregations and weightings apply to 'core' and 'non-core' countries in the final index
Data sources	Two-thirds of the data derives from Executive Opinion Surveys (11,000 responses in 2008–9) and one-third comes from sources such as the United Nations
Coverage	134 countries in 2008–9

Source: author's own compilation based on the Global Competitiveness Report 2008–9.

Table 4.4 World Economic Forum and its global competitiveness rankings of selected Asian countries, 2004–8

	Index 2008	Rank 2008	Rank 2004
United States	5.74	1	2
Singapore	5.53	5	7
Japan	5.38	9	9
Hong Kong	5.33	11	29
South Korea	5.28	13	21
Taiwan, China	5.22	17	4
Malaysia	5.04	21	31
China	4.47	30	46
India	4.33	50	55
Indonesia	4.25	55	69

Source: World Economic Forum, Global Competitiveness Reports 2007–9.

Development Bank (IADB)'s Multilateral Investment Fund for SME competitiveness, and the Asian Development Bank's Asian Development Outlook 2003. My chapter focuses on Asia and discusses two ways in which the competitiveness discourses have been recontextualized by sub-hegemonic actors such as the Asian Development Bank (ADB), the Asian Institute for Competitiveness (ACI) in Singapore and strategy firms (see Tables 4.3 and 4.6).

The ADB, which is a regional counterpart of the World Bank as a knowledge bank (Plehwe 2007), spearheaded and adapted 'competitiveness' in 'developmental terms'. In Section III of its *Asian Development Outlook 2003*, Porterian ideas were recontextualized in terms of 'catch up competitiveness'. With the electronics sector as its shining example, 'catch-up' in East Asia was narrated thus:

> The nature of catch-up competitiveness in the NIEs contrasts sharply with the traditional definition of technological innovation, namely the production of new (or improved) products, based on R&D...
>
> Furthermore, the stages model captures the fact that innovation occurs, not just in technological terms but also, and very importantly, in institutional terms. The technological change which took place in East Asia in electronics probably could not have occurred with such rapidity without the OEM and, later, ODM systems.
>
> Similarly, the increase of MNC-led growth was also a critical development. MNC investment on such a large scale was new to Southeast Asia and allowed parent companies to transfer foreign technology to local subsidiaries. These were then able to systematically learn the technological arts of electronics production. MNC subsidiaries provided a route into international markets and enabled continuous, routine technological learning to occur within local plants. The 'master-pupil' relationship described by Cyhn (2002) in case studies of East Asian OEM mirrors the relationships that developed between parent and subsidiary plants in Southeast Asia.

The exploitation of MNC investment began in Singapore (Goh 1996) and was imitated by other countries wishing to export to OECD countries. Although FDI occurred prior to 1960s, the electronics industry brought with it a huge expansion of FDI in Southeast Asia, leading to the development of several industrial clusters. For example, the computer disk-drive cluster in Thailand is the largest of its kind in the world. Similarly, in Penang, Malaysia, the semiconductor assembly and testing cluster is the largest exporter of semiconductors worldwide.

> (www.adb.org/documents/books/ADO/2003/part3_3–7.asp, accessed on 26 January 2009)

This narration portrays and normalizes East Asian countries as 'laggards' (with their own internal hierarchy). Their imagined 'niche' was to 'catch up' by engaging in process and product innovation, educational provision and market-friendly institutions. Profiling Singapore as the export-oriented, MNC-led and FDI-driven growth model, industrial development through thematized clusters (e.g. the 'computer disk-drive' cluster in Thailand) was advocated as the export-oriented policy strategy for Asian countries. Such export-oriented clusters are then tied to the 'global value chains' (GVCs) with the following 'beneficial' relationship:

> International production chains are likely to benefit firms in countries where they can go into GVCs in sectors including furniture, footwear, textiles and garments, and electronics, in three main ways. First, by increasing the set of internationally traded goods, GVCs increase opportunities to benefit from the gains from trade by allowing the participants greater room for specialization in the labor-intensive stages of manufacturing processes (which overall might be technology or capital intensive). Second, by broadening the scope for gains from trade, it renders protectionist, import-substitution, or anti-foreign investment policies even less effective. Third, given that this kind of production and trade tends to occur in tightly knit 'just in time' global networks, it gives added impetus to the need for improving the efficiency of transport and communications infrastructure and for a stable business environment.
>
> (Yeats 1998: 2)

GVCs can enable firms to enter global production networks more easily, allowing them to benefit from globalization, climb the technology ladder, and gain wider access to international markets. GVCs provide firms with a wide spectrum of options to operate in global markets with a view to staying competitive. In theory, GVCs offer a way for local enterprises in developing countries to engage in international markets at their own level of capability. In practice, however, it is often extremely difficult for a firm to secure an initial order, and only if a firm has a proven track record with a buyer is it likely to win a major contract. Entry into GVCs is easiest when an agglomeration of local buyers and manufacturers already exists, so that newcomers can learn from the established players. Sometimes, new entrants emerge as spin-offs from existing local firms or from MNC subsidiaries with whom they establish a new GVC linkage. For countries and groups of firms outside successful clusters, accessing GVCs can be difficult. For very poor countries with little engagement of or prior experience in GVCs (especially high-technology GVCs), entry can pose major developmental challenges to policy makers and business leaders alike.

(www.adb.org/documents/books/ADO/2003/part3_3–5.asp, accessed on 26 January 2009)

Framed as being 'beneficial' and offering 'opportunities', participation in global value chains offer regional 'clusters' access to global markets via restructuring. Nations, regions and localities are recontextualized and co-constructed by official organizations (e.g. Asian Development Bank Institute, USAID), research/training centres (e.g. Singapore's ACI), strategy firms (e.g. Hong Kong's Enright, Scott and Associates Ltd.), think tanks (e.g. Hong Kong's 2022 Foundation), and the business media (e.g. *Straits Times*). Each of these institutions has its own spatial focus and practices in organizing thematized clusters in the region (see Table 4.5).

The Harvard brand is thereby mapped onto the region's development policy through macro-regional, national and local sub-hegemonic actors, discourses and practices. This resonates what neo-Foucauldians called the technology of agency (Cruikshank 1999), which combines participation, capacity-building and control. These institutions co-construct and share knowledge in cluster building as one form of knowledging technology and thereby produce 'competent' actors equipped to perform their constructed but eventually self-guided role in promoting competitiveness. But these discourses and practices also map/control the organization of regional space, the policy for exercising agency and types of agency (see Table 4.6).

The cluster metaphor encourages actors to treat these spaces as (potential) clusters in which companies, suppliers, service providers and associated institutions interact to form export-led production- and/or service-oriented nodes (e.g. fruit, transport and logistics, finance, electrical/electronic products etc.) that are opened to FDI and MNC-dominated global value chains. It also stipulates the types of public and private agencies – world-market-oriented, catalytic government bodies and self-responsibilized entrepreneurial subjects – who should reorganize themselves through training and affective-pragmatic identification with the competitiveness project. Though some are ambivalent and even resistant, others may identify themselves as competitiveness subjects and relays through participation in local training courses, seminars, overseas aid/funding or simple observation of the everyday routines and requirements of 'catch-up competitiveness'.

The 2008 financial crisis and loss of 'competitiveness'?

Use of 'index' measurements and the 'cluster-and-chain' metaphors and their related technologies of power highlights how 'competitiveness' has become a

Table 4.5 Institutions and practices in organizing thematized clusters in Asia

Institutions	Spatial focus	Practices	Examples of themed clusters
Asia Development Bank Institute, United State Agency for International Development (and Institute for Industrial Policy and Strategy in Vietnam)	Transitional economies in Asia (e.g. Vietnam)	Seminars, lectures, pilot projects, funding, technical cooperation etc.	*Cluster-Based Industrial Development Workshop* 2006 • Vietnam: software/ICT, fruit, ceramics, and agricultural products (rice, coffee, pepper, rubber etc.)
Asia Competitiveness Institute (Singapore)	ASEAN countries	Reports, information repository, training courses (for postgraduates and executives) etc.	Report on *Remaking Singapore* 2008 • Petrochemical, transport and logistics, finance, information technology and biopharmaceuticals
Enright, Scott and Associates Ltd.	Hong Kong and Pearl River Delta	Consultancy reports, conferences, seminars etc.	Report on *The Hong Kong Advantage* 1997 • Business and financial services, transport and logistics, light manufacturing and trading, property and construction, and tourism. Report on *Hong Kong and the PRD: the Economic Interaction* 2003 • Pearl River Delta: electrical/electronic goods, software, toys, furniture, telecommunication products, plastics, clothing, port services, ceramics etc.

Source: author's own compilation based on various websites, www.abdi.org/conf-seminar-papers/ 2007/04/04/2226.vietnam.cluster.dev/, www.spp.nus.edu.sg/ACI/home.aspx, www.2022foundation.com/ index.asp?party=project1 (accessed on 26 January 2009).

crucial element of the neoliberal hegemonic logic. Though the Harvard-based transnational knowledge brand is influential, regional and local actors also act as nodes of translation and centres of persuasion in diverse global-regional-local construction relays. The resultant technologies are sutured across different scales/sites via the operations of heterogeneous institutions, agents, ideas and practices that cut across different scales and sites. The resultant sutured coherences of the hegemonic logic incur surpluses that allow for negotiations and shifting compromises when faced with challenges from labour unions and social movements related to minimum wage legislations, corporate social responsibility and environmental stewardship. Since mid-2008, sub-prime debts, declining stock prices, the credit crunch, export sluggishness, production downturns,

Table 4.6 Technology of agency that organize regional spaces, policies and population

Sites of organizing agency	Ways of controlling/mapping agency
Regional space	• Market- and FDI-promoting • Export-oriented clusters • Thematized clusters tied to global value chains
Policies	• Governments playing catalytic or supply-side roles • Promotion of technology, innovation, education and training
Population	• Competitive, entrepreneurial and self-responsibilized individuals for 'catch-up' development

factory closures, unemployment etc., have reinforced these tendencies (Blackburn 2008; Klein 2008; Gowan 2009). The crisis-related events have affected, albeit unevenly, regional finance clusters, with knock-on effects on production clusters in Asia and elsewhere. This has heightened fears about 'loss of competitiveness'. Accordingly there is a clamour to fix the 'international financial architecture' and develop alternative imaginaries, which range from 'responsible economy' to the 'Green New Deal'. The latter, for example, is promoted by a discursive network comprising green groups, the United Nations Environment Programme and a European-funded Green Economy Initiative. It involves Keynesian creation of green investment and jobs to revive the world economy and avert environmental disaster in time of deep financial crisis. Given the pervasiveness of competitiveness discourses, it is currently being (re-)negotiated and ideas, such as 'green' and 'responsible competitiveness', are available that could reinvent neoliberalism, remake hegemony and reorganize bloc building at this conjuncture.

Conclusion

Adopting a CPE approach, this chapter goes beyond the usual approach to neoliberalism in terms of 'what' and 'with what results' questions to ask 'how' and 'who' questions. It focused on mechanisms (e.g. knowledge apparatuses and technologies) that secure the hegemony of neoliberal logic(s) in and across diverse institutional orders and civil society (e.g. business schools, strategy firms, think tanks, business press, international organizations, regional organizations, aid agencies etc.). It shows how this process is mediated by transnational knowledge brands that are recontextualized at different scales and sites. Mundane and everyday practices helped make competitive subjects and common sense through the working of knowledge apparatuses (e.g. indexes, outlooks, pilot projects, seminars, training) and related technologies of power (performance, judgement and agency). Such hegemonic logics are not unique to a given site or scale but are typically developed and recontextualized at different sites and scales in relation to different regional, national and local conjunctures. Constructions ranging from the Global Competitiveness Index of the WEF to cluster development programmes promoted by the Asian Development Bank, research institutes, think tanks, consultancy firms and business media. Their knowledge apparatuses and technologies are sutured together in the ongoing production of neoliberal (sub-)hegemony across sites and scales. These involve the intermingling of different technologies sustained by articulation of different elements of indexes, numbers, clusters and chains. These technologies, especially those promoted as knowledge for development, help to remake and reorganize common sense and everyday rationalities/consciousness of policy-makers and citizens. Nonetheless, these approaches to cluster building connected with global value chains illustrate the variegation of the world market, i.e. the co-existence, complementarity and structural coupling of varieties of capitalism and other economic formations in the global economy (see Chapter 2, this volume).[4] It does this by:

1   mapping specific clusters and chains in the world economy and identifying their distinctive features (e.g. finance, toys, fruits, electronics etc.);
2   allowing MNCs and MNBs to (out-)source to and integrate the different production and service sites within a given cluster/chain;
3   specifying how these spaces, policies and people can be organized through specific technologies and practices to enable them to 'catch up'; and
4   decomposing societies into factors of competitiveness that should be governed through export-promotion, FDI, development aids, plans, funding, seminars, training and related measures to enable them to integrate into the world market.

This approach to the interaction among discourses, governmentalities and structure in the production of (sub-)hegemony is characteristic of the CPE approach. Though this chapter focuses on knowledge brands and knowledging technologies, a fuller CPE account should analyse their material preconditions and effects. These include the capacities to construct, select and disseminate these discourses, how they mediate alliance-building in particular sites, their impact on class, gender, place and nature (e.g. sweatshops that exploit migrant women workers, environmental damage, land use favouring particular clusters/ groups etc). Such displacements marginalize some groups; and unsurprisingly, invite resistance from labour organizations, social movements, place-based communal groups and consumer activism that demand greater equality and protection for local communities and the environment, and respect for the body politics of workers and families. The maturing of the current – financial crisis has aggravated pre-existing tensions through its impact on the financial and real economies around the world. At the time of writing, competitiveness discourses and practices are being reinvented yet again as struggles continue over the future of a (post-)Washington Consensus world (dis-)order.

Notes

1 Clusters are made visible via the technique of 'cluster charts' which identify local industries based on export statistics and use the diamond model to test selected cases to establish a pool of unique clusters.
2 For a summary of this debate, see Martin and Sunley (2003).
3 In short, there is no global 'conspiracy' involving all the actors that help to reproduce the discursive power of the competitiveness discourses.
4 While varieties of capitalism are often analysed in isolation from each other as if each were viable in its own terms, variegated capitalism explores the links among varieties of capitalism within the world market – whether due to their respective specializations in the international division of labour, their respective modes of regulation and forms of state, their respective temporalities, their respective positions as creditors and debtors etc. This perspective excludes the generalization of one variety to the whole world market as well as simplistic forms of regime shopping, in which social forces seek to combine features of different varieties of capitalism to seek the optimum balance among them (personal communication from Bob Jessop, 25 September 2008).

References

Arvidsson, A. (2005) *Brands: Meaning and Value in Media Culture*, London: Routledge.
Bernstein, B. (1990) *The Structuring of Pedagogic Discourse: Class, Codes and Control*, London: Routledge.
Blackburn, R. (2008) 'The Subprime Crisis', *New Left Review*, 50: 63–106.
Cruikshank, B. (1999) *The Will to Empower*, Ithaca: Cornell University Press.
Dean, M. (1999) *Governmentality*, London: Sage.
Enright, M., Scott, E. and Dodwell, D. (1997) *The Hong Kong Advantage*, Hong Kong: Oxford University Press.
Gowan, P. (2009) 'Crisis in the Heartland: Consequences of the New Wall Street System', *New Left Review*, 55: 5–29.
Jessop, B. and Sum, N.-L. (2006) *Beyond the Regulation Approach*, Cheltenham: Edward Elgar.
Klein, B. (2008) 'The Great Crash in China', *Far Eastern Economic Review*. Online, available at: www.feer.com/economics/2008/october/The-Great-Crash-of-China (accessed on 26 January 2009).
Krugman, P. (1994) 'Competitiveness: A Dangerous Obsession', *Foreign Policy*, March 73: 342–65.
Martin, R. and Sunley, P. (2003) 'Deconstructing Clusters: Chaotic Concept or Policy Panacea?', *Journal of Economic Geography*, 3: 5–35.
Miller, P. and Rose, N. (1990) 'Governing Economic Life', *Economy and Society*, 19: 1–31.
Plehwe, D. (2007) 'A Global Knowledge Bank? The World Bank and Bottom-Up Efforts to Reinforce Neoliberal Development Perspectives in the Post-Washington Consensus Era', *Globalizations*, 4 (4): 514–28.
Porter, M. (1980) *Competitive Strategy: Techniques for Analyzing Industries and Competitors*, New York: Free Press.
Porter, M. (1985) *Competitive Advantage: Creating and Sustaining Superior Performance*, New York: Free Press.
Porter, M. (1990) *Competitive Advantage of Nations*, Basingstoke: Macmillan.
Sum, N.-L. (2004) 'Towards a Cultural Political Economy: Discourses, Material Power

and (Counter-)Hegemony', EU Framework 6 DEMOLOGOS project. Online, available at: http://demologos.ncl.ac.uk/wp/wp1/disc.php (last accessed on 15 June 2007).

Sum, N.-L. (2009a) 'A Cultural Political Economy of Transnational Knowledge Brands: Porterian "Competitiveness" Discourse and its Recontextualization in Hong Kong/ Pearl River Delta', *Journal of Language and Politics* (in press).

Sum, N.-L. (2009b) 'The Production of Hegemonic Policy Discourses: "competitiveness" as a Knowledge Brand and its (Re-) Contextualizations', *Critical Policy Studies* (in press).

Sum, N.-L. and Jessop, B. (forthcoming) *Towards a Cultural Political Economy*, Chelten-ham: Edward Elgar.

Yeats, A. (1998) 'Just How Big is Global Production Sharing?', The World Bank, Policy Research Working Paper No. 1871.

5 Socially responsible investment and neoliberal discipline in emerging markets

Susanne Soederberg

One of the most striking trends in global development finance over the past decade has been the rise in private equity financing in middle-income countries. Equity financing, which refers to the method by which publicly traded corporations in the emerging markets raise long-term capital through the sale of shares (equity) to investors, has been a central feature in boosting private debt levels in emerging markets in the new millennium (World Bank 2006). Because they are major suppliers of capital to emerging markets, US pension funds have played a leading role in monitoring and measuring financial risk – or what is known in the industry as 'benchmarking' – through the inclusion of non-financial or social risk factors such as good human rights policies. Although many institutional investors would not deem their use of non-financial indicators as socially responsible investing (SRI), which is often associated with the rise of ethical awareness, the discourse and objective driving the inclusion of social factors mirrors the same concern as SRI, namely: the reduction of risk exposure. Over the past several years, the investment community has expanded their narrow economic perspective regarding risk calculations. According to the United Nations Principles for Responsible Investment, for instance, 'There is a growing view among investment professionals that environmental, social and corporate governance issues can affect the performance of investment portfolios' (www.unpri.org/about).

Despite the increasing use of social indicators as a method of reducing risk, pension funds have not been subjected to critical analysis. This chapter addresses this neglect in the literature by providing a critical analysis of the non-financial risk factors employed by the California Public Employees' Retirement System (CalPERS). With a market value of about $240 billion, CalPERS represents one of the largest pension funds in the world. CalPERS is also well known for its proactive benchmarking system, most notably its Permissible Country Index (hereafter PCI or Index). The Index incorporates both financial and social factors when calculating the risk levels in 27 emerging markets. On the surface, the PCI has been celebrated to be a progressive means of encouraging middle-income countries to adhere to the principles of the International Labour Organisation, or freedom of the press. Indeed, some authors have suggested that the PCI has led to positive change, in that governments of emerging markets attempt to improve on social criteria so as to make their countries more attractive to large, foreign investors like CalPERS (cf. Hebb and Wójcik 2005). Viewed at a deeper level, I argue that the PCI reproduces the neoliberal-led development paradigm, by naturalising 'development' as largely an uncontested, market-driven phenomenon (Soederberg 2009). The Index does this primarily through coercive measures, such as exit strategies (or, removing a country from its Index), as well as through attempts at constructing specific forms of knowledge that act to normalise the expansion and restructuring of spaces of capital in the global South.

The remaining chapter is divided into the following three sections. The next section discusses the general emergence of SRI with regard to United States and outlines the non-financial risk factors of the PCI. The following section then provides a critical analysis of the PCI by identifying three main characteristics underpinning the Index that serve to naturalise the neoliberal development paradigm. The final section concludes by revisiting the argument and drawing out future implications of the Index.

Non-financial risk metrics and the PCI

In its first version of the PCI, which was established in 1987, the decision by CalPERS' Board of Directors to commission their financial advisors, Wilshire Consulting, to devise an Index to screen countries that demonstrated unfavourable economic and financial conditions was motivated by shareholder activism driven by waves of mergers and acquisitions, and the associated abuses of corporate management in the United States, as well as the high-profile fight against the apartheid regime in South Africa. It was not until 1999 that CalPERS' Board of Trustees insisted that Wilshire Consulting revise the Index to include non-financial risk measurements when assessing the stability and profitability of investment opportunities in developing countries. The amendment to the Index took into account two broad sources of risk:

1 country factors, which concentrated on a narrowly defined concept of political risk, and
2 market factors, which related to issues such as market liquidity and volatility, market regulation/legal system/investor protection, capital market openness, settlement proficiency/transaction costs.

In the wake of the spate of financial crises in emerging market economies during the latter half of the 1990s, and corporate accounting scandals in the United States and elsewhere in the early 2000s, CalPERS' Board of Trustees insisted that the definition of 'country factors' or social risk be broadened to encompass the following points:

1 transparency;
2 productive labour practices; and an expanded understanding of
3 political stability (see Table 5.1).

The latter, for instance, was to embrace several sub-factors including:

1   civil liberties;
2   independent judiciary and legal protection; and
3   political risk.

CalPERS shocked the investment community by pulling out of investments of four East Asian countries – the Philippines, Thailand, Indonesia and Malaysia – on the basis of social issues and human rights. In the words of Verité, the pension fund's third-party verification company, 'We looked at the laws and then we looked at what was really going on – child labour, force labour, freedom of association and discrimination' ('US Pension Fund Quits Asian Countries', BBC News, 21 February 2002).

The politics of naturalising neoliberal-led development

The neutrality and universality of development

Aside from recent critiques that the Index has led to the exclusion of CalPERS from 'burgeoning' stock markets such as China, and which have resulted in the loss of about $401 million since 2002 ('CalPERS Emerging Market Policy Hit', *Pensions & Investments*, 5 March 2007), the content of the Index has remained above critical reproach. One reason for this is that its categories resonate well with deep-seated, Western, common-sense understanding that economic growth leads to progress. As Gilbert Rist observes, this understanding – which has permeated the official development project up to the so-called post-Washington Consensus (Fine 2006) – 'offers the promise of general abundance, conceived in biological imagery as something natural, positive, necessary and indisputable'

Table 5.1 Permissible Country Index/CalPERS country and market macro-factors

Country macro-factors (or political risk factors)	Weight (%)	Market macro-factors	Weight (%)
Political stability	16.7	Market liquidity and volatility	12.5
Transparency	16.7	Market regulation/legal system/ investor protection	12.5
Productive labour practices	16.6	Capital market openness	12.5
		Settlement proficiency/transaction costs	12.5
Total assigned weight	50		50

Source: adapted from Wilshire Consulting, 'Permissible Equity Markets Investment Analysis'. Prepared for The California Public Employees' Retirement System. Santa Monica: Wilshire Consulting, 2005, pp. 4 and 11.

(Rist 2002: 214). The debates have remained silent on the question of how and why the knowledge contained in the PCI is readily accepted by policy-makers, the media, shareowners and scholars as some objective fact.

To transcend the technical and economistic treatment of the Index, it is important to question the assumption of progress, as this highly political concept beats at the heart of the official understanding of development. Progress is defined in terms of material prosperity, which is, in turn, generated by economic growth. According to the PCI, the ability of countries to attract equity finance assists in the achievement of growth. The International Financial Corporation (IFC), a branch of the World Bank Group, insists that harnessing the power of private capital and free enterprise – represented as 'positive' power – is necessary to bring about *needed change* in the developing world (IFC 2006, my emphasis). This change will in turn reduce economic risks and protect shareholder value by ensuring that the 'underdeveloped' countries strive toward establishing 'good' (read: Anglo-American) corporate governance practices through, for example, implementing 'well-functioning' (universal) legal and political systems, modernising stock exchanges, stabilising capital market flows, decreasing commission rates and other transaction charges, and so forth. The questions that emerge here, who benefits from this change? And, what social, political and cultural dislocations are associated with this change, and why?

To address these questions it is useful to combine the capitalist nature of the PCI with an interrogation of its cultural dimensions of knowledge and production of social space. This strategy allows us to grasp that the key sources of power of the PCI lie not only in the coercive features of the Index (exit strategies, blacklisting 'bad' investment sites, cure periods), but in its ability to normalise, and therefore reproduce, the knowledge rooted in official development discourse and policy. What is at stake here is concealed by the neutrality of the term 'development', namely the production of knowledge and exercise of power over the Third World (Escobar 1995). As Arturo Escobar argues,

> The forms of power that have appeared act not so much by repression but by normalisation; not by ignorance but by controlled knowledge ... As the conditions that gave rise to development became more pressing, it could only increase its hold, refine its methods, and extend its reach even further.
> (Escobar 1995: 53)

The space within which the knowledge underpinning the PCI is both produced and reproduced reflects dominant capitalist interests in the United States. In an attempt to deal with the effects of the tendency toward capital overaccumulation, and its primary manifestation of a surplus of capital, especially in the form of money-capital, US institutional investors, such as CalPERS, expand geographically into new regions by exporting capital extending towards the creation of what Marx referred to as the world market (Marx 1981). David Harvey describes as this as a process of a spatial displacement of capital (Harvey 1999). The latter refers to a strategy in which capitalists seek to find outlets for their surplus capital by 'opening up new markets, new production capacities and new resource, social and labour possibilities elsewhere' (Harvey 2003: 64). As Marx suggested, 'If capital is sent abroad, this is not done because it absolutely could not be applied at home, but because it can be employed at a higher rate of profit in a foreign country' (Harvey 1999: 434). Despite its public commitment to the PCI, CalPERS, for instance, has employed private equity firms to circumvent the limits in the Index such as China, Pakistan, Russia and so on, i.e. instead of directly investing in these blacklisted countries, private equity firms, such as Genesis, do so on their behalf (Soederberg 2009). Second, as discussed above, equity finance is not an object, but has its base in money, which is viewed here as an integral moment of the social relations of capital. Seen from this perspective, money, and by extension, equity finance, wields social power. Those who wield this social power, according to Harvey, also seek to cultivate command over spatial organisation, and authority over the use of space becomes a crucial means for the reorganisation and reproduction of social power relations (Harvey 1989). This command over space, and subsequent power struggles to resist this command, is concealed in the discourse and policy of the PCI, as money which takes the form of equity financing is reduced to a neutral object.

Key aspects of the Index's 'country factors' involve changing national legal and political systems, so as to protect private property, liberalise financial and flexibilise labour markets. However, the political and legal systems of a country are not undifferentiated, ahistorical features of 'investment sites'; rather, they are complex historical products of class-led struggles rooted in nationally specific colonial and post-colonial power relations. Thus, a basic prerequisite for the Anglo-American reforms contained in the PCI to be implemented, would entail a fundamental reorganisation of the total social relations of production and exchange in a given social formation. For instance, given the high concentration of family-owned, publicly run corporations in East and Southeast Asia, minority shareholder rights cannot be guaranteed by mere technical changes, without ensuring major social and political struggle and dislocation through the implementation of neoliberal forms of social engineering (Zhuang *et al.* 2000). The naturalised understanding of 'development' allows the PCI (or, more specifically, the money managers and Board of Trustees of CalPERS) to conceal its role in promoting imperial practices required to guarantee the expanded reproduction of capital in the context of Third World countries.

Economics as 'scientific' knowledge

Despite its emphasis on country factors (or political factors), the PCI grants primacy to the market. Both the means and end of the Index is to promote a well-functioning market by granting it as much freedom from government intervention as possible. This position is firmly rooted in the hegemonic understanding of economic growth and the material prosperity it generates, which we discuss in more detail below. For our purposes here, suffice to say that the theory that the hegemony of market rule reduces all aspects of life to the needs and proper functioning of the market serves to remove and therefore sanitise the political, material and cultural aspects of societies and recast them ahistorically in terms of the neutral realm of science. In doing so, economics is represented as somehow embodying a scientific and therefore accurate representation and truth about the world (Escobar 1995). As Arturo Escobar notes, there is a close, albeit distorted, connection drawn between the scientific knowledge of economics, and its implicit claims to neutrality, and what he refers to as the 'cultural code', or cultural discourse of economics. 'Economists do not see their science as a cultural discourse. In their long and illustrious realist tradition, their knowledge is taken to be a neutral representation of the world and truth about it' (Escobar 1995: 59).

One of the main reasons why economics is treated and largely understood as a science is due to the fact that it places rationality as a dominant value in its paradigm. This is evident in the country and market factors that comprise the PCI. Within the parameters of the Index, the market or the economy is viewed in harmonious terms, without politics, social power or history, an utterly rational world, made even more abstract with the application of mathematical tools used to gauge the quality of investment potential of a country (Escobar 1995: 65). The basic premise driving this view is that the economy is comprised of rational actors, whose behaviour can be readily explained and understood through observation, measurement and prediction. It follows from this that rational behaviour is innate and therefore only alterable if and when external forces to the market, such as the state, distort the competitive environment through, for example, rent-seeking activities or weak legal systems that fail to protect private property. The assumption that markets are inherently rational, as long as they are left to their own devices, is an important feature of the cultural code of economics, and serves as the cornerstone of the Index's ability to recreate the status quo by neutralising and thus normalising disciplinary relations of exploitation and domination. It does so in the following two ways.

First, the understanding that markets are inherently rational depoliticises, and therefore naturalises, the knowledge upon which the PCI attempts to exercise its disciplinary power, as it removes any problematic issues, such as social conflicts, contestation over material power, and so forth, from the political and cultural realms and recasts them in terms of the sanitised and neutral realm of science. While CalPERS claims that its revised Index gives equal weight to market and country factors, for instance, it should be underlined that the country factors have been selected to encourage governments of emerging markets to pursue the neoliberal utopia of unregulated freedom of the market. Country factors are scored on the basis of how well national governments provide the proper conditions (e.g. legal entitlements, sound economic policy based on fiscal austerity, financial deregulation and trade liberalisation, and so on) for the market actors to flourish under the conditions of competition in order to promote economic growth.

Second, the assumption of the rationality of the market allows CalPERS to continue to place the blame for economic crises or slowdown at the door of the developing world, thereby justifying ever more intrusive forms of surveillance and control through neoliberal knowledge. Given the assumption of rational and efficient behaviour of financial actors, such as CalPERS, the occurrence of crises is largely blamed on internal factors of state failure or, in neoliberal parlance, poor governance structures and lack of sound macroeconomic fundamentals of developing countries. As we saw above, the PCI was subject to revision each time a major crisis occurred, whether it originated in the Third World (East Asian crisis) or in the United States (corporate accounting scandals of the early 2000s) (see Soederberg 2009). The underlying assumption in each revision of the Index, and paralleling one of the basic assumptions driving the reformulation of the Washington Consensus, i.e. the post-Washington Consensus (Fine 2006), was not merely an acknowledgement of market failure, but rather of state failure to provide a free-market environment. Crony capitalism, rent-seeking behaviour and weak legal systems, for example, were believed to have led to the distortion of the competitive tendencies of rational economic actors.

An important consequence of this neoliberal knowledge, which is rooted in the 'economics as a science' assumption, has served to naturalise further the efficiency and desirability of Anglo-American forms of corporate governance (Soederberg 2004). One criticism of the high concentration of family ownership of indigenous, publicly listed corporations, for instance, is that the management and board of directors are effectively insulated from market discipline, due to, for example, their lack of exposure to outside voices, such as minority shareholders. The assumption here is that, in the presence of good governance structures, such as the democratic and legal systems found in the United States, there will be less chance of market failure. The 2001 Enron-style debacles and sub-prime mortgage and credit crises in the United States towards the end of the 2000s have revealed that the same short-term, speculative and irrational 'herd-behaviour', as well as 'bad' corporate governance practices, are alive and well across the globe (Soederberg 2009).

There is an important feature of the cultural code of economics that Escobar overlooks, however. While the assumption of rationality appears to legitimise the reductionism that occurs in the portrayal of economics as a science, it also helps to cloak the social power inherent in capital by treating the latter as some sort of neutral object or thing. The ability of CalPERS' investment in publicly listed corporations in the developing world to increase in value is believed by neoclassical economists to occur through harmonious and equal relations (both of which take place on a level playing field) between rational market actors (buyers and sellers). The latter conditions are predicated on the ability of the state to provide the right policy and institutional atmosphere (good governance), so as to encourage free market competition by ensuring, for example, that universal laws apply to both foreign and local capitalists regarding the protection of private property, the expression of 'voice' in the management of corporations, sound macroeconomic policy framework (liberalised financial system), the avoidance of formulating policy that encourages rent-seeking behaviour, and so forth.

There are at least two immediate and interrelated outcomes in treating capital as an object as opposed to a social relation. First, the dominant treatment of capital as an entity devoid of social power fails to acknowledge the exploitative relationship that occurs between capitalists and labour in the creation of surplus value. Investors, like CalPERS, hold titles of ownership and receive interest (dividends). The latter are not generated in thin air but, in order to share in future surplus value production, must at some point confront labour (Harvey 1999). Second, by treating capital as a thing, the cultural code of economics conceals the role and class nature of the bourgeois state, and thereby depoliticises and declasses the gloss of good governance in which the country factors of the Index are encased. While so-called good governance practices acknowledge the role of the state in creating the ideal conditions for the untrammelled freedom of the market, they do so by representing the state as a set of neutral institutions and policies, thereby concealing its repressive and ideological functions. Thus the content of the Index masks the capitalist nature of the state and its role in recreating the conditions for expanded reproduction of capital accumulation, through, for example, the establishment of good governance principles. The technical and economic aspects of the Index also downplay how the historical configuration of relations of power within a particular national formation can delimit the degree to which Anglo-American forms of good governance can be effectively and swiftly implemented, for example, through the one year of 'cure period' granted by CalPERS, without deeper social conflicts and/or possible threats of economic and political destabilisation.

Following Marx, capital (or, in the case of equity finance, money circulating as capital) is not a thing, but a social relation that takes on historically specific meaning in a class-based society in which the means of production rest in one class (capitalists). Within this societal context, capital cannot increase in value, or turn a profit, without confronting labour through exploitative and unequal relations. Profit is not generated in a conflictless relationship between labour and capitalists, but instead is fraught with social antagonisms. Seen from this perspective, the bourgeois state is required to intervene in order to mediate struggles and thereby recreate the conditions of accumulation. As David Harvey argues:

> The free market, if it is to work, requires a bundle of institutional arrangements and rules that can be guaranteed only by something akin to state power. The freedom of the market has to be guaranteed by law, authority, force, and, *in extremis*, by violence.... Free markets, in short, do not just happen. Nor are they antagonistic to state power in general though they can, of course, be antagonistic to certain ways in which state power might be used to regulate them.
> (Harvey 2000: 178)

Cultural homogenisation and objectification

The act of denying a country its individual history, culture and political characteristics objectifies national social formations, so that 'scientific' assessments of its investment potential can be undertaken. This process of 'othering' also permits capitalists to control social space within these countries by naturalising the importance of reducing all economic, political and social activities to the goal of convincing investors that the country is a good investment site. The country categorisation of the Index is rooted in cultural imperialism that feeds off of, and is reinforced by, what Edward Said refers to as 'orientalism' that occurs through the spatial (re-)organisation of capital. An example of this process may be found in the manner in which the PCI establishes two main investment categories involving 24 'developed' countries and 27 'emerging markets' (Said 1979). This representation demarcates and re-creates geopolitical space or imaginative geographies that showcase the evolutionary phases of 'progress' across the globe. For instance, a large majority of the world's population (approximately 140 countries), who fall outside the two categories of the PCI, are viewed not only as high risk, and therefore unworthy investment sites, but also as failures of development, due to their unwillingness and/or inability to embrace Western expert knowledge, technology and management skills (www.un.org/Overview/unmember.html).

The PCI does not allow for any differentiation between the various countries. Take, for example, the term 'emerging market economies', which was constructed by the International Financial Corporation, a branch of the World Bank Group, in 1981 to encourage foreign investment in select countries in the global South. It has reduced the historically distinct cultural, social and political characteristics of entire countries to a potential investment site, or simply 'financial markets'. Yet, as Escobar suggests, this 'discursive homogenization (which entails the erasure of the complexity and diversity of Third World peoples, so a squatter in Mexico City, a Nepalese peasant, and a Tuareg nomad become equivalent to each other as poor and underdeveloped)' is necessary to exercise power over the Third World (Escobar 1995: 53). An important consequence of discursive homogenisation has been the objectification of countries that are rated by Wilshire through the PCI. The 'political risk factors' of the Index (i.e. political stability, transparency and productive labour standards), for instance, are presented in an unproblematic fashion as embodying the universalised understanding of how markets and states should be optimally organised, not to meet the social, physical, spiritual and mental needs of people working and living in the Third World, but instead to support the requests of foreign capitalists by constructing stable political and legal systems, so that their investments are made to feel safe and secure (Soederberg 2006).

The benefits of creating a better investment climate are portrayed by the Index not only as a win-win situation for developing countries and foreign investors, but also as universal. According to the World Bank,

> investment climate improvements are the driving force for growth and poverty reduction. A good investment climate is one that is better for everyone in two dimensions. It benefits society as a whole, not just firms. And it expands opportunities for all firms, not just large or influential firms.
>
> (World Bank 2004: 35)

The knowledge entailed in the prescription of desirable investment sites is further normalised by portraying the interests and goals (material gains) of foreign investors and (apolitical and asocial) markets of (homogenised) Third World countries as fundamentally the same, and thereby side-stepping issues of power, struggle, class, contestation, gender and race.

Viewed against the above backdrop, the SRI dimension of the PCI may be seen as a social construct that reflects and bolsters the ultimate goal of development: expanded reproduction of capital. The 'political risk or country factors' of the PCI are not designed to address humanitarian concerns, but have been crafted, first and foremost, to assist in the establishment and reproduction of good investment climates for US institutional investors. The significance of transparent and impartial governments and legal systems vis-à-vis 'development' are not new, however. In several of its World Development Reports, the World Bank has stressed the importance of 'good governance' in the creation and maintenance of well-functioning markets (Fine 2006). Corruption and lack of property rights are seen as hindering the state's ability to provide market-supporting institutions, due to the absence of effective restraints on arbitrary behaviour of public officials (World Bank 2001). In other words, Western-based institutional investors reject certain forms of regulating the market, particularly those that do not provide them with enough power once in the host country, such as the structures of the development state model. Economic and political inequality, which are brought about by poor labour standards and lack of basic human rights, lead to economic inefficiency, political conflict (and therefore instability) and institutional frailty – all of which act to hinder poverty reduction and growth (development) (World Bank 2005). To obtain the latter goal, the political risk factors of the PCI, such as civil liberties, human rights, freedom of the press and independent judiciary and legal protection, need to appear neutral, desirable and universally applicable.

Conclusion

I have argued that when we look behind the progressive veil of responsible investing strategies of the third largest pension fund in the world we are able to observe disciplinary features associated with the normalisation and legitimation of the neoliberal development agenda. In 2007, the Board of Trustees of CalPERS actively debated the future of the Index, especially in light of the fact that the exclusion from profitable, yet 'impermissible', investment sites such as Pakistan, China, Egypt, and so forth, was believed to have led to a loss of performance of about $401 million from August to December 2002. Whatever the fate of the PCI, its neoliberal content and disciplinary features mirror a wider tendency towards expanding meanings of corporate governance, or what has been referred to as the 'corporate governance-socially responsibility nexus' or 'cross-over proposals', which is embodied in the United Nations Principles of Responsible Investment (UNPRI). CalPERS, along with some of the largest pension funds in the world, are signatories to the UNPRI. The UNPRI and the corporate governance–SRI nexus continue to smooth over the contradictions and contestation linked to the highly uneven and exploitative nature of global capitalism, especially in its neoliberal form.

This is not to suggest that SRI, or 'cross-over proposals', is an ineffective form of resistance to the growing power of corporations over all aspects of social life. Indeed, there have been important victories by stakeholders applying pressure to the Board of Directors of large corporations to change investment decisions and strategies. Nonetheless, we must remain wary and critical of SRI-based strategies that are devised and employed to judge 'objectively' whether countries are worthy of either receiving foreign investment or divestment (i.e. blacklisting a country from the Index). More fundamentally, while the reduction of financial risk to the investor will remain a central feature of SRI and cross-over proposals, care must be taken to question the tendency toward the marketisation of social concerns, i.e. the reduction of social issues to economic criteria. This process of resisting the neoliberal tendency of establishing institutional conditions to foster economic growth, which lies at the heart of the PCI and, by extension, the post-Washington Consensus, can only be realised, however, within an alternative accumulation paradigm (see the Introduction to this volume).

References

Escobar, A. (1995) *Encountering Development. The Making and Unmaking of the Third World*. Princeton: Princeton University Press.

Fine, B. (2006) 'The New Development Economics', in K.S. Jomo and Ben Fine (eds) *Development Economics: After the Washington Consensus*. London: Zed Books, pp. 1–20.

Harvey, D. (1989) *The Urban Experience*. Boston: Johns Hopkins University Press.

Harvey, D. (1999) *The Limits to Capital*. London: Verso.

Harvey, D. (2000) *Spaces of Hope*. Berkeley: University of California Press.

Harvey, D. (2003) 'The 'New' Imperialism', in Leo Panitch and Colin Leys (eds) *Socialist Register*. London: Merlin Press.

Hebb, T. and Wójcik, D. (2005) 'Global Standards and Emerging Markets: the Institutional Investment Value Chain and CalPERS' Investment Strategy'. *Environment and Planning A*, 37(11), pp. 1955–74.

International Finance Corporation (2005) 'Emerging Markets Heading for Banner Year in 2006: IFC Notes Progress, Development Challenges Ahead'. Online, available at: www.ifc.org/ifcext/home.nsf/Content/Emerging_Mkts_2006 (accessed 14 December 2005).

Marx, Karl (1981) *Capital Volume 3*. London: Penguin.

Rist, G. (2002) *The History of Development: From Western Origins to Global Faith*. London: Zed Books.

Said, E. (1979) *Orientalism*. New York: Vintage Books.

Soederberg, S. (2004) *The Politics of the New International Financial Architecture: Reimposing Neoliberal Domination in the Global South*. London: Zed Books.

Soederberg, S. (2006) *Global Governance in Question: Empire, Class, and the New Common Sense in Managing North-South Relations*. London: Pluto Press.

Soederberg, S. (2009) *Corporate Power and Ownership in Contemporary Capitalism: The Politics of Resistance and Domination*. London: Routledge.

World Bank (2001) *World Development Report 2002: Building Institutions for Markets*. New York: Oxford University Press.

World Bank (2004) *World Development Report 2005: A Better Investment Climate for Everyone*. New York: Oxford University Press.

World Bank (2005) *World Development Report 2006: Equity and Development*. New York: Oxford University Press.

World Bank (2006) *Global Development Finance 2007 – The Globalization of Corporate Finance in Developing Countries*. Washington, DC: World Bank Group.

Zhuang, J., Edwards, D., Webb, D. and Capulong, M.V.A. (2000) *Corporate Governance and Finance in East Asia: A Study of Indonesia, Republic of Korea, Malaysia, Philippines, and Thailand*. Manila: Asian Development Bank

6 Global unions and global capitalism

Contest or accommodation?

Seyhan Erdoğdu

The stage of the internationalisation and restructuring of capitalism starting around 1980 can be named globalisation, and neoliberalism has been both the social philosophy and the political strategy of this capital-driven globalisation. The basic reason behind this transformation in the world economy is the crisis that emerged in the mid-1960s due to the intensive post-war capital accumulation and monopolisation in developed economies. The way to overcome the crisis was through the elimination of the obstacles to the free movement of goods, services and capital on a global scale, and downsizing of the public sphere. Since the 1980s, neoliberalism began to dominate the economic policies of governments around the world.

As part of this process, trade unions worldwide have witnessed the globalisation of the problems of their existing and potential members. In most countries, the trade unions gradually lost members while their traditional means of struggle at national level, including collective bargaining and strikes, as well as their involvement in domestic politics, became less effective. These processes lent support to the view that solutions to these global problems should also be global. The impact of globalisation on the trade union movement was widely discussed, and trade union policies and programmes began to change in this new environment. One of the elements brought under consideration was the level of union organisation, where it was increasingly argued that global solutions could be found only through the international trade union movement, representing the national trade unions as organisations of the real movement of the working classes.

Since the 1990s, the capacity of the international trade union movement to represent trade unions worldwide has increased considerably as a result of new affiliations from the ex-socialist countries and the developing world, as well as through mergers at the international level. With this increased capacity of representation, the international trade union movement is able to play an increasingly significant role creating a global labour movement. While globalisation brings changes in the international trade union movement, the movement in turn can influence the process of globalisation through its social practices. This chapter analyses the policy and actions of the international trade union movement in the process of globalisation. The analysis is based mainly on the examination of

World Congress reports and publications of international trade union organisations between 1980 and 2006, as well as interviews conducted with international trade union leaders.[1]

International trade union organisations

The term 'international trade union organisations' refers mainly to the International Confederation of Free Trade Unions (ICFTU), which merged with the World Confederation of Labour (WCL) in 2006, and was renamed as the International Trade Union Confederation (ITUC), and to international industry-based federations which cooperate with it. In 2006, the ITUC was a global international trade union centre representing 168 million workers and 311 organisations from 155 countries, and there were 11 industry-based federations, formerly known as International Trade Secretariats (ITS), which are now called Global Union Federations (GUF).

Of course, the international trade union movement was not historically confined to the ICFTU and its predecessors, the International Secretariat of National Trade Union Centres (1902–12), International Federation of Trade Unions (1912–44) and World Federation of Trade Unions (1945–9). The First International (1864–76) included trade union organisations; the Second International (1889–1914/23) accepted affiliation by trade unions; the Red Trade Union International was founded in Moscow under the influence of the Third International (1921–37); the International Federation of Christian Trade Unions/International Confederation of Christian Trade Unions/World Confederation of Labour (1919–46–68–2006) and the World Federation of Trade Unions (WFTU) (1949–) were all international organisations leaving their imprint on the history of international trade union movement with their specific organisational, political and ideological specificities (Işıklı 1990). However, what remains from these movements in the era of globalisation are the ICFTU and the industry-based federations under its umbrella. The ICFTU and the industry-based federations have been dominated by a Europe-centred social democratic reformism despite the different trade union approaches among them.

Historical background

After the Second World War the capitalist world, alarmed at the possibility of recurrence of trade wars, financial crises and depression, sought new solutions in line with liberal economic thought. These policies were influenced by social forces seeking to build defences against the disasters brought about by unregulated capitalism during the Great Depression. The political centres planning the post-war world economy rearranged international economic relations within the framework of a consensus based upon an interventionist state, or an embedded liberalism. Thus, the post-war economy of the developed capitalist countries was built on the principles of multilateralism at the international level, accompanied by national economic policies geared towards the provision of stable and secure lives for their own citizens. In other words, international liberalism was supported by domestic interventionism. The measures intended to maintain stability in the national economies should not become an obstacle to the new international economic relations (Cohn 2000: 86–7). In the backdrop of this combination of liberalism and intervention, there was a class compromise between labour and capital.

In the period of the Bretton Woods system, the target was to revitalise international trade in a stable environment for foreign exchange transactions. Speculative capital movements were blocked, in order to preserve the fixed exchange rate system and free trade (Cohn 2000: 141). The post-war policies of the ICFTU were shaped by interventionist liberalism. In terms of politics, the most salient feature of the period was the Cold War between communist states and the Western world, the latter being led by the United States. The international trade union approach of the ICFTU was built on anti-communism. Led by Western trade unions, the ICFTU was not an organisation for the international solidarity of labour, but an organisation used by the trade unions of the developed countries to promote the economic interests of their members. This policy led the unions within the ICFTU to support of the foreign policies of their national governments. Consequently, political differences – particularly between the US and British trade unions – came to the fore in all ICFTU activities (Carew 2000).

After the withdrawal of the US confederation AFL-CIO from the ICFTU in 1969, the latter evolved as an European international where the trade unionism of continental Europe gained more and more influence, in contrast with the AFL-CIO dominance in the Latin American regional organisation ORIT. Taking into account the political weight of continental social democracy, the ICFTU tried to develop a global Keynesian approach in order to confront the neoliberal globalisation taking shape in the late 1970s and early 1980s.

Global Keynesian approach

During the 1980s, the consensus in the advanced capitalist countries incorporating democracy and the welfare state started to weaken. This period is also marked by the debt crisis which devastated many developing countries who were compelled to bow before the neoliberal policies of globalisation, and the collapse of the Soviet Bloc and its inclusion in the expansion and restructuring of capitalism. The international trade union movement stepped into this process of globalisation with a structural and historical legacy already one century old, and found itself in a position to develop new strategies and means of action while defining globalisation in the light of this legacy.

In the early 1980s, the ICFTU and its industry-based federations came up with a global programme for 'Full Employment and an End to Poverty', against the monetarist policies that were being promoted as a panacea (ICFTU 1983). This programme derives from the strategy for the establishment of a new international economic order, adopted by the Independent Commission on International Development Issues (1977–83), known as the Brandt Commission

(Independent Commission on International Development Issues 1980, 1983). The Brandt Report was based on the idea that the stagnation faced by the developed countries at the beginning of the 1980s and the debt crisis faced by the developing countries could be overcome through the national and international regulation of capitalism. According to the Commission, the governments of the developed countries could surmount the crisis and social tensions through far-sighted approaches accompanied by national and international reforms. Failing to do so would risk the collapse of democracy and of the global economy. It would still be necessary to launch reforms at that point, but only after suffering significant losses. In short, the Brandt report says 'reform, either today or tomorrow'. There is no scope for a third possibility, that is, global capitalism securing economic growth and social welfare out of its own workings, since there is no tendency towards internal harmony. On the contrary, unless it is managed, capitalism brings crisis and discord. Harmony at both national and international levels can be achieved through negotiations between nations and classes, which can lead to solutions serving the interests of all parties. Only then would classes and nations abandon their short-term selfish interests and move ahead with the reforms that could yield long-term benefits to everyone.

This stance can be summarised by the transfer of social democracy in politics and Keynesianism in economics up to global level (Loxley 1984). Including a significant representation of peripheral countries, the Brandt Commission also stood for the democratisation of the international organisations. Just as post-war social democracy regarded the state as the regulator of capitalism at national level, the Brandt Commission considered democratised international organisations to be regulators of global capitalism. The task of trade unions within this framework would be to avert the extremes of capitalism. This approach has gained influence on the international trade union movement, especially through the European trade unions.

According to the ICFTU (1983), the main reason for the stagnation of the world economy was the restrictive policies adopted by the industrialised countries against the oil shocks. These policies led to falling growth rates, which spread in waves not only among the industrialised countries but also among the socialist and developing countries. The appropriate response would be to abandon the deflationary policies imposed after the two oil shocks, and return to Keynesian interventionist policies since market economies presumably could not achieve full employment spontaneously. Given the level of integration of these economies and the depth of the stagnation, it had become virtually impossible for any economy to return to expansionist and demand-driven policies or to confront the adverse consequences of national Keynesianism on the exchange rates and the balance of payments. The return to Keynesian policies should take place at the global level, and in a coordinated manner. Public investment should be given priority, and investments in transport, energy, health, education and local development should be the key in overcoming the recession in the industrialised and the developing countries.

The increase in governments' non-wage public spending should boost the world economy through a multiplier effect. Since two-thirds of world output and

80 per cent of world trade rest within the OECD and, particularly, seven of them (the United States, Japan, Germany, France, Great Britain, Italy and Canada), it was considered that their macroeconomic policies would have a disproportionate impact on the world economy. Therefore, the struggle for the return of Keynesian policies was seen as the main task of the trade unions in these countries. The AFL-CIO's return to the ICFTU and the rallying of most trade unions in the industrial countries around demands for an interventionist capitalism brought along an environment more conducive to the introduction of these policies. The ten articles in the Declaration 'Ensuring Full Employment and an End to Poverty', adopted by the ICFTU World Congress in Oslo in 1983 laid down the basis of this global strategy (ICFTU 1983).

In the fourteenth Congress period (1983–8), the ICFTU maintained its ten-article global Keynesian strategy through international and regional meetings as well as various reports submitted to international organisations. During this period, and in the framework of developing a global strategy, the ICFTU pursued policies which prioritised the debt crisis and criticised the structural adjustment programmes advocated by the creditor countries as solutions to the crisis. This stance of the international trade union movement appears more radical than the approach of adding a social dimension to globalisation, which was adopted by the ICFTU and most industry-based federations in the 1990s. Indeed, this radical stance was even more salient during the regional meetings of developing countries and conferences organised by women.

The declaration 'First the People and then the Debt' adopted by the trade unions of Latin America and the Caribbean participating in the ICFTU/ORIT meeting on debt and development in Buenos Aires (24–6 September 1986), which was approved by the ICFTU Governing Body (ICFTU 1988a: 224–9), envisaged radical measures regarding foreign debt and structural adjustment. These measures included the cancellation of external debts; cancellation of loans to illegitimate governments; limits on the share of debt service paid from export revenues; the right of crisis-stricken countries to suspend debt service if people are unemployed and hungry; a moratorium on resource transfers to industrial countries and financial organisations; the reduction of interest rates; sustaining the united front of Latin American indebted countries launched at the 1984 Cartagene Conference and abandoning IMF structural adjustment policies. The same radicalism can also be observed in the 1984 Dakar Declaration (ICFTU 1988a: 229–32) and the ICFTU's Fourth World Women Congress Declaration (1985), which adopted a strong statement against privatisation (ICFTU 1988a: 206).

Liberal reformist approach

The core document prepared for the 1988 Congress of the ICFTU was 'The Challenge of Change: Tasks Ahead for the International Free Trade Union Movement' (ICFTU 1988b). This report signals first steps towards a liberal reformist approach. Coining 'change' in 1988 and 'globalisation' in 1996 as challenges for the trade union movement means that unions are facing tests, and they have to demonstrate their skills steering change through positive channels (Kyloh 1998). Since it is virtually impossible to stop these changes, the trade unions must learn to keep up with them. This includes new technologies, economic internationalisation, liberalisation of trade and capital movements, the shrinking sovereignty of nation-states, and increasing the influence of international organisations on national economies.

In such an environment of 'change', the task of trade unions is to protect the democratic rights and interests of their members and other workers. Since the international movement was dominated by the trade unions of the industrialised countries, their preferred policies became disproportionately influential. Issues coming to the fore during this period included the modernisation of trade unions; organising the women and youth; unionisation of the growing number of unorganised workers; restructuring and the spread of flexible employment; defending trade union rights in developing countries, particularly in export processing zones; the struggle against child labour, partly in order to prevent capital flows to countries where labour costs are much lower, and the limitation of the process of de-industrialisation (ICFTU 1992a). As we moved into the 1990s, additional challenges faced by the ICFTU included the further liberalisation of commodity and service flows, the elimination of obstacles to capital movements, the implementation of privatisation and structural adjustment policies, and the transition of former socialist countries. The ICFTU moved further away from its former Keynesian approach, and closer to a liberal reformist stance.

Although some industry-based federations considered globalisation as a 'threat' as well as a 'challenge', including the Public Services International (PSI), whose affiliates were public sector unions which directly experienced the consequences of privatisation (PSI 2000, 2001), most international trade unions, especially the ICFTU, developed a tendency to regard neoliberal globalisation as irreversible, especially during the first half of the 1990s, after the collapse of the Soviet system. This view of globalisation led to the conditional acceptance of neoliberal policies by the international trade union movement, including privatisation, pursued under the titles of 'reform' and 'restructuring'. Although trade union publications occasionally included some radical critiques against these policies, especially from the trade unions in developing countries, the overall policy of the ICFTU and industry-based federations was based on the perception of capitalist globalisation not as a threat for working people and humanity in general, but as a 'challenge' which may eventually yield its benefits to many nations, the poor and the excluded. According to the ICFTU and the federations, what is needed in order to reap these benefits of globalisation is to ensure the participation of trade unions to the processes of privatisation, reform and restructuring, and to convince transnational capital, developing country governments and intergovernmental organisations to accept minimum labour standards.

In the early 1990s the strategy of the international trade union movement, based on involvement in the process of change in order to mitigate the worst consequences of globalisation, was also advised to the emerging trade unions of the former socialist countries. The role these potential members, as well as the ICFTU, industry-based federations and the European Trade Unions Confederation (ETUC) might have mitigating some of the social problems arising in the transition of the above economies seemed to accentuate the importance of the task of adding a social dimension to globalisation (ICFTU 1992b).

The ICFTU and the federations focused on the protection of workers' rights in cases of privatisation, and avoiding privatisation in some social services areas. The ICFTU agreed that trade and financial liberalisation will bring along growth and employment, and that competition will create a strong incentive for more efficient use of resources. What the ICFTU argues against is competition on the basis of lower labour costs through additional pressures, exploitation and discrimination targeting workers at these enterprises.

While maintaining collective bargaining is one way of halting the minimisation of labour costs, another way is to accept core labour standards. In the face of rather comprehensive agreements on international trade and financial flows, the ICFTU's objection is not against these agreements as such but against the absence of any agreement making international recognition of core labour standards and rights a legal obligation. Just as 'economic flexibility and social security are twin obligations' to be observed at enterprises for a harmonious economic and social progress (ICFTU 2000a: 353), so are trade and financial liberalisation and internationally sanctioned labour rights.

The ICFTU also deems structural adjustment to be the natural outcome of globalisation. In a competitive global market, economies have to engage in a continuous process of restructuring. However, this structural adjustment creates social problems which, in turn, damage international cooperation. The global system has to develop responses in the field of social priorities. The ILO should play a significant role in this regard. Also important are the roles of organisations such as the IMF, the World Bank and the World Trade Organisation (WTO). What falls to the ICFTU is to act as a catalyst prompting the architects of globalisation to develop responses to social problems. Towards the mid-1990s, the international trade union movement realised that no progress could be made in giving a social dimension to the process of globalisation. Yet, this did not bring any modification to the liberal reformist policy line.

In its report *The Global Market – Trade Unionism's Greatest Challenge*, prepared for the Sixteenth World Congress held on 25–9 June 1996, the ICFTU identified the core problem in the agenda of the trade union movement in the twenty-first century as the protection and promotion of workers' rights in an environment of social crisis created by the globalisation of the world economy (ICFTU 1996a). The ICFTU Report gives a detailed account of deepening worldwide inequalities in the process of globalisation; the plight of Africa despite its natural resource wealth; the impact of the debt crisis in Latin America; the violation of trade union rights and poor working conditions underlying the so-called 'Asian miracle'; poverty and unemployment reaching unprecedented dimensions in the former socialist countries; growing inequalities and social exclusion in the industrialised countries; and the weakening of collective bargaining by changes in job organisation and management which are, in turn, triggered by new technologies. The identification of these problems, which became apparent as a result of financial crises, brought no radical change to the strategic approach of the ICFTU, and globalisation was still seen as a process which could be corrected by adding a social dimension to it. As the leading instrument in adding this social dimension, the social clause which was to be given importance particularly within the WTO left its imprint on the policies of international trade union movement. The elimination of child labour was identified as an important element in the social clause and consequently, the ICFTU and other international trade union organisations launched campaigns against child labour.

Adopting the report *The Global Market – Trade Unionism's Greatest Challenge*, the Sixteenth World Congress formulated its resolutions capitalising on the analyses embodied in it. The resolution 'Free Trade Unionism in the 21st Century: Priorities for the ICFTU Action' (ICFTU 1996b: 491–552) reiterated that globalisation had already reached an advanced stage and offered promising opportunities, but it also highlighted some of the problems the trade unions should tackle. The role of the international trade union movement in the collapse of the Soviet system was underlined and it was stated that now free from the rivalry of the WFTU, the ICFTU would proceed for a single trade union centre by furthering cooperation with the WCL. The major areas in which efforts would concentrate were identified as protection of trade union rights, campaigning for employment-creating measures and international labour standards, policies to be pursued vis-à-vis multinational companies, enlarging trade union membership, and gender equality.

The ICFTU invited the IMF Director Michel Camdessus to its Sixteenth World Congress. While inviting Camdessus to rostrum, ICFTU President Trotman (Barbados) made flattering remarks about the IMF Director including how he helped to reduce the number of workers to be laid off as required by Barbados' structural adjustment programme, facilitated the adoption of a price and income policy while wages were frozen as well as a productivity programme which could be considered as a model. He also stated that Camdessus had been in dialogue with the international trade union movement since 1992, that the trade unionists had learned much from him, and that he was 'respectful' to the views of trade unions on the IMF programmes. Taking the rostrum after this introduction, Camdessus made a long speech defending IMF policies (ICFTU 1996b: 165–76). There were few speakers in the Congress raising objection to the presence of Camdessus and the substance of his address. One of them was Luis Anderson (Panama), the Secretary General of the ORIT who ran for the post of ICFTU Secretary General then held by Bill Jordan, but failed due to lack of support from delegates. The following statement by Anderson shows how the liberal reformist strategy clashes with the interest of working people of the south:

> The President, the General Secretary and others have indeed indicated that a process of globalisation can have some positive aspects. What I want to tell

you is that this process of globalisation which workers are suffering from and which the peoples of the whole world are suffering from does not represent progress in any way, either for the workers or, in particular, for the peoples of the southern part of our planet ... Mr Camdessus, I am sure, has seen the statistics of the United Nations Programme for Development which said that if one takes only Brazil one finds that there are 5 million boys and girls under 14 years of age who are today exploited by multinational corporations and by the traders of the streets of Rio and Sao Paolo – exploited in the countryside and exploited every hour of their living day. This is a situation that exists in Latin America and in Africa where hundreds of millions of people live in total poverty. These will all be directly affected, and negatively, by the process of structural adjustment ... Brothers and sisters, we need to overcome the Eurocentrism which at present prevails in the organisation and develop a more horizontal, more democratic and more planetary leadership. If we do not succeed in doing this, the danger is that within our own great organisation we may be basically sowing the seeds of our downfall and our disappearance over time.

(ICFTU 1996b: 195–7)

Indeed, considering that it had started its Thirteenth World Congress with the 'International' (ICFTU 1988b: 32), the Sixteenth World Congress of the ICFTU had made a significant turn away from the socialist tradition of the European trade unionism. The ICFTU developed its policy of negotiating with the IMF and the World Bank in cooperation with affiliated federations in this period, and eventually opened an office in Washington, DC in 1994 (ICFTU 1996c: 49).

The Seventeenth World Congress document of the ICFTU is titled *Globalising Social Justice, Trade Unionism in the 21st Century* (ICFTU 2000b). This document identifies six major problem areas for twenty-first-century trade unionism. The first one is related to the spread and deepening of democracy in the process of globalisation. Trade unions are to play important roles from enterprise level to local level and then to international level in achieving this end. It is stated that, while globalisation has the potential to eliminate poverty and unemployment, it is instead deepening divisions within society and that the modern market economies have to be balanced through democratic governments. Where non-democratic governments exist, the 'international community' is called to impose economic sanctions (ICFTU 2000b: 7). However, while the international system, UN Security Council, IMF and World Bank are entitled to intervene in national contexts when it comes to human and trade union rights either through military force or economic sanctions, there is no comprehensive suggestion for the democratisation of these institutions themselves.

The second concern is giving a human face to globalisation. For this, it is suggested that good governance comprising transparency, accountability and participation should be established at all levels from workplaces and nation-states up to international organisations. At the workplace level, the ILO 'Decent Work' programme (ILO 1999) should be the starting point. At the national level, the governments should provide social protection in line with internationally set rules in order to enhance the potential benefits of expanded trade and investment in the process of globalisation and to reduce the social cost of rather swift change. Finally, at the international level, the poverty alleviation programmes of the IMF and World Bank are considered positive steps to supplement the structural adjustment programmes.

The major rearrangement suggested in regard to international macroeconomic policies is the regulation of the financial markets of developing countries. As to ways of introducing these regulations and arrangements, there is some mention of initiatives to reform international finance following the Asian crisis, and the IMF patented codes and guides are deemed as public intervention to global economy. Reduction of the debts of the most impoverished countries and making this conditional upon the observance of human rights and core labour standards constitute another policy line suggested. The liberalisation of trade and investment is to be supported provided that the social clause is incorporated into the agreements of WTO and a future MAI (Multilateral Agreement on Investment), and that education and health sectors are excluded. Complementing the MAI with a 'development clause' reflecting the demands of developing countries is defended as a way of increasing the transparency of the system and preventing individual governments from placing in open-ended exemptions. Privatisation is criticised only in cases where it is 'badly planned and hasty' (ICFTU 2000b: 15).

The third problem area is securing trade union rights and core labour standards. This specific area is elaborated mainly in reference to violations in trade union rights particularly in developing countries, child labour, forced labour, poor working conditions in free trade zones and problems deriving from the informal sector. Female, young, migrant and elderly workers as well as the disabled are mentioned as groups that suffer discrimination. The fourth problem area is ending discrimination at workplaces. The fifth one is related to getting workers organised in multinational companies. The policies related to multinationals include: drawing a multilateral framework for investment by multinational companies with an improved MAI that features a social as well as an environmental clause; social dialogue with multinational companies; making use of company codes of conduct; cooperation of trade unions with multinationals in fighting corruption; social management of pension funds and organisation of investor initiatives; establishment of advisory bodies at company level; international trade union campaigns focusing on multinationals; and unionisation in the informal end of the production chain. It is suggested that irregular forms of employment created by flexibility, atypical work and informality in the global production chain should be regulated with rights equivalent to those in formal employment and new strategies should be developed for the unionisation of workers in informal employment. The sixth and the last issue concerns the new strategies and tactics that the trade union movement of the twenty-first century needs to develop for confronting the impact of globalisation. On the basis of problem areas mentioned in the ICFTU document, the Seventeenth World Congress resolutions identified the priorities of the trade union movements in the new century with respect to the right of organising, organising the unorganised, equality at work, 'decent jobs' for all, alliances for ensuring the accountability of multinationals, and adaptation of trade unions to changing working life.

The trade unions of advanced capitalist countries, the winners of globalisation, have been influential in the adoption of the liberal reformist strategy in the international trade union movement. The liberal reformist policies of the international trade union organisations reflect the search of their quantitatively and qualitatively dominant members, i.e. the unionised workers of the advanced capitalist countries, for their national and sectoral interests that cannot be achieved through national action.[2] Nevertheless, there are ways open to the trade unions of developing countries, the losers of globalisation, to influence and give shape to the Congress resolutions of the ICFTU and global union federations. The term 'resolution machines' is used for international trade union organisations (Wedin 1974: 11). Indeed, these organisations have adopted too many resolutions which have little or no practical meaning. Still, the Congress resolutions bear importance in reflecting trade unions' political tendencies at least in broad lines. According to the ICFTU Constitution, the programme and the main policy line of the organisation are both established by the World Congress. The same holds true for the industry-based federations. Congress resolutions are shaped through a participatory mechanism well in advance of Congresses, leaving the final decision to the Congress itself. It is beyond doubt that the experts in the ICFTU secretariat who draft resolutions as well as the trade unions in industrialised countries play a more important role in this mechanism. Yet, this fact per se does not alter the participatory structure in the drafting of resolutions.

In the period discussed above, the trade unions from developing countries did not come up with draft resolutions within the framework of a global union strategy alternative to the liberal reformist policy line adopted by the ICFTU and its industry-based federations. Why the trade unions of the developing countries are not the owners of the ICFTU resolutions cannot be explained only by the dominance of the trade unions of the developed world in the international trade union organisational structures. If the members and delegates from developing countries were to exert pressure regarding, say, the total rejection of privatisations and structural adjustment programmes, democratisation of the governing bodies of international organisations, the impositions of capital controls and the defence of public investments, it is inevitable that this pressure would find its reflections on the international trade union movement despite the weight of industrialised countries in the composition of delegations. However, for the time being, it is not possible to speak about such pressure in the congresses of the ICFTU or industry-based federations.

While the root cause of this shortcoming deserves a separate study, some possible explanations can be given here: the weakness of trade unions in developing countries in terms of membership; the fact that these unions too represent worker groups that can be considered as 'privileged' in the context of their respective countries; failure to develop radical solutions against globalisation as a coherent whole; the indebtedness that holds these countries back from developing policies alternative to globalisation; inability to allocate sufficient personnel and resources to international relations; the fact that trade unions still conceive short-term economic interests of workers only within national boundaries and the atmosphere created by a Europe-centred trade union movement which precludes the active participation of trade unions from developing countries.

Instruments of action of the international trade union movement

The tool which is credited with the greatest importance in implementing the liberal reformist strategy adopted by the ICFTU and industry-based federations is the inclusion of a social clause which covers the core labour standards in rules set for the liberalisation of trade and investments at both regional and international levels. Hence, it is expected that with the liberalisation of commodity, service and capital flows and protection of intellectual property rights, rights of labour are to be protected. It is demanded that these core labour standards expressed as a social clause are tied to trade sanctions within the WTO or included in the loan qualifications of international finance organisations.[3] Influencing the management of 'Pension Funds' and organising 'Investor Initiatives' are other types of special initiatives intended to shape the flow of financial capital on the basis of social clause. However, the contradictory nature of these initiatives also called 'Workers' Capital' prevents them from being effective instruments of international trade union pressure.

Another major approach of the international trade union movement is to exert pressure on intergovernmental organisations, foremost among them the IMF and the World Bank, and to establish an institutional and permanent cooperation with these organisations with structural and functional prerogatives. It must, however, be stated that while the international trade union movement claims to be working for an international-level social democratic milieu and practices of social corporatism, even the unions in continental Europe with strong social corporatist structures have faced the negative pressures from the neoliberal environment. While drifting farther away from its social content, the corporatism is now assuming the function of an instrument to negotiate concessions from the working masses with the threat of unemployment under the conditions of capitalist restructuring. The global social corporatism that the international trade union movement claims to be creating is in contradiction with the new liberal structuring of global capitalism. Indeed, it is not possible to say that the meetings with such intergovernmental organisations as the IMF, World Bank, WTO and OECD and the pressures exerted through various channels have so far resulted in any notable change in the economic and social policies of these organisations. On the contrary, it can be said that within the process of governing the antagonistic relation between capital and labour, efforts by the international trade union movement to move towards an institutionalised cooperation with the WTO, IMF and World Bank with structural and functional prerogatives will be instrumental not in a 'global social corporatism' but in the 'global governance' in favour of the interests of the multinational capital.

Another set of instruments that global trade unions are trying to develop is related to multinational companies. Sheer economic size as well as organisational structure of these companies gives them an upper hand in their global activities, especially in developing countries, before national governments and workers' organisations. International trade union movements support initiatives such as Global Contract, Social Accountability 8000 Standards, Corporate Codes of Conduct, Social Labelling and Social Certification, which are hoped to be functional in making corporations more sensitive to their social responsibility. However, the common feature of all these initiatives is that they depend upon the voluntary compliance by multinationals. It is expected that multinationals which do not recognise their social responsibilities will lose by shrinking market share or lower shareholder value. It should be stressed that most social responsibility instruments voluntarily adopted by multinational companies are merely loose texts devoid of implementation and supervision mechanisms, and even when such mechanisms exist, they cannot be effectively implemented as a result of the fragmented nature of global production and trade.

Basic instruments envisaged by the Global Trade Union Federations (World Company Networks, trans-boundary organisations, framework agreements, transnational industrial actions), in their global trade union activities run parallel to the traditional organisation, collective agreement and industrial action lines of national trade unions.

Parallel to the revival of the concept of global trade unionism in the 1990s, a similar rise was also observed in the activities of World Company Councils and Networks. What is expected of these Councils/Networks is to create environments in which workers in different countries can learn about each other's working conditions, learn the structure and policies of their respective companies, inform each other about developments in company restructuring and, if needed, engage in solidarity actions. Examples of trans-boundary organisation come to the fore as a different form of international solidarity in the era of globalisation. Yet, such organisational initiatives constituting a part of multinational company campaigns are viewed mainly as symbolic instruments supporting national level organisations.

Another field of activity of the Global Union Federations is the signing of framework agreements with multinationals based on the provisions of the social clause. While such international framework agreements are not intended to replace national level collective agreements, the very nature and mechanism of implementation of these agreements are not conducive to such replacement anyway. When compared with the corporate codes of conduct, framework agreements are more effective instruments in forcing companies into socially responsible behaviour. Still, unless accompanied by trade union power at national level, they cannot play a significant role in improving industrial relations and where there is local trade union power there is less need for framework agreements.

It can be said that the international trade union movement is far from materialising primary collective action in multinational companies. As for secondary collective action at the international level, examples are rare and what exists is far from being truly global. It must however be added that, starting from the 1990s, international trade union solidarity and action against violations by multi-national companies is on the rise.

As tools of action for global trade unionism, organisation in multinationals, framework agreements and global solidarity actions bear the potential of becoming more effective with the active participation of trade unions from developing countries. In so far as they are supported by multinational company networks and global solidarity actions, global framework agreements appear as instruments that global trade unionism must develop further.

From liberal to social reformism?

During the globalisation of the 2000s, it has become impossible to ignore facts such as rising unemployment; deepening inequalities worldwide; the plight of Africa despite its richness in natural resources; Latin America suffering a collapse brought along by the debt crisis, structural adjustment and privatisations; violation of trade union rights and heavy working conditions all over the world; rising poverty and unemployment in many of the former socialist countries; ever-spreading inequalities and social exclusion in industrialised countries; and collective bargaining regimes weakened by changes in job organisation and management (ILO 2004).

Consequently, the ICFTU's liberal reformist approach characterising the period until the 2000s, which focused on the potential benefits of globalisation, has started to give way to a social reformist tendency which emphasises the 'threats' of the same process with ever-deepening problems of worldwide unemployment, poverty and social exclusion, and suggests a fair globalisation. Discourse on globalisation which was initially welcomed as a process to the benefit of all parties, has started to change when it became apparent that it actually fuelled the polarisation of the rich and the poor and triggered social crisis. The first hints of this change emerged in the Eighteenth World Congress held in 2004 (ICFTU 2004) and the discourse turned even harsher during the merging Congress of 2006 (ICFTU 2006). Indeed, the 2006 World Congress no longer talked about giving a human face to globalisation but *'changing it fundamentally'* (ITUC 2006: 1).

Debt cancelling, restructuring and review of standing debts so as to identify the responsibilities of debtors and creditors are the ways suggested for the solution of debt crisis. Other suggestions include reforms of the governing structures of the IMF, the World Bank and the WTO, maintaining dialogue with these organisations for the purpose of giving effect to fundamental changes in their policies, and standing against them when they act contrary to the interests of the working people and the poor. It is now declared that a sustainable and socially fair development alternative can be built against the IMF and the World Bank policies which are obsessed with privatisation and liberalisation of trade and capital flows, the de-regulation of labour markets and undermining the capacity of national governments, all detrimental to the interests of the working people and the poor.

Standing against the free trade model adopted by the WTO which aggravates exploitation, inequalities and environmental destruction; supporting developing countries in their strategy to develop local industries; demanding a strengthened position for them in the decision-making processes of the WTO; and calling for urgent exclusion of education, health, water supply, public transportation and other essential services from the scope of liberalisation are other elements in the new discourse. The ITUC also adopted a more radical language against the multinational companies and called for combat against their corruption and illicit activities, and for introducing mechanisms of supervision and sanctioning through the adoption of binding national and international arrangements concerning the multinationals. It was also underlined that legislation and collective agreements came before the policy of corporate social responsibility. Nevertheless, what was summarised above is merely discourse and it is not clear when and through which means this discourse will translate into action. It shall be seen in years to come if and how this social reformist discourse finds its reflections in practice and whether the instruments of action geared to alter capitalist globalisation fundamentally can be created or not.

Notes

1 See Erdoğdu (2006).
2 For a theory if international trade union movement along these lines see Logue (1980).
3 The World Bank's private-sector arm, the International Finance Corporation (IFC), since May 2006, has required that all enterprises borrowing from IFC abide by the core labour standards.

References

Carew, A. (2000), 'Towards a Free Trade Union Centre: The Confederation of Free Trade Unions (1949–1972)', in M. van der Linden (ed.), *The International Confederation of Free Trade Unions*, Bern: Peter Lang, pp. 187–339.
Cohn, T.H. (2000), *Global Political Economy, Theory and Practice*, New York: Longman.
Erdoğdu, S. (2006), *Küreselleşme Sürecinde Uluslararası Sendikacılık, (International Trade Unionism in the Era of Globalisation*, Ankara: İmge Publishers.
ICFTU (1983), *Report of Thirteenth Congress*, Brussels: ICFTU.
ICFTU (1988a), *Report of the Fourteenth World Congress*, Brussels: ICFTU.
ICFTU (1988b), *Decisions of the Fourteenth World Congress*, Brussels: ICFTU.
ICFTU (1992a), *Report of the Fifteenth World Congress*, Brussels: ICFTU.
ICFTU (1992b), *Free Trade Unions for a Democratic World Order: The Role of the ICFTU*, Brussels: ICFTU.
ICFTU (1996a), *The Global Market – Trade Unionism's Greatest Challenge*, Brussels: ICFTU.
ICFTU (1996b), *Report of the Sixteenth World Congress*, Brussels: ICFTU.
ICFTU (1996c), *Report on Activities, Financial Reports, 1991–1994, Sixteenth World Congress*, Brussels: ICFTU.
ICFTU (2000a), *Report on Activities and Financial Reports 1994–1998*, Brussels: ICFTU.

ICFTU (2000b), *Globalising Social Justice, Trade Unionism in the 21st Century*, Executive Summary, Brussels: ICFTU.

ICFTU (2000c), *Decisions of the Congress, 17th World Congress of the ICFTU*, Brussels: ICFTU.

ICFTU (2004), *Globalising Solidarity, Building a Global Union for the Future, Final Resolution, 18th World Congress*, Brussels: ICFTU.

ICFTU (2006), *Report on Activities of the Confederation and Financial Reports, for the Period 2004–2006*, Brussels: ICFTU.

ILO (1999), *Decent Work, Report of the Director General*, Geneva: International Labour Office.

ILO (2004), *A Fair Globalisation, the Role of the ILO*, Report of the Director General on the World Commission on the Social Dimension of Globalisation, International Labour Conference, 92nd Session, Geneva: International Labour Office.

Independent Commission on International Development Issues (1980), *North-South, a Programme for Survival*, Cambridge: MIT Press.

Independent Commission on International Development Issues (1983), *Common Crises: North-South Cooperation for World Recovery*, Cambridge: MIT Press.

Işıklı, A. (1990), 'Uluslararası Sendikal Örgütler', *Cahit Talas'a Armağan*, Ankara: Mülkiyeliler Birliği Vakfı, pp. 293–320.

ITUC (2006), *Programme of the ITUC, Adopted by the Founding Congress of the ITUC Vienna, 1–3 November 2006*, www.ituc-csi.org.

Kyloh, R. (ed.) (1998), *Mastering the Challenge of Globalisation: Towards a Trade Union Agenda*, ILO Bureau for Workers' Activities, Working Paper. Geneva: International Labour Office.

Logue, J. (1980), *Toward a Theory of Trade Union Internationalism*, Kent, Ohio: Kent Popular Press.

Loxley, J. (1984), 'Saving the World Economy', *Monthly Review*, September, pp. 22–34.

PSI (2000), *Report of Activities 2000*, Ferney-Voltaire: Public Services International.

PSI (2001), *Report of Activities 2001*, Ferney-Voltaire: Public Services International.

Wedin, A. (1974), *International Trade Union Solidarity. ICFTU 1957–1965*, Stockholm: LO/Prisma.

7 Neoliberalism and the politics of war

The case of Iraq

Filiz Zabcı

The occupation of Iraq by the United States is a striking example of the relationship between war and politics, as it demonstrates that war has become a key mechanism for the expansion of neoliberal policies and financialisation. During the Clinton administration, many indirect military interventions have been legitimated by the strategy called 'humanitarian intervention'. The Bush administration planned a new national security strategy which included a doctrine of 'pre-emptive war' against 'terrorist and hostile states'. This strategy paved the way to the occupation of Afghanistan and Iraq. It is obvious that, as a strategy 'pre-emptive war' shifted the US foreign policy towards a more aggressive stance.

From a critical point of view, it is possible to claim that by this strategy the United States aims not only to access but also to control the energy resources; that is, the control of the direction of pipelines and production. At the same time, pre-emptive war is a strategic element of the general policy of expansion of corporate capitalism to regions and countries in which neoliberal policies yet to be implemented. In the case of the invasion of Iraq, the war became an instrument of toppling Saddam's interventionist state and implementing neoliberal economic policies. The new economic agenda and new economic laws (especially the Iraqi oil law) paved the way for privatisation of Iraqi oil and opened the market for foreign oil companies. This chapter examines the relationship between the expansion of neoliberal globalisation policies and the strategy of pre-emptive war by focusing on the implementation of radical liberalisation policies and realisation of sweeping advantages of multinational corporations in Iraq after the invasion.

New wars, new politics

The Prussian General Carl von Clausewitz has describes war as a continuation of politics in another level and with other tools.[1] Clausewitz underlines that organised war based on armed conflict is a significant part of politics. Indeed, we can define war as a form of daily existence of capitalism as well as its style of preservation. Let us think about economical life. Every day, there is a cruel war between capitalists: commercial wars, stock market wars, productivity and profit wars etc.[2] In addition, there are wars that are not based on armed forces: diplomatic wars, armament race, technological superiority wars, wars for taking over national or international markets, wars for establishing cultural hegemony etc. Each of us is like a warrior wearing a helmet and aiming to beat our rival. This competition reveals the structure of capitalism that curtails us from being free human beings. This section will not deal with such a war panorama; it attempts to provide some information and data concerning the new shapes it acquired recently, i.e. harsher and barbarian types of war.

According to the information provided by the historians, the twentieth century is the bloodiest and the most murderous century of written history. The number of people who died due to wars is 187 million and this number corresponds to 10 per cent of world's population in 1913.[3] In the aftermath of the Second World War, the 'Cold War' period started. This was a temporary peace condition in which hot wars were replaced by ideologies. After the Cold War, the world has entered into a period in which several conflicts have been witnessed. The wars in Europe, Africa, Western and Eastern Asia have shown that peace is as far away at the end of the century as it was at the beginning of the century. When these wars are considered geographically, it is seen that wars among states have disappeared from Europe since 1945, which was the main battlefield until then. During the Cold War period, wars have been experienced in the Middle East and Southern Asia yet they were not at the global scale. However, war has returned back to Eastern Europe since the 1990s.[4]

One of the most important features of the twentieth century wars was the expansion of the boundaries of the wars from armed forces to civilians. The number of civilians affected by wars has increased continuously.[5] While only 5 per cent of the victims of the First World War were civilians, this increased to 66 per cent in the Second World War. Today, 80 to 90 per cent of those affected by wars are civilians.[6] The problem of civilian deaths in Iraq is very dramatic: according to a declaration made by US experts in October 2006, since the beginning of the occupation in 2003, 50,000 civilians have died.[7]

These features of wars continued in the last decade, but there has been a new tendency of handing the right to violence to private hands, therefore a huge private military industry is emerging. The private military industry includes many different groups: mercenaries, private armies, private security and private military companies. Private military companies, which are the most important part of this industry, generally serve the colonialist purposes of the major capitalist states and operate particularly in key strategic zones and in the weak states. Because they do not face any restrictions in terms of national or international law, they can easily violate human rights.[8] Post-9/11, especially the Iraq War, marks a turning point for some private military companies. The biggest military power in Iraq after the United States is such companies. 'The recent conflict in Iraq has drawn the attention of the media to the emergence of private military and security firms, with an estimated 20,000 staff member in the war-torn country'.[9] Private military companies provide a wide range of services, from intelligence, military training, technical aid and logistic support to attack and defence in battlefields.[10] These private military actors make us ponder on the concepts of traditional state and the 'special and temporal' boundaries between war and peace.[11]

When the armies are privatised, it is assumed that the use of legitimate violence is beyond the possession of the states, although we have not yet entered into such a period completely. Legitimate violence, based on legal-rational authority, is a significant feature of the modern state. In other words, the conditions and limits of the use of violence can only be determined by rational laws of state authority. This is an accepted principle in the international system; however the attacks made by the United States on Afghanistan and Iraq are based on a moral ground that is not 'legal' in terms of traditional state warfare. Especially the legitimacy of the military violence during and after the attack by the United States on Iraq is moved to some universal values as democracy, human rights and freedom. Previously in the military intervention made by UN soldiers in Kosovo, 'human rights' was used as a reason to justify violence and this was registered under the name of 'humanitarian intervention'.[12] Actually it is necessary to state that violence is justified not only on a moral but also on a 'religious' basis. The notion of 'just war',[13] which has been forgotten after the placement of the use of violence onto a secular basis, has now become a very important instrument to legalise imperialist violence that would help the capitalist system to perpetuate. While the United States commits violence, parties of conflict are reformulated as 'West' and 'Islam'. This makes us remember the 'clash of civilisations' thesis of Huntington; however there is a difference, as oppositions are not drawn from both parts using the same measurements. 'West' is a geographical term and 'Islam' is a religious term so that civilisation and religion are shown as two main conflict points. Here, is it necessary to emphasise that the West is represented as the civilised party?

Another characteristic of the twentieth century concerning wars is that the boundaries between war and peace, between civil wars and international wars, have been blurred thoroughly. The main principal of the international system was that one country does not have the right to make a military intervention to the land of another. However, examples such as Yugoslavia, Kosovo, Afghanistan and Iraq showed that this principle does not work anymore and we have to review our traditional approaches to war.[14]

As the conventional distinction between war and peace becomes increasingly unclear, war tends to expand even farther, becoming more continual. Today, the blurring of this distinction and the new nature of war, that is its interminable and permanent nature, suspends the international legal framework determining the use of power. What is at stake here is no doubt war as a concept which develops and changes in time. The US policies and especially the strategy of pre-emptive war as a concrete form of these policies create the conditions which mark the continual and uninterrupted exercise of power and violence. In other words, pre-emptive war strategy developed by the United States in 2002 (also known as the Bush Doctrine)[15] is not a symptom of this change; on the contrary, this strategy itself provides the political climate in which politics becomes interlocked with war. Then, what is pre-emptive war strategy and for which purpose it is shaped? This question will bring forth the relation between war and the expansion of neo-liberal capitalism in accordance with the imperialist purposes of the United States.

Pre-emptive war strategy

Pre-emptive war strategy has been formed in the National Security Strategy document of September 2002. The most important aspect of this strategy is that the US military forces could act without any real as well as foreseeable threat. Thus, the Iraq occupation has been justified by establishing such an understanding. Indeed, the threat perceived by the pre-emptive strike has no place in international law.[16] As of 17 March 2006, national security strategy was updated and the Bush administration has emphasised that it is not possible to retract from pre-emptive war. According to the document, although a country may not have a hostile attitude, it could be conceived as a threat or a potential threat and thus this perception could bring the United States to a point to justify its attack. Therefore, although the use of force is justified even if there is complete uncertainty concerning the place and time of the enemy attack, the use of force before any attack constitutes the basis of this strategy. By this feature, pre-emptive war strategy is indicative of a return to 'just war'.[17]

There are many effects of the pre-emptive war strategy. One of them, as mentioned above, is turning war into something permanent and perpetual: its target as well as its reason is not definite. For the use of power, it is sufficient for the United States only to perceive any country or a group as a potential threat. Since the enemy is indefinite, it is possible to create an enemy figure appropriate to the very situation and condition. Thus, Iraq has been declared as an enemy in the National Security Strategy Document of 2002. The reason behind this is that this country had weapons of mass destruction that threatened world peace. This time round, in the updated version of the document, the enemy is defined as Iran. The reason is the hidden nuclear armaments of Iran. This strategy prepares the conditions of war to be permanent as well as perpetual today. Therefore, by a definition, which does not exist in international law, a strategy has been formed to present the use of military power for the desired region and during the desired period as legitimate.[18]

Second, this also prepares an appropriate ground for the expansion of the neo-liberal economic programme. The countries, which are insistent on central and statist economic programmes or national interests, are easily defined as evil states or a threat, according to this strategy, and thus there appears to be a right for the United States to use power against them. In the words of Bush, Iran is perceived as a threat beyond the nuclear problems since it is helping the terrorists, threatening Israel, hindering the settlement of peace in the Middle East, disturbing democracy in Iraq, rejecting people's demands for freedom. The Bush administration emphasises this point in the National Security Strategy Document:

The nuclear issue and our other concerns can ultimately be resolved only if the Iranian regime makes the strategic decision to change these policies, open up its political system, and afford freedom to its people. This is the ultimate goal of US policy.[19]

Hence it would not be incorrect to argue that the presentation of nuclear weapons as a threat does not seem realistic, and that the real aim of the United States is a 'regime change' in Iran. Therefore, in 2006 when the strategy was renewed, the theme of spreading democracy became prominent and the aim of the strategy has been formulated as abolishing tyrannies all over the world. As Baker says,

Without saying what action would be taken against them, the strategy singles out seven nations as prime examples of despotic systems: North Korea, Iran, Syria, Cuba, Belarus, Burma and Zimbabwe. Iran and North Korea receive particular attention because of their nuclear programs, and the strategy vows in both cases to take all necessary measures to protect the United States against them.[20]

The United States aims to reshape the world in a manner which will best suit its interests and thus the Greater Middle East Project is the story of redesigning the borders in this region. Apart from the Middle East, South, Central and Eastern Asia are all defined as regions having vital importance by the Bush administration. It is also mentioned in the same document that Africa is gaining ever-increasing geo-strategic importance and remains one of the priorities of the administration. The United States uses the 'nation building' concept as a means of opening the country to free market and trade, which it invades or performs an armed intervention. For nation-building, first of all, a 'regime change' is required, which implies a puppet government fulfilling the requirements of the United States. Regime changes are accomplished by military means in the cases of Afghanistan and Iraq, whereas in Georgia and Ukraine they were accomplished by means of civil disturbances. In fact, after a regime change, no matter how it takes place, conditions become available for a rapid privatisation as well as opening the country to free trade and foreign countries.

Hardt and Negri presented nation-building as 'one central example of the productive project of bio-power and war'.[21] In their book war appears as a political agent which has a global project actually undertaken by an imperialist state.[22] Nation-building should be understood as a project of playing over political borders as well as the implementation of neoliberal programme. It is obvious that here the objective is not to create a new nation. For example, in the case of Iraq, the Provisional Coalition Government which was formed after the military occupation has not made the country a powerful nation-state. On the contrary, conflicts between ethnic and religious groups persist and even they are actually provoked in a controlled manner by the occupant forces, benefitting from the advantages of instability.

This process of nation-building on the part of the United States in Iraq or Afghanistan can be interpreted as a stylized presentation of the redesigning of borders in this region. This practice, which has frequently been observed in the experiences of the imperial states, comes into being now in the restructuring of the political geography of the Middle East. According to Chossudovsky, the assassination of Benazir Bhutto in Pakistan is a part of the project of redrafting the borders through 'Balkanizing Pakistan' and such ethnic conflicts soon lead the country to political instability. He also points out that the separatist movement (the Baluchistan Liberation Army) in Baluchistan Province, which has wide oil and natural gas reserves, has been supported by the United States and Britain. Washington is in pursuit of the establishment of 'Great Baluchistan' in the territories separated from Iran, Pakistan and Afghanistan, thus provoking Belluci nationalism.[23]

Reconstruction or sharing?

Economic reconstruction, which is the other step of nation-building, implies the re-establishment of the market economy and of the infrastructure which were devastated after the war in Iraq, and also opening the region to foreign companies, the IMF and free trade. Two months before the occupation of Iraq in 2003, the economic programme to be implemented in Iraq was prepared by the consulting company of Bearing Point Inc. on behalf of the Bush administration. This company at the same time signed a contract of US$250 million with the government for building economic infrastructure.[24] Not only this corporation but also academic institutions, special investigation companies and consulting companies have presented plans as well as proposals concerning the revitalisation and restructuring of the Iraqi economy. The most remarkable example among them is the study prepared by the Heritage Foundation. This study, which attracted the attention of the political circles of Washington, presents a road map for the Iraqi economy and especially the privatisation of oil industry. However, beyond all these assumptions, the fundamental parameters of this neoliberal economic programme to be implemented after the war in Iraq are determined in a USID/US Treasury document titled 'Moving the Iraqi Economy from Recovery to Sustainable Growth'. The main elements of the strategy include:

- privatisation of Iraq's industries;
- modernisation of the Baghdad stock exchange;
- giving the Central Bank independence in pursing monetary policy;
- establishing a new currency;
- providing Iraqi businesses with fresh credit;
- creating a legal framework compatible with private ownership, production and distribution;
- rewriting the tax and tariffs system.[25]

Within the framework of the strategies mentioned above, the Iraqi economy is transformed from a central-planning dependent economy to a market economy.[26] First of all, Iraqi military powers were abolished and nearly half a million soldiers become unemployed and, thus, many of them joined resistance organisations. Furthermore, Bremer separated 120,000 bureaucrats from ministries, hospitals and schools. By the new laws enacted in the short term, all the economic assets apart from oil were opened to privatisation and almost all parts of the 'reconstruction' contracts were drawn up by US companies. Laws enabled a decrease in taxes by 25 per cent for the foreign companies. Foreign companies become free in owning all the company shares in Iraq and taking their profits out of the country without making one cent's worth of investment in the Iraqi economy. All the laws regulating the areas of banking, foreign investment, patent rights, copyrights, taxes, mass media, agriculture and trade were changed.[27]

Contracts having a total of more than US$50 billion were drawn up by 150 American companies. Of these 150 companies, Halliburton, with a contract of US$12 billion, has taken the largest share. Thirteen other companies have contracts with a value of US$1.5 million. Those companies undertake reconstruction in areas such as electricity, roads, water systems, bridges, hospitals and sewerage systems.

After a while, complaints of extravagance, abuse, forgery and misuse of authority were made against these companies and as a result a series of contracts were cancelled.[29] One of them is Parsons Corporation, which signed a contract of US$243 million for the construction of 150 health centres. It elapsed more than two years ago and US$186 million was spent on only six centres. Only two of them provided service for the patients. Furthermore, Parsons signed two more separate contracts for the construction of two prisons. These were also cancelled.

> The Bechtel Corporation was dropped from a US$50 million contract for the construction of a children's hospital in Basra after it went US$90 million over budget and a year-and-a-half behind schedule. These contracts have since been turned over to Iraqi companies.[30]

As a result of the inspections conducted by government officers, KBR, which is the subsidiary company of Halliburton and also a military company known worldwide, was accused of forgery and misuse of authority. Furthermore, the investigations conducted demonstrated that companies performing in the electric sector did not even accomplish the half of the projects that they carried out. Therefore, the Iraqi people could use electricity for only 11 hours. Electricity could only be given to Baghdad, the heart of Iraq, for about four to eight hours. Before the war, Baghdad had 24 hours of electricity. A similar tragedy has been experienced in the health sector where only 36 per cent of the projects have been completed.

Although there were some private banks operating in Iraq before the war, the banking system was under the authority of the two state banks. These two state banks, which kept 90 per cent of the assets in the banking sector, had 340 branches all over the country in 2003. Each branch of those banks became the target of plundering after the war. The commercial bank law enacted towards the end of 2003 paved the way for not only the setting up of private banks in the country as well as increasing their assets, but also enabling foreign international banks to open branches and purchasing 50 per cent of the banks already operating in Iraq.[31] Changes in banking sector were followed by new arrangements such as the opening of Iraq's borders to imports, the encouragement of foreign investments and the building up of an economy dependent on dual-currency.[32]

As well as the close relationship of high-ranking officials of the Bush administration with the gas and energy sector, the key positions that the former members of this sector occupy in the government have been the main reasons for the interest in Iraqi oil. According to the studies conducted between December 2002 and April 2003 before the occupation, it is stated that Iraqi oil should be opened to international petroleum companies as soon as possible[33] and Production Sharing Agreements (PSAs) were recommended as a way to realise this.[34] Those agreements were preparing the worst scenario for oil-rich countries. The ownership of oil is left for the government. However, the most profitable areas, namely searching and manufacturing, are left for the private companies with quite favourable conditions.

Undoubtedly the most significant step of the opening up of Iraqi oil for the international companies is the Oil and Gas Law[35] that was formed as a draft in December 2004 and submitted to the parliament by the Iraqi government in May 2007. Not only the Bush administration but also the multinational oil companies pressurised the Iraqi government to enact the law as soon as possible. The draft law is still waiting in the parliament due to the disagreement between the different provinces and parties. The failure in enacting the law arises from the demand of the Northern Iraqi Kurds who want to manage oil fields under their authority. Iraqi oil fields are mainly located in the Northern and Southern regions, where the Kurds and Shiites inhabit respectively. The draft envisages the allocation of oil resources between all the ethnic and religious groups including the Sunnis. The US authorities hope for the urgent enactment of the law. An important issue, which is underlined by the Middle Eastern oil experts, is that although the Provisional Coalition Administration does not want to give the image that they are affecting this law directly; they are, in fact, giving a great importance to the legal arrangement in the oil industry. The occupation authorities did not take the initiative of setting up such legal frameworks for other industrial sectors in Iraq. By the help of a 'shock therapy', they rapidly caused the collapse of several sectors, especially the public sector, under the name of restructuring.

> However, the different approach adopted toward the oil industry was predicated upon intervention of a longer-term nature. The occupation authorities attempted to control the oil industry without destroying it. This included direct security control and abortive attempts to enfranchise foreign companies and personnel.[36]

Besides, the major international companies are not entering into long-term contracts without having any legal framework that provides assurance.

The draft law concerning the future of Iraq was not opened to public discussion for a long time. Furthermore, there exists no mechanism or platform for opening it to public discussion. This emanates not only from the failure of parties and political structures but also from prevailing violence in daily life and thus the inability to ensure security.[37]

The content and possible results of the draft having 42 provisions could be summarised as follows:

- Iraqi oil is left to the foreign companies by the contracts, which could be extended to 30 years. This could enable the use of oil for longer periods in the interests of the foreign companies. Furthermore, this provision has a content of binding the future Iraqi governments and keeping them to control their resources as well as forming a new oil law.[38]
- Iraq will cancel its OPEC membership since it could not determine the oil amount to be produced. The representatives of international oil giants such as Exxon Mobile, Shell and BP, shall be present in the Iraq Federal Oil and Gas Council to be established. This implies that foreigners shall govern which type of contracts will be agreed. Iraq National Oil Company shall continue its existence. However, this company shall have the control of 17 oil regions out of 80.

The draft law does not oblige the foreign companies to invest the money they earn from Iraq in Iraq, make partnerships with the Iraqi companies or employ Iraqi workers and allocate technologies.

The draft law gives the final word to the regional administrations on the issue of how to use the oil in their regions. If the central administration does not use the veto right, then the regions do not encounter any intervention concerning the agreements made with the foreigners. Therefore, this could lead to the division of Iraq into three by increasing inter-regional competition.[39]

Foreign companies are attaching greater importance to the enactment of the oil law than to ensuring security in Iraq. For the first time the law shall give the rights over oil searches in Iraq to national as well as international companies. In reality, whether there is a law or not, the race between the companies concerning the allocation of oil in Iraq is still continuing.[40] Whether there is a new oil law or not, contracts concluded with the companies are still an issue of debate concerning their legacy and sustainability. However, this does not constitute an obstacle to attempts to realise a new contract. For example, in recent period, it has been reported that the 'Chinese oil firm CNPC is in talks with US energy companies to team up to bid for oil and gas deals in Iraq'[41] or that the Russian oil firm LUKOIL is interested in bidding for at least two of the fields in Iraq, West Quma and Rumaila. 'Rumaila is the largest field on offer and alone accounts for nearly 15 percent of Iraq's oil reserves, the world's third largest.'[42] Furthermore, newly discovered but underdeveloped regions of Iraq are opening up to foreign firms one by one. For example, for the Nasiriyah oil field in Dhi Qar, which is located 320 km south-east of Baghdad and is rich in oil, three companies, Italy's Eni SpA, Spain's Repsol and Japan's Nippon Oil, are competing for the service contract.[43]

Conclusion

Iraq has become an instrument of the United States in imposing neoliberal capitalism in the Arab world. The mechanism of these is ensured by the Middle East Free Trade Area (MEFTA), which was initiated by the Bush administration and developed in 2003. This proposal is presented as a part of the US strategy of the war on terrorism following 9/11.[44] In fact, MEFTA should be considered as the economic transformation programme which will be extended throughout the region as a 'civil' intervention chain.

The Bush administration adopted a special negotiation strategy for MEFTA. Rather than negotiating with the countries as a block, it accepted free trade agreements in pieces by negotiating individually. Then, those minor agreements are merged inside MEFTA. If it becomes successful, then MEFTA shall be accomplished in 2013 and include 20 countries: Algeria, Bahrain, Cyprus, Egypt, Palestine, Iran, Iraq, Israel, Jordan, Kuwait, Lebanon, Libya, Morocco, Oman, Qatar, Saudi Arabia, Syria, the United Arab Emirates, Tunisia and Yemen.[45]

So far, the Bush administration signed 13 Trade and Investment Framework Agreements. Those are the agreements that demonstrate the acceptance of a country into MEFTA as well as constituting a fundamental step for the Free Trade Agreement. Those steps were rapidly taken after the occupation of Iraq. Algeria and Bahrain signed agreements before the occupation of Iraq. However, Lebanon, Tunisia, Saudi Arabia, Kuwait, Yemen, United Arab Emirates, Qatar, Egypt, Morocco, Oman and Iraq signed the agreement after the war.[46]

Iraq is transformed into a laboratory in which neoliberal policies are implemented and which constitutes the starting point of a wider project towards the region. After the occupation, the Iraqi economy experienced a major collapse. The rate of inflation was 31.7 per cent by the end of 2004[47] and the rate of unemployment was estimated between a range of 28 to 40 per cent as of the end of 2004.[48] It is not only Iraq and the Middle East, but in fact the major part of the world population, that has become impoverished by the profit-seeking capitalist market. Pre-emptive war strategy is functioning smoothly in legitimising the military intervention and in expanding the neoliberal policies towards the resisting regions in terms of US policies and at the same time by choosing the intended targets without any justification.

Notes

1 Clausewitz (2008).
2 When considered theoretically, as Magdoff states, in the neoclassical economy peace is a dominant theme; but war is a 'derivative' variable damaging the universal balance of economy.

> One of the distinguished features of Marxist thought, on the other hand, is the conviction that economic processes must be understood as part of a social organism in which political force plays a leading role and in which war is at least as typical as peace.

> (Magdoff 1970: 237).

3 Hobsbawm (2002).
4 As Hobsbawm points out, the twentieth century can be chronologically regarded as three periods: 'the era of world war centreed on Germany (1914 to 1945), the era of confrontation between the two superpowers (1945 to 1989), and the era since the end of the classic international power system' (2002).
5 For a study presenting a wide analysis framework examining philosophical arguments developed in terms of wars, humanity norms and protection of civilians, see Slim (2003).
6 Hobsbawm (2002).
7 Brown (2006).
8 Carbonnier (2006).
9 For the claims concerning the Blackwater company which becomes a current issue with illegal activities in Iraq within the recent period, see Risen (2008).
10 Concerning this issue see Zabcı (2007).
11 At the end of the eighteenth century, it was important to establish the difference between state and society, public and private, economical and political and civil and military in order to make the modern state gain specific features. See Kaldor (2006: 22).
12 Hardt and Negri (2004: 45); Chomsky (1999: 1–23).
13 For the moral justification of the wars and for philosophical and religious foundations of the 'just war', see Rockmore (2004).
14 Hobsbawm (2000).
15 There are very different ideas for the reasons that drag the United States to war. Popular theories can be collected under four headings:

 1 Neo-con militarists drag the United States to an adventure for one-sided military power.
 2 Effect of Zionist management on the US administration in order to realise the geo-political benefits of Israel.
 3 The wish to provide cheap gas and petrol and to control the pipes in Middle East and Middle Asia.
 4 Political and ideological insufficiency of G.W. Bush.

 See Hossein-Zadeh (2006). Hossein-Zadeh states that classical or economical imperialism fails to understand the reasons of wars and militarism in today's world and develops the term 'parasitic military imperialism' and states that the war and militarism is an aim in itself.
16 North (2006).
17 See Lopez (2004).
18 One of the most significant aspects of this strategy is that the intelligence concerning the capacity and intentions of the enemy is accepted as sufficient for the legitimisation of pre-emptive war.
19 North (2006).
20 Baker (2006).
21 Hardt and Negri (2004: 23).
22 Discussing their analyses concerning war could be the subject of another study. However, it would be suffice to mention here that seeing war like an 'active subject' in the international arena creates a methodological problem.
23 Chossudovsky (2007).
24 Juhasz (2004).
25 See McDougall (2003).
26 Furthermore, this process is realised without having any economic policy.

 Since the fall of Saddam's regime, attention by the CPA and Governing Council (GC) as well as foreign business communities has focused on rebuilding the country's infrastructure, especially oil production, electricity and water, and identification of the available investment opportunities. Little attention has been given to the role of economic policy.

(Zire Al-Saadi 2004)

27 Juhasz (2007).
28 The unemployment ratio in Iraq is very high, especially amongst the young. 'More than a fourth of Iraq's young men are out of work, a situation that is likely to worsen and threatens the country's long-term stability, according to a dismal economic forecast Sunday from U.N. and nongovernmental agencies' (Susman 2009).
29 Transparency International prepared a report including warnings concerning the probability of the greatest corruption scandal in Iraqi history occurring due to weaknesses in public openness as well as in the transparency of the contracts signed with the foreign companies. See, 'Iraq Facing Corruption Threat', 16 March 2005 (available at: http://news.bbc.co.uk/2/hi/business/4353491.stm).
30 Juhasz (2007).
31 Foote *et al.* (2004: 21).
32 Foote *et al.* (2004: 22–4).
33 Oil reserves of Iraq are arousing the interests of the foreign companies. 'With potential reserves of 160 billion barrels, Iraq would rank second in reserves behind only Saudi Arabia's 260 billion barrels of proven reserves (25) and ahead of neighboring Iran, which has reserves of about 136 billion barrels' (Sakmar 2008).
34 For further information see Muttitt (2005).
35 For the full text of the draft law see: www.al-ghad.org/wordpress/wp-content/uploads/2007/02/iraqi_oil_law.pdf.
36 Mahdi (2007: 15).
37 Mahdi (2007: 13).
38 Searching and production which are the profitable areas are left to the companies although their ownership belongs to the state.
39 'Bribery for Petroleum Law by US!', *Radikal Newspaper*, 4 February 2008.
40 An ambiguous situation is appeared in terms of the foreign companies that signed the agreement especially with the Kurdistan Regional Government after the submission of the draft law to the parliament. See Crooks and McNulty (2007). Those agreements do not have a legal status but they are accepted as valid.
41 'CNPC Talks the US Firms on Iraq Oil Bids-source', 16 February 2009 (available at: www.iraqog.com/page1.cfm?ser=1858).
42 'Russia's LUKOIL Eyes Two Iraq Oilfields-sources', 13 February 2009 (available at: www.iraqog.com/page1.cfm?ser=1847).
43 'Official: Iraq to Award Oil Contract in March', *International Herald Tribune*, 18 February 2009 (available at: www.iht.com/articles/ap/2009/02/18/business/ML-Iraq-Oil.php).
44 See 'Middle East Free Trade Area: Progress Report', 3 July 2006 (available at: http://opencrs.com/document/RL32638/2006–07–03).
45 Juhasz (2007).
46 Juhasz (2007).
47 The Central Bank of Iraq (available at: www.cbi.ig).
48 Campbell and O'Hanlon (2008).

References

Baker, Peter. 'Bush to Restate Terror Strategy', *Washington Post*, 16 March 2006.
Brown, David. 'Study Claims Iraq's "Excess" Death Toll Has Reached 655.000', *Washington Post*, 11 October 2006.
Campbell, Jason H. and Michael E. O'Hanlon. 'Iraq Index-Tracking Variables of Reconstruction & Security in Post-Saddam Iraq', The Brooking Institution, 5 January 2008 (available at: www.bespacific.com/mt/archives/017039.html).

Carbonnier, G. 'Privatisation and Outsourcing in Wartime: The Humanitarian Challenges', *Disasters*, 2006, vol. 30, no. 4, pp. 402–16.

Chomsky, Noam. *The New Military Humanism, Lessons from Kosovo*, London: Pluto Press, 1999.

Chossudovsky, Michel. 'The Destabilisation of Pakistan', *Global Research*, 30 December 2007 (available at: www.globalresearch.ca/index.php?context=va&aid=7705).

Clausewitz, C. Von. *On War* (trans. C.J.J. Graham), in *The Complete Art of War*, Radford: Wilder Publications, 2008.

Crooks, E. and S. McNulty. 'Big Oil Plays Waiting Game Over Iraq's Reserves', *Financial Times*, 19 September 2007.

Foote, C., W. Block, K. Crane and S. Gray. 'Economic Policy and Prospects in Iraq', *Public Policy Discussion Papers*, Federal Reserve Bank of Boston, 4 May 2004 (available at: http://papers.ssrn.com/sol3/papers.cfm?abstract_id=887920, last accessed 12 February 2009).

Hardt, Michael and Antonio Negri. *Multitude: War and Democracy in the Age of Empire*, London: Penguin Books, 2004.

Hobsbawm, Eric. 'War and Peace' (in conversation with A. Polito), *The New Century*, London: Abacus, 2000.

Hobsbawm, Eric. 'War and Peace', *Guardian*, 23 February 2002.

Hossein-Zadeh, Ismael. *The Political Economy of US Imperialism*, New York: Palgrave Macmillan, 2006.

Juhasz, Antonia. 'Ambitions of Empire: The Bush Administration Economic Plan for Iraq (and Beyond)', *Left Turn Magazine*, 20 January 2004 (available at: www.globalpolicy.org/security/issues/iraq/after/2004/0120ambitions).

Juhasz, Antonia. 'Spoils of War: Oil, the US-Middle East Free Trade and the Bush Agenda', 14 January 2007 (available at: www.inthesetimes.com/article/2979/spoils_of_war).

Kaldor, Mary. *New and Old Wars: Organised Violence in a Global Era*, Cambridge: Polity Press, 2006.

Lopez, George. 'Just? Unjust? The Bush Doctrine of Pre-emptive War Opened a New Front in the Debates Over "Just War" Theory', *Sojourners Magazine*, May 2004 (available at: www.sojo.net/index.cfm?action=magazine.article&issue=soj0405&article=040520).

McDougall, Paul. 'BearingPoint Gears up for Iraq Rebuilding', *Information Week*, 4 August 2003 (available at: www.informationweek.com/news/management/showArticle.jhtml?articleID=128081).

Magdoff, Harry, 'Militarism and Imperialism', *American Economic Review*, 1970, vol. 60, no. 2, pp. 237–42.

Mahdi, Kamil. 'Iraq's Oil Law: Parsing The Fine Point', *World Policy Journal*, summer 2007, vol. 24, no. 2, pp. 1–23.

Muttitt, Greg. 'Production Share Agreements: Oil Privatisation by Another Name', 26 May 2005 (available at: http://platformlondon.org/carbonweb/documents/PSAs_privatisation.pdf).

North, David. 'Bush Administration Renews "Pre-emptive War Strategy"', World Socialist website, 17 March 2006 (available at: www.wsws.org/articles/2006/mar2006/nsec-m17.shtml).

Risen, James. '2005 Use of Gas by Black water Leaves Questions', *New York Times*, 10 January 2008.

Rockmore, Tom. 'On the So-called War on Terrorism', *Metaphilosophy*, April 2004, vol. 35, no. 3, pp. 386–401.

Sakmar, Susan. 'The Status of the Draft Iraq Oil and Gas Law', *Houston Journal of International Law*, spring 2008 (available at: www.entrepreneur.com/tradejournals/article/180517175.htm, last accessed 10 February 2009).

Slim, Hugo. 'Why Protect Civilians? Innocence, Immunity and Enmity in War', *International Affairs*, 2003, vol. 79, no. 3, pp. 481–501.

Susman, Tina. 'IRAQ: Unemployment Bad and Getting Worse', *Los Angeles Times*, 16 February 2009.

Zabcı, Filiz. 'Private Military Companies: "Shadow Soldiers" of Neo-Colonialism', *Capital and Class*, summer 2007, no. 92, pp. 1–11.

Zire Al-Saadi, Sabri. 'Iraq's Post-War Economy: A Critical Review', *Middle East Economic Survey*, April 5 2004, vol. 47, no. 14 (available at: www.mees.com/postedarticles/oped/a47n14d01.htm, last accessed 15 February 2009).

Part II
Country experiences

8 State, class and the discourse

Reflections on the neoliberal transformation in Turkey

Pınar Bedirhanoğlu and Galip L. Yalman

Introduction: the need to challenge the dominant paradigms

Political sphere in modern bourgeois societies has always been one in which political and social implications of capital-labour contradiction are confined and redefined within the limits posed by capitalist interests in particular historical conjunctures through the mediations of law and money, two crucial transnationally operative forms (Clarke 1992: 136). While the content as well as the success of political and ideological strategies to manage this contradiction might have varied according to the historical specificities of different countries, the concern to put an end to class-based politics can be identified as a persistent feature of the alienated bourgeois sphere at different scales. Neoliberalism as a particular class-based response to the global capitalist crisis of the 1970s has not been an exception. Hence, while it has been historically shaped, practiced and managed unequally as well as contingently at local, national, international and transnational levels since the early 1980s, the reconfiguration of the political sphere has been an integral and constitutive aspect of neoliberal transformation processes.

On this basis, a cursory review of the debates – which have dominated the academic as well as the political agenda since the 1980s, at least until the global crisis in 2008 – about the role of the state in a capitalist economy, would highlight two particular deficiencies. First, there is the dominance of a dualistic conception of state/market and/or state/society relationships in so far as these spheres are perceived as being externally related, if not as ontologically distinctive domains, with their own logics and principles. Second, there is a tendency to approach the relations between states and markets in terms of alternative 'paradigms', thus reproducing varieties of relativism, if only to reiterate the validity of a theoretical edifice with universalistic aspirations.

An adherence to the philosophy of external relations could also be detected in attempts to develop 'non-reductionist' accounts of state–society relations with an emphasis on 'institutional orders' operating according to their distinctive rules and priorities as a characteristic feature of modernity. Two extremely influential, though equally misleading, corollaries follow: that the relations of domination are not inherent in the capitalist relations of production; and that a capitalist market economy faces instability because of exogenous interventions rather than its inherent systemic characteristics. The former not only implies an identification of the state with coercion per se, but also as something external to consciousness. It also indicates the lack of a conceptual apparatus to come to terms with the fact that not only the outcome of human actions, but also the human actions themselves have a material aspect which cannot be reduced to their conceptual aspect and/or subjective meaning. In particular, it indicates a refusal to acknowledge the historical-social nature of the categories which would have provided one avenue to escape their reification.

Against these dominant tendencies, it is imperative that a proper analysis of capitalism should be grounded on the methodological premise that the state and the economy do not 'exist' as externally related entities, one of which is determining and/or dominating the other. For, in the neoliberal era as ever, state power is integral for the constitution *and* the reproduction of the market economy as a 'form' of the capitalist relations of production. Concomitantly, there is the need to come to terms with the constitution of social classes in general, and the bourgeoisie in particular, 'within and through the state', if one is to avoid the relationship between the state and social classes being viewed as one of externality. It would also underline the importance of treating the state as an 'empirically open-ended' concept that can be employed to come to terms with the relational and the historical character of social reality rather than a *sui generis* reality and/or absent concept.

A better understanding of the relations between states and markets can thus be realised if they are conceived in terms of alternative strategies of capitalist development rather than paradigmatic differences as has been the case with particularistic arguments which contemplate the institutions of a society as if they were the expressions of a primary essence.[1] This, in turn, underlines the methodological imperative to approach the determination of social forms as an historical process whose dynamic is internal to it so as to come to terms with the relational and the historical character of social reality. In short, it becomes essential to explain why this particular form has taken the form it has in that particular context. By the same token, the modalities of these relations that could be observed over the last two decades in many of the so-called emerging markets as they have experienced economic and political crises while going through different phases of financial liberalization could be contemplated as alternative strategies of adjustment to the vagaries of international financial markets rather than manifestations of a single project of restructuring attributed, *inter alia*, to globalization (cf. Cerny 1997; Robinson 2002). Yet, at the same time, it is also crucial to come to terms with these strategies as hegemonic projects to the extent that they fulfil certain functions in the reproduction of particular forms of social relations in historically specific contexts.

Neoliberal policies have led to sharp political and social confrontations wherever they have been introduced. Disenchantment with Keynesian and/or developmentalist policies in line with the neoliberal ideology has led to a process that has made not only labouring classes, but also different capitalist interests increasingly more dependent on the market to survive. In this regard, crisis management and/or prevention has become a central concern of the neoliberal reformers in many countries so as to mitigate the adverse consequences of the market reforms. Several Gramsci-inspired studies have conceived neoliberal transformation processes in different countries as 'passive revolutions' which have comprised attempts to co-opt, assimilate or dissolve opposition to reforms through policies that might have ranged from violent suppression of organized labour to innovative welfare transfer mechanisms such as conditional cash transfers and/or corruption.[2] The necessity to form 'winning coalitions' has been another intensively debated strategy to proceed with neoliberal change in the Northern and Southern countries (Evans 1992), while transition debates of the 1990s constituted attempts to lock in the trajectory of social transformation in the former Eastern Bloc into one of either shock or the gradual move to a market economy. Putting an end to class-based politics by dissolving class alliances through such strategies has hence been one of the central concerns of not only the neoliberal reformers but also the states – a task which has become ever more challenging due to the aggravating poverty and exclusion of the labouring masses.

While conscious strategies to dissolve opposing class alliances have always been integral aspects of bourgeois power struggles, the process of putting an end to class-based politics in the neoliberal era should not simply be understood as an outcome of such strategies only. Indeed, the very success of the neoliberal project lies in its ability to isolate the reform process from the transformative impact of such social criticisms or pressures, and turn it into one which has primarily been proceeding under the discipline of finance. Strengthened by neoliberalism's anti-state rhetoric, the financialization of everyday life has thus played a central role in delegitimating class-based struggles in many countries. This has proved to be an effective process in the reproduction of the separation of the political and the economic in contemporary capitalism for it helps to 'construct new public perceptions concerning the "neutrality" … of the state' (Burnham 2000: 22) on the one hand, and the 'self-regulating market' on the other. Once the protective armour of capitalist relations of production has been strengthened in this way, arguments emphasizing the importance of class struggles might easily lose ground against such others that underline the role of competition states, or identities, or civil societies in social change.

The neoliberal transformation process in Turkey, though acquiring historically specific characteristics, has been in line with these general trends observed elsewhere. This chapter aims to identify the processes and strategies that have served to put an end to class-based politics in the neoliberal period in Turkey by focusing on the implications of the 1980 coup d'état, post-1989 capital account liberalization, the rise of identity-based politics and conflicts, and the anti-statist hegemonic discourse. It will be argued that the neoliberal authoritarian form the state had acquired as early as the 1980s has persisted since then through the powerful articulation of these economic, political and cultural processes into each other. This argument will obviously be in contrast to those perspectives that tend to identify the Justice and Development Party's (AKP) government since 2002 as an historical opportunity to initiate a rupture in Turkish politics.[3] Instead it will be maintained that to the extent that the AKP promises to reproduce neoliberal authoritarianism in Turkey, it represents more continuity than radical change in terms of state–class relations whilst claiming to initiate radical changes in state–society relations. Therefore, it will be much more realistic to assess the phenomenon as an example of how the political Islam adjusted to neoliberal restructuring project within the process of globalisation.

A bird's eye view of Turkish neoliberal transformation

It would be naive to think that the change from the so-called Washington Consensus to the post-Washington Consensus after the mid-1990s in the neoliberal agenda was shaped by the lessons drawn from the neoliberal reform process. Gamble mentions the coexistence of two different but complementary conceptions of market, namely the 'free' and the 'social' market understandings in neoliberal ideology since its inception. The free market ideology, for Gamble, underlines the importance of the strong state in eliminating the barriers in front of the free play of market forces, whereas the social market ideology attaches crucial roles to states in the construction of the institutions within which the market forces would properly play (Gamble 2006: 21–2). Interestingly enough, these conceptions seem to have shaped the two consequent periods of neoliberal consensus. Hence, the first period up to the mid-1990s saw the implementation of financial and trade liberalization policies through deregulation in many countries, a process which brought about greedy capitalist concerns to capture the newly privatized public assets either to enjoy the already available profits or to dissolve them in order to oligopolize world markets. The succeeding post-Washington Consensus period on the other hand has highlighted capitalist concerns to protect their gains through institutional structures and constitutional guarantees at the expense of those social forces that resist and would resist neoliberal change.

The development of the neoliberal reform trajectory in Turkey largely overlaps with this historical periodization. The first generation of neoliberal reforms were launched in the country in the early 1980s within a context of the 1970s world capitalist crisis. The state had felt this crisis in the form of economic default and loss of political legitimacy due to the concurrent hegemonic crisis. Within such a political context, the neoliberal rupture was facilitated by the 1980 military coup's violent suppression of all social opposition – the left being still the primary target – the two stand-by agreements signed with the IMF, and Turgut Özal's capability to develop an expansive hegemonic project in support of neoliberalism (Tünay 1993: 17; Boratav 2002: 145–50).

It can be argued that financial liberalization within the context of deregulation has provided the Turkish state with both opportunities and further problems in administering neoliberal change. But the 1989 capital account liberalization has created a very volatile economy in Turkey vulnerable to financial speculation, reflected in its weakness in the 1994, 1998 and 2001 financial crises, and the ongoing global crisis.

The institutionalization process has acquired a new momentum after AKP's coming to power in the 2002 general elections, a development which was arguably the outcome of the extraordinary post-2001 crisis atmosphere. The Islamic-oriented AKP, having felt its vulnerabilities within the internal power structure in Turkey, has powerfully played in the hands of the United States and the EU to strengthen its rule, and attempted to accelerate neoliberal institutionalization under the guidance of the IMF and the EU 'anchors', particularly during its first four years in power.

Putting an end to class-based politics in Turkey

From structural adjustment to 'twin crises'

It is worth remembering that Turkey is a country where the need for adjustment has emerged periodically since the end of the Second World War. Indeed, it had become almost a self-fulling prophecy to expect not only a stabilization programme to be put into effect so as to respond to the macroeconomic instability that ensued from the efforts to achieve rapid economic development; but also a change in political regime shortly thereafter. Curiously, the civilian governments which were rather reluctant in adopting the stabilization packages were forced out of office by military interventions. This cycle of events seemed to repeat itself at every ten years or so for more than two decades. But the launching of the 24 January 1980 stabilization programme was hailed in the international financial community as well as in political and business circles within the country as a turning point. The specificity of the programme, it was argued, lay in its alleged aim to go beyond standard stabilization and to achieve structural adjustment by changing the development strategy that it followed for several decades. According to a discourse reflecting the neoliberal aspirations which has become particularly effective in Turkey especially during the first half of the 1980s, the twin long-term objectives would be an export-oriented trade and development strategy based on the neoclassical principle of comparative advantages, and a more market-directed system of resource allocation (cf. Baysan and Blitzer 1990: 10; Krueger and Turan 1993: 356). Put differently, the programme is said to signify a radical change *both* in the mode of articulation of the Turkish economy with the world economy and in the nature of the state–economy relationship prevalent within the social formation, at least since the end of the Second World War. This would, in turn, make Turkey 'the darling of the [World] Bank' as the total commitments of the latter had exceeded a billion dollars a year during the 1986–8 period under successive Structural Adjustment Loans (SALs) which had been initiated from 1980 onwards (World Bank 2005a).

By the end of the 1980s, however, the early optimism about the success of Turkish policy-makers in creating an exemplary model of a 'market economy' seemed to have been largely evaporated. There were increasingly critical, albeit conflicting, accounts of what actually has been taking place since the 1980s. But one thing was quite clear, the disenchantment has not stemmed from any disappointment about the adverse distributive impact of the policies pursued, since the 1980–8 period was characterized by a severe suppression of wage incomes (Boratav *et al.* 2001). The culprit would rather be identified stemming from the belief that the Turkish society has been dominated for decades, if not centuries, by a 'strong state', whether civilian or military in complexion. This would have sounded as the death-knell of the initial structural adjustment strategy to the extent that its main objective was understood as the replacement of a 'traditional statist system by a market system' (Williamson 1990), since it was held that 'the reforms of the 1980s' have not changed this decisive feature of the Turkish society (Mosley *et al.* 1991: 147). Indeed, it was assumed that the presence of a long-standing 'state tradition' has influenced the actual course of these reforms in significant respects (Öniş 1992). The World Bank, too,

> became concerned that the failure to get macroeconomy under control and to build on the earlier policy changes was likely to lead to a crisis. [It would thus] decide not to provide additional adjustment loans until Turkey could demonstrate progress on the structural problems destabilizing its economy.
>
> (World Bank 2005a)

While gains made by Turkey in opening up to new markets and in increasing the volume of its international trade were considered as positive developments, these were hardly implying a mode of articulation with the world economy as envisaged by the leading proponents of the structural adjustment policies. For the initial success in the export orientation of the manufacturing industry had less to do with the positive effects of structural adjustment policies than the competitive edge gained by real effective depreciation of the currency and other measures, such as subsidies, promoting exports (IMF 2003). In short, the pattern of investment behaviour on the part of the domestic private sector firms as well as the multinational corporations would hardly be in compliance with the objective of 'transforming the economy into an export-oriented, technology-intensive production structure' (World Bank 2003). As the failure to undertake structural reforms would continue to disappoint the Bretton Woods institutions, the need to focus on higher value added goods and services away from low quality, labour-intensive products would continue to be an acknowledged, yet elusive objective for the Turkish industrialists.[4] Indeed, Turkish industry had continued to specialize in sectors of production with standard technologies and relatively low production costs[5] as part of its export-oriented, but not necessarily export-led, growth strategy.[6]

In line with the perception of the state in general, and the Turkish state in particular, as an impediment to achieving optimal economic outcomes, as a source of macroeconomic instability and business uncertainty as well as a fetter on civil society, the state was promoted as dysfunctional not only for the reproduction of the capitalist relations on a national scale, but also for enhancing the new mode of articulation of the Turkish economy with the world economy. Even the critical accounts of the neoliberal transformation seemed to concur, as they argued that 'the state apparatus turned into a bastion of privilege as it assumed a regulatory role in the creation and absorption of the economic surplus, while the fiscal balances have taken the major brunt of adjustment' (Boratav *et al.* 2001). It is noteworthy that such a tendency to avoid the necessary fiscal adjustment through the monetization of deficits has been characterized in the Latin American context as an accommodation to the disapperance of external sources of finance in the wake of the 1982 debt crisis (Cardoso 1992). Yet, it also turns out to be a characteristic of the exemplary case of structural adjustment for which creditworthiness remained the primary objective.

The main problem facing heavily indebted countries, whether in Latin America or in Turkey, then turns out to be debt refinancing and the funding of current-account deficits created by capital service payments (interest and profits). The balance-of-trade deficit becomes less important by comparison with the permanent, growing deficits seen in the financial and factor services accounts (Frenkel 2001). Hence, the proliferation of episodes where increasing financial inflows and current account deterioration were matched with an ongoing real appreciation of the currency; thereby undermining the contemplation of competitiveness as a viable policy objective (Rodrik 2001; Palma 2000). Neoliberal response would be rather inconsequential as it would tend to put the blame once again on the recipient governments for neglecting the fact that capital flows are 'pro-cyclical'.[7] In other words, they ought not to have used these short-term funds for financing budget and/or current account deficits. It would also provide an excuse for the IMF against the criticisms of incompetence. Hence the contention that 'the IMF's influence was particularly limited by the general strength of capital flows to emerging markets in the period preceding the crisis'.[8] This was, in fact, nothing but a reiteration of the IMF's age-old objection to the availability of external sources of finance as a means of avoiding adjustment.

The decision to complete the capital account liberalization in the summer of 1989 with the declaration of the Turkish lira as fully convertible in foreign exchange markets, in fact signified the increasing dependence of the economy on private financial sources. This decision which was, in fact, in line with the classical sequencing strategy of liberalization, effectively put an end to the policy of enhancing the export capacity of the economy by the real effective depreciation of the currency. For the dependence on the so-called hot money flows necessitated a higher return on domestic assets as compared to the rate of nominal depreciation of the Turkish lira (Balkan and Yeldan 2002: 47). While this policy stance led to a considerable growth of the country's international reserves, it would also raise eyebrows about the sustainability of the policy, since it would be at the expense of 'fast-growing short-term foreign indebtedness' as well as 'slow-growing foreign exchange earnings'. What is worse from a neoclassical perspective, the overvalued currency, albeit by default, would return to haunt the policy-makers.

If the evidence of economic health is assessed by the ability to sustain the current account deficit through foreign investment, without increasing the debt stock, then clearly the Turkish experience of the post-1989 opening of the economy to global financial competition was hardly encouraging. In particular, the reliance upon portfolio investments as the main source of money creation made the economy susceptible to the vagaries of the international financial markets, as increasing creditworthiness through higher 'country risk assessment' by the rating institutions of the international financial world became critical. More fundamentally, what the Turkish experience highlights is that the process of financial liberalization would not necessarily put an end to the functioning of the state as an 'asymmetric risk holder', whilst the mechanisms that have tended to 'socialize' the risk for the entrepreneurs might be changing. The increase in public debt has, in fact, been indicative of a transfer of resources to the private sector in a variety of forms ranging from several subsidy and bailing-out schemes to a series of tax policy changes which have deliberately favoured the corporate sector.[9]

Yet, the neoliberal-cum-statist accounts continued to put the blame on the continuity of the statist tradition, thus negating any inclination to hold the underlying theory responsible for the perceived mishaps of the neoliberal policy agenda. It has been contended that the liberalization process in Turkey was introduced within an institutional environment marked by excessive discretion and pervasive rent-seeking. Liberalization of the economy was said not to have prevented policy oscillations, short-termism, arbitrary and wasteful expenditure of state resources for legitimacy and patronage purposes, thus causing significant macroeconomic instability (Öniş and Bayram 2008: 52; Eder 2004). In other words, the alleged continuity of the state tradition and/or the lack of a regulatory state implied, in the popular jargon of the neoliberal political economy, the domination of political rationality over economic rationality. This, in turn, would have adverse consequences for the growth prospects of the economy since it perpetuates incentive structures that generalize 'rent-seeking' behaviour (Lafay and Lecaillon 1993). Thereby, the presentation of the state as an impediment fulfils a methodological service for the neoclassical theory, as it implies that there is nothing inherently wrong about the theory underlying the structural adjustment-cum-stabilization efforts in terms of the linkages that it prescribes between macroeconomic stability and growth (cf. World Bank 1990).

Nonetheless, this did not bode well for the neoliberal theoretical framework, in so far as the establishment of a stable macroeconomic environment is envisaged as a prerequisite for a successful transition to sustainable economic growth (cf. World Bank 1987: 23). The state is thus held responsible for preventing the economy from moving closer towards the competitive ideal of a long-run equilibrium of internal and external balance, signifying a more efficient use of resources, deemed necessary for sustainable long-term growth. The presentation of the state as a source of instability and uncertainty as well as of rent-seeking behaviour purports, at the same time, to provide an explanation for the lack of investment on the part of the market agents (cf. Buğra 1994; Öniş 1992). Additionally, the repercussions of the increasing dependence on hot money flows in the context of capital account liberalization and the ensuing macroeconomic instability were to be explained away by the lack of 'the necessary institutional environment to supervise and regulate the high liquidity of international flows' (Öniş and Bayram 2008: 53).

This presentation of the state as 'a spanner in the works', so to speak, of the economy both at the national and global levels (cf. Grindle 1991), has a further, more direct, political and ideological significance. It serves to delegitimize political activity in as much as the state is seen as the main arena of struggle for the pursuit of particularistic interests whether perceived and/or presented in terms of class or clientelistic relationships. It also feeds into the misperception that the real antagonism within the society is between the state and the individual and/or the market agent, personified in its institutional form by the private sector firms. Thereby, this mispercuation not only contributes to the perpetuation of the conception of the relations between the state and capital as confrontational, but also helps to conceal the real transfer of income from labour to capital that has been taking place in the course of the structural adjustment process.

Hence the calls for the withdrawal of the state from the economic domain with a renewed emphasis. From the 1990s onwards, however, this would be formulated as the need for 'regulatory reforms' for 'enhancing market openness'.[10] In other words, the initial anti-state, market fundamentalist stance would give way to the acknowledgement of the need for state interventions provided that they become 'market-friendly'. In the Turkish context, it is noteworthy that the chief architect of the structural adjustment policies, late President Turgut Özal had been claiming in retrospect that there has been a 'mutation' in (the conception of) the state (which has been prevailing in the society), i.e. from a 'dirigiste/etatist' to a one more in line with the neoliberal prescriptions.[11] Others would regret that whatever its achievements, the process of market reforms failed to initiate any change in the mindset of the Turkish people.[12] Yet, it is plausible to say that the processes of financial liberalization since the 1980s with their ensuing crises helped to redefine discursively the boundaries between the state and the market in Turkey. It has also brought along another euphemism, the 'depoliticization of economic management', in a bid to bring to an end the domination of political rationality over economic rationality.[13]

The age of globalization, if one is to go by the promises made until the ongoing global crisis, was supposed to bring economic growth, prosperity and stability for the participants of the post-Cold War international economic order. But ironically, it has been so far plagued with a series of financial crises which posed a threat to the stability of the financial system. More significantly, it wreaked havoc with the contention that the policies of financial liberalization in general, of capital account liberalization in particular, would constitute the lynchpin of political and economic stability. The Turkish case provides an exemplary illustration of the fallacy of this contention as 'the economy was trapped within mini cycles of growth-crisis-stabilisation'. This would, in turn, lead many to conclude that 'the 1990s had been a lost decade for Turkey', since in per capita terms Turkish GDP was just about its 1990 level by the end of the decade (Yeldan 2002: 1; Taylor 2005: 12).[14] This was to be acknowledged by a World Bank study in the following manner:

> the country has not yet achieved the momentum needed to bring the great majority of its poor and economically vulnerable population into economic mainstream. Progress in reducing poverty and vulnerability, while significant, has been uneven and painfully slow.
>
> (World Bank 1999: i)

As a matter of fact, the intermittent financial crises (1994, 1998, 2000–1) have become the main driving forces to ensure neoliberal transformation since the liberalization of capital accounts in 1989. It is, therefore, impractical to consider the financial crises of the era of globalization as 'dysfunctional' moments which the states of the crisis-ridden economies, or the IMF for that matter, as rationalizing instance, simply attempt to 'avoid' (cf. Poulantzas 1975: 171–2). Rather, it highlights once again that the economic crises of capitalism are 'organic moments' in the reproduction of social relations of production as well as in the reassertion of the hegemony of the dominant class in the absence of credible counter-hegemonic alternatives. Indeed, it has been contended that

> it was the combination of a major financial crisis and the possibility of EU membership that helped to create a suitable environment for the restructuring of the neo-liberal model [in the Turkish context] in such a way as to make it far more compatible with the objective of sustained economic growth.
>
> (Öniş 2006a)

While the periodic crises of the post-war era had primarily manifested themselves as crises of balance of payments, the November 2000–February 2001 crisis in Turkey showed all the distinctive features of the so-called 'twin crises', in which a balance of payments crisis triggered by capital outflows took place simultaneously with a banking crisis.[15] In a sense, it also revealed the inadequacies of the IMF's approach in the wake of criticisms that it failed to anticipate and/or prevent 'the capital account crises', or worse actually contributed to these crises with its recommended policies. This gained significance particularly in the Turkish case, since the twin crises in Turkey occurred during the implementation of the IMF stabilization programme which was put into effect in December 1999, and identified the exchange rate as a nominal anchor of an anti-inflation strategy. This particular episode also highlighted the policy dilemmas facing the policy-makers, dubbed the 'Unholy Trinity', that is, the mutual incompatibility of exchange-rate stability, capital mobility and autonomy of national monetary policy.[16] The adherence of the policy-makers to the IMF programme was retrospectively criticized for forcing the Central Bank to operate like a quasi-currency board, thus limiting its monetary policy autonomy, as the interest rates were determined by the market forces while the Central Bank was unable to respond to the liquidity crisis of the banking sector (Öniş 2003).[17] In other words, the pursuit of such an anti-inflation programme with capital free to move, did not only deprive the policy-makers of control over domestic monetary conditions, it also made the country hostage to policies shaped elsewhere.[18] The domestic repercussions of the crisis, on the other hand, was very much in line with the so-called Mishkin thesis that the credit crunch resulting from sharp contractions in domestic bank credit following financial crises has been instrumental in aggravating these crises and reducing investment and economic activity (Rogoff *et al.* 2003).

Yet, the 2001 crisis was going to be celebrated for paving the way for a new phase of neoliberalism in Turkey. Through the implementation of 'regulatory reforms' in the wake of a severe and prolonged crisis, a restructuring of the state in line with the requirements of a globalized market economy was finally considered within reach of a 'pro-reform' constituency emboldened by the promise of an accession to the European Union (EU).[19] Put differently, it implied the internationalization of the Turkish state in the sense of its cooperation in taking responsibility for global accumulation within its borders and its cooperation in setting the international rules for trade and investment.[20] However, this was a process already initiated since the end of the Second World War, albeit experienced under different strategies of capital accumulation, though the discursive treatment of the state as an impediment had tended to portray it otherwise, as we have tried to illustrate. It is noteworthy that the perception of the Turkish economy has undergone successive stages. From being a problem country of the 1970s to a model debtor of the 1980s (Celasun and Rodrik 1989: 209), and once again a crisis-ridden country of the 1990s, turning into an 'investors' paradise'[21] in the wake of a yet another catastrophic crisis at the turn of the century. Yet, the constant of the Turkish political economy is continued to be portrayed as its intransigent state, hopefully, to be constrained this time, with a double external anchor, namely simultaneous IMF and EU discipline.

Politics of neoliberalism from the 1980 military coup to the present

It is commonplace to note that the way the structural adjustment episode in Turkey was carried out was due largely to the brutal military regime which facilitated the elimination of the potential sources of resistance to this rather savage experiment of wholesale economic and political restructuring. As it was aptly described, it was the intention of the military junta that came to power on 12 September 1980 'to de-politicise society, so as to render any future military intervention unnecessary' (Ahmad 2004: 150). While the military rule itself was relatively short-lived compared to its counterparts in Latin America or elsewhere in the developing world, the return to civilian rule in the context of the 1982 constitution 'was to be a democracy without freedoms' (Ahmad 2004: 151).

In line with the discourse of the continuity of a state tradition, however, there is a widespread tendency to portray the authoritarian nature of this constitution as a reflection of 'the tutelage of the state over the society'.[22] Hence, the characterization of the Turkish state *à la* Samuel Huntington as a *praetorian republic* to underline the influence of the military in dictating the actual course of the political regime (İnsel 2007).[23] Moreover, in line with the tradition of the institutionalist analysis from Huntington's critique of the political development approach in the 1960s to the 'transition to democracy' studies of the 1980s, there is an exclusive focus on the nature of the political regime so as to render the social classes as rather ineffective agents of social transformation.[24] In short, the post-1980 coup political regime in Turkey tends to be accounted for within the problematic of modernization-cum-institutionalist framework so as to highlight the continuity rather than change in the nature of the relations between the state and the society.[25]

This emphasis on the military as the self-declared protector of the republic not only tends to a rather misleading identification of the state per se with one of its repressive apparatuses, it also entails the conceptualization of the state as an agent, which can be abstracted from class contradictions.[26] In short, it is yet another argument for 'the emergence of a state emptied of its class contents', rather misleadingly alluded to Marx's conceptualization of Bonapartism.[27] Thus, it becomes almost impossible to grasp the state as a specific form assumed by the social relations within a historical process, which does not exist independently from the power struggles within the society.

Furthermore, it also seems to accentuate yet another version of Turkey's 'exceptionalism'. While the era of globalization, coinciding with the end of the Cold War, would be marked by a tendency to 'move beyond praetorianism' especially in Latin America, the military's increased role in Turkish politics has continuously been in the limelight.[28] Turkey is, thus, said to represent a paradox in civil–military relations for the post-Cold War era during which military perceptions, strategies and institutional structures have been radically altered (Uzgel 2003).

The fact that the national-security regime was entrenched by the 1982 constitution in Turkey demands a fundamentally different explanation from those that have been purportedly provided so far by these, to put it that way, 'state-centered though anti-state' accounts. First of all, it is imperative to note that the transformation process after the 1980 military coup has had two important features which are at the same time defining features of neoliberal hegemony in general. On the one hand, the state is being subjected to a continuous process of restructuring in relation to the definition of its role in the economy, as discussed above. On the other hand, it entailed a crucial change in the balance of class forces within society, which the state played a crucial role in constituting rather than simply registering in itself. In other words, the military coup of 1980 signified not only a change in the political regime but also a change in the form of the state in both senses that were alluded by Nicos Poulantzas to that rather critical concept. For the state forms concerned are nothing but the 'crystallisation of different class strategies' which 'must be reproduced in and through class struggle'. Hence the need to analyse the state form in its institutional materiality with its specific patterns of strategic selectivity and state power as a form-determined condensation of the balance of forces in various historical contexts.[29]

This is why it is necessary to characterize the post-1980 regime in Turkey in relation to an authoritarian form of state which remained in effect after the return to civilian rule. It thus becomes possible to come to terms with the changing nature of the state–class relations and the attempts to develop a new hegemonic strategy so as to provide a long-term solution to the hegemonic crisis of the Turkish bourgeoisie in the pre-1980 period. Return to civilian rule did not pave the way, however, for a removal of the limitations on the democratic rights and freedoms of the working classes that have been engrained in the 1982 constitution and the related legislature enacted by the military regime. These limitations have crippled the capacity of the trade union movement to defend the interests of their membership, let alone promote them. Accordingly, it would be apposite to depict the core of the new hegemonic strategy accompanying the restructuring of the state in the post-1980 period as *putting an end to class-based politics*.[30]

There is yet another dimension of restructuring of the state in line with neo-liberal understanding. The success in putting an end to *class-based* politics had a consequence, perhaps not anticipated at the time but furnished by the debates among the Western liberal intellectuals such as multiculturalism and the politics of recognition. This is the substitution of class-based politics with *identity-based* politics in the post-1980 period. While it is true that class-based politics has hardly been the defining feature of political struggle within the atmosphere of limited democratic rights and freedoms in Turkey, even under the relatively speaking more democratic 1961 constitution, the identification of social class became at best one identity among others in the context of post-1980 politics with severe implications for the process of further democratization of the country. Thereby, concepts such as democracy, freedom and equality, which have vital importance in terms of defending the rights of workers, are hollowed out to a great extent and started to be used in line with the aims of the identity-based politics. Put differently, they tended to assume new connotations as hegemonic apparatuses of the projects striving to achieve a variety of identity-based political objectives.

It has to be underlined that while these identity-based demands have challenged the long-claimed unitary character of the Turkish Republic more than ever and led to deep legitimacy crises starting from the early 1990s, the transformation of the nature of political struggle as such has substantially disabled the reintroduction of class considerations into the political agenda, hence enabling the reproduction of the alienated form of state/politics as an autonomous sphere. In a sense, it can be surmised that the belated discovery of the civil society in the context of the post-1980 authoritarian form of the state tended to entrench the neoliberal hegemony rather than paving the ground for the emergence of social movements that would challenge that hegemony. The uninterrupted character of neoliberal transformation in Turkey within such a political context shows how the articulation of ethnic, religious and/or nationalist identities into politics might enable a risky but an effective implementation of neoliberal policies.

By way of conclusion: AKP and the political Islam's articulation with neoliberalism

The need for an institutional turn in the neoliberal reform process which started to be voiced with the start of the Customs Union with the EU in 1995, gained pace from December 1999 onwards with the signing of three year stand-by agreement with the IMF, and the granting by the EU at its Helsinki summit of candidate status to Turkey. This has acquired a new momentum after the Justice and Development Party (AKP)'s coming to power in the November 2002 general elections. The latter had led to a reconfiguration of the political scene, with the annihilation of the electoral credibility of the political parties which had formed the coalition government that had to bear the brunt of the 2001 crisis.

Ironically, AKP governments would strongly adhere to the neoliberal policy agenda set by the so-called 'programme for transition to a strong economy' put in place after the twin crises by the discredited coalition government in May 2001. It is also noteworthy that this programme which was instrumental in initiating a period of economic recovery was supported by a new three year stand-by agreement which terminated the use of the exchange rate as a nominal anchor. It thereby signified a new phase in the Turkish economy's neoliberal transformation characterized by a process of fiscal adjustment targeting a *primary surplus*[31] (6.5 per cent to the GDP) on the one hand, and high rates of growth of GNP accompanied by high rates of unemployment, on the other. This pattern, which tended to perpetuate the dependence on massive inflow of foreign finance capital, necessitated a continuation of the high rates of return on domestic assets, reflected in real rates of interest higher than those prevailing in most 'emerging market' economies.[32] This was going to be reinforced by an ambitious acceleration of the process of privatization by the AKP government, thus making the country, as already mentioned, an 'investors' paradise' from the perspective of international finance capital.

The seemingly loyal stand of the AKP to the neoliberal agenda should not however lead to the illusion that the Party has taken all the expressed targets of the post-Washington Consensus seriously in the 2000s; this can better be interpreted as the articulation of different political projects into each other. To give some examples; while the neoliberal anti-poverty agenda has very well matched with the conservative Islamic community- and charity-based anti-poverty strategy of the AKP, the neoliberal privatization agenda has helped the Party create its own capital base through transferring public assets to a selected list of 'green' companies, a process which has led ultimately to the aggravation of corruption claims in Turkey. At this point, it is important to mention that the privatizations of the large-scale profitable state enterprises have helped strengthen the negotiation capability of the AKP vis-à-vis powerful capital groups in Turkey.

In macroeconomic terms, the Turkish economy under AKP rule has been manifesting the symptoms of what is referred as 'jobless growth' as the increases in labour productivity have not been accompanied by an improvement in either real wages or labour participation rates.[33] While a modicum of macroeconomic stability would be achieved with inflation brought under control, the economy would also be saddled with soaring current account deficits, at a time when most of the emerging market economies have been recording current account surpluses. This is, in short, how the IMF anchor functioned as a mechanism of crisis management as well as of prevention, as the Turkish economy remained strongly moored to the dock of neoliberal policy prescriptions.

As for the EU anchor, it seems that its salience was more political than economic, as the economic criteria of the Turkish pre-accession process simply reinforced the conditionalities entailed in IMF stand-by agreements (Yalman 2007: 234). With the coming to power of the AKP, the process of Europeanization in the Turkish context seemed to have taken a new twist. Indeed, it has become quite trendy among the liberal intelligentsia both in Turkey and the West, to attribute a new and unprecedented quality to it. Hence, the EU accession process has been celebrated for transforming an Islamist political movement into a party that embraces the norms of liberal democracy. The latter, in turn, is said to have played a key role in the further democratization and Europeanization of the Turkish political system. It is worth noting that the EU anchor has been attributed a dual function. On the one hand, it has been described as being instrumental in 'helping to soften the underlying secular versus Islam divide in Turkish society' (Öniş 2006b). On the other hand, it has been argued that this so-called anchor has also been instrumental in achieving 'a system of democratic governance, within which Islamic social and political forces would be regarded as legitimate players' (Aydın and Çakır 2007).

There seemed to be an underlying assumption that a window of opportunity for subjecting the state–society relations to a fundamental transformation was opened with AKP coming into power. In this context, the AKP government was put on the stage, not only as the provider of political and economic stability which Turkey could not reach for years, but also as the bearer of a project for democratization defined on the basis of market-oriented reforms and multiculturalism. It can be claimed that AKP followed a political strategy which coincided with this role in its first five years of power, during which the political criteria for EU accession process was decisive to a great extent. In accordance with the neoliberal understanding of the state, it is pretended that the state's tutelage over society will be eroded as the hold of the state over the economy will be diminished through the policies of privatization.

Furthermore, there is the issue of the AKP's stance vis-à-vis the political Islam as the carrier of the neoliberal project of globalization as a mechanism of transforming state–society relations. It is a fact that the AKP has been purporting to distance itself from its Islamist origins by labelling itself as a conservative democrat party, more or less in the same mould with the Christian Democrat parties of Western Europe.[34] However, it is not necessarily a convincing argument since it is generally acknowledged that political Islam has been strengthening through the process of globalization.[35] In other words, the adherence to the neoliberal project by itself does not entail a qualitative transformation in terms of a break from Islamic tradition. There is also the need to come to terms with the ways in which the internal contradictions and uneven nature of capitalist development in Turkey have contributed to the articulation of identity-based feelings of exclusion for different political projects.[36]

What is more striking is the attribution of a further mission to AKP, that of extricating Turkey from the regime of 12 September.[37] However, while in power the AKP had made it clear that it had no intention to assume such a mission to the chagrin of those who had such expectations. What is more conspicuous however is the tendency of those who attributed this mission to the AKP to conceive the state as a subject which dominates politics but one that can be driven out of it. There is also an evident negligence to recognize that neoliberal policies, which have been implemented worldwide since the 1980s, have tended to endanger the democratic form of the state. Racism, various forms of social exclusion, unregistered labour exploitation in 'flexible' labour markets, and repressive policies put in practice in the name of combating terrorism are common problems of both the Southern and the Northern countries today. These problems are expected to be aggravated within the context of the ongoing global capitalist crisis. However, identifying the AKP rule in Turkey as enhancing the prospects for a liberal democratic opening, tends to reproduce yet another version of relativist understanding as reflected with its emphasis on Turkey's 'exceptionalism' in underscoring the compatibility of Islam and democracy.[38] Rather, it is imperative to understand that the AKP represents more continuity than radical change in terms of the authoriarian form of the state that has been the defining feature of the Turkish political economy in the neoliberal era, in that its policies and practices can be best summed up with Gramsci's notion of *transformismo*.

Notes

1 See Yalman (2001) and (2009) for a critique of such a tendency in the Turkish context.
2 See Tünay (1993); Yalman (2001) and Morton (2007).
3 See İnsel (2003) and Barkey and Çongar (2007) as examples of such a perspective.
4 See Yalman (2009) for a detailed analysis of the investment behaviour of the domestic capital groups and multinational corporations in Turkey during that period.
5 According to a report (BSB 2006), prepared by Independent Social Scientists (BSB), an academic group critical of the neoliberal policy agenda in Turkey, this continued to be a persistent characteristic of the Turkish manufacturing industry well into the twenty-first century.
6 For the characterization of Latin American experiences as 'export growth but not export-led growth', see Mortimore and Peres (2001).
7 See Erdem (2007) for a comparative analysis of hot money flows in three different contexts.
8 Independent Evaluation Office, 'Evaluation Report: IMF and Recent Capital Account Crises: Indonesia, Korea, Brazil', 28 July 2003. Online, available at: www.imf.org.
9 See also Köse and Yeldan (1998: 70).
10 See OECD (2002).
11 The late President Turgut Özal's Inaugural Speech to the Third Izmir Congress of Economics, 4 June 1992.

12   For decades, the administration has favoured a paternalistic approach in making and implementing laws while interest groups could exert influence through informal and political channels. The frequently suspicious attitude of officials against the private sector has been underpinned by an overall lack of understanding of the private sector.... Some more established and open consultation procedures have recently emerged but public consultation still appears as a new concept in Turkey. Further development in that direction entails a deep change in mindset, both in the administration and the private sector, to move away from mutual distrust towards co-operation needed to create a more competitive regulatory environment for business.

(OECD 2002)

13 As Burnham (2000) argued, this euphemism implied a shift in state policy formation from discretion to rule-bound so as to redefine state bureaucracies' relationship with the political authority through the mediation of the market, which has been promoted as a self-regulating sphere.
14 See also Akyüz and Boratav (2003) for a detailed analysis of this cycle of intermittent crises, and Boratav *et al.* (2001) for its implications for the income distribution during the 1990s in the Turkish context.
15 See Independent Evaluation Office, 'Evaluation Report: IMF and Recent Capital Account Crises: Indonesia, Korea, Brazil', 28 July 2003. Online, available at: www. imf.org.
16 Cf. Cohen (2008).
17 See also Balkan and Yeldan (2002: 51); Yeldan (2002: 14).
18 See Cohen (2008) for an assessment of the Asian experiences along these lines in the aftermath of the Asian crisis in 1998.
19 Öniş (2003 and 2006a).
20 Cf. Panitch and Gindin (2008).
21 *International Herald Tribune*, 'Turkey is Looking Like an Investor's Paradise', 23 February 2006.
22 See İnsel (2003).
23 See Huntington (1968) for the characterization of the national-security regimes that dominated the political scene especially in Latin American countries during the 1960s as 'praetorianism'. In this perspective, it becomes necessary for the armed forces to impose order on turbulent, modernizing societies where and when social mobilization instigated by economic growth was not channelled through legitimized political institutions.
24 While some institutionalists (see, for example, Schmitter and Schneider 2003) tend to concede that no single set of institutions and/or rules defines political democracy, there is nonetheless a preoccupation with the procedural aspects in attempts to differentiate between phases of liberalization, transition and consolidation in a democratization process.
25 'The praetorian nature of the republic in Turkey is inherent in its foundation' (İnsel 2007).
26 Hence one is confronted with the conceptualization of the state both as an instrument and as a subject with its own independent will, that is, a methodological trap which Nicos Poulantzas had warned against and developed his alternative conceptualization of the capitalist state as a condensation of power relations. See Martin (2008: 20) for a reminder of this rather vital methodological issue with immense political significance.
27 See Jessop (2008: 83).
28 See Ropp (1998) for a rather sceptic review of this assessment for Latin America.
29 See Jessop (2008: 33, 126).
30 See Yalman (2001) for an elaboration of this argument.

31 'The predominant objective of fiscal policies has become servicing the rising levels of public debt and reducing the risk of default' (Boratav 2007: 11).
32 Indeed, it has been contended that 'the main adjustment mechanism of the post-crisis IMF programme was embedded in maintaining a significantly high rate of real interest' (Yeldan 2006).
33 Yeldan (2006); cf. World Bank (2005b).
34 See Hale (2006).
35 See Bayat (2008) and Atasoy (2007).
36 See Aydın (2005: 183).
37 Ahmet İnsel, 'Olağanlaşan Demokrasi ve Modern Muhafazakarlık', *Birikim* 163/164, November 2002 and '12 Eylül'den Çıkış Kapısı', *Radikal-2*, 10 November 2002.
38 See Rabasa and Larrabee (2008).

References

Ahmad, F. (2004) *Turkey: The Quest for Identity*, Oxford: One World Publications.
Akyüz, Y. and K. Boratav (2003) 'The Making of the Turkish Financial Crisis', *World Development*, 31: 9, 1549–66.
Atasoy, Y. (2007) 'The Islamic Ethic and the Spirit of Turkish Capitalism Today', *Socialist Register 2008.*
Aydın, S. and R. Çakır (2007) 'Political Islam in Turkey', CEPS Working Document, 265/April. Online, available at: www.ceps.eu.
Aydın, Z. (2005) *The Political Economy of Turkey*, London: Pluto Press.
Balkan, E. and E. Yeldan (2002) 'Peripheral Development under Financial Liberalisation: The Turkish Experience', in N. Balkan and S. Savran (eds), *The Ravages of Neoliberalism: Economy, Society and Gender in Turkey*, New York: Nova Science Publishers, 39–54.
Barkey, H. and Y. Çongar (2007) 'Deciphering Turkey's Elections, The Making of a Revolution', *World Policy Journal*, 24: 3, 63–73.
Bayat, A. (2007) 'Islamism and Empire', *Socialist Register 2008.*
Baysan, T. and C. Blitzer (1990) 'Turkey's Trade Liberalisation in the 1980s and Prospects for its Sustainability', in T. Arıcanlı and D. Rodrik (eds) *The Political Economy of Turkey: Debt, Adjustment and Sustainability*, London: Macmillan.
Bedirhanoğlu, P. (2004) 'The *Nomenklatura*'s Passive Revolution in Russia in the Neoliberal Era', in Leo McCann (ed.) *Russian Transformations: Challenging the Global Narrative*, London: RoutledgeCurzon, 19–41.
Boratav, K. (2002) *Türkiye Iktisat Tarihi, 1908-2002*, Ankara: Imge Yayinevi.
Boratav, K. (2007) 'Net Resource Transfers and Dependency: Some Recent Changes in the World Economy', in A.H. Köse, F. Şenses and E. Yeldan (eds) *Neoliberal Globalisation as New Imperialism*, New York: Nova Science Publishers, 1–19.
Boratav, K., A.H. Köse and E. Yeldan (2001) 'Turkey: Globalization, Distribution and Social Policy', in Lance Taylor (ed.) *External Liberalization, Economic Performance and Social Policy*, Oxford: Oxford University Press.
BSB (2006) *Turkey and the IMF: Macroeconomic Policy, Patterns of Growth and Persistent Fragilities*, Penang, Malaysia: Third World Development Network.
Buğra, A. (1994) *State and Business in Modern Turkey: A Comparative Study*, Albany: State University of New York Press.
Burnham, P. (2000) 'Globalisation, Depoliticization and Modern Economic Management', in Werner Bonefeld and Kosmas Psychopedis (eds) *The Politics of Change: Globalisation, Ideology and Critique*, Basingstoke: Palgrave.

Cardoso, E. (1992) 'From Inertia to Megainflation: Brazil in the 1980s', in M. Bruno, S. Fischer, H. Helpman and N. Liviatan (eds) *Lessons of Economic Stabilisation and Its Aftermath*, Boston: MIT Press.

Celasun, M. and D. Rodrik (1989) 'Turkish Experience with Debt', in J. Sachs (ed.) *Developing Country Debt and the World Economy*, Chicago: The University of Chicago Press, 193–211.

Cerny, P. (1997) 'International Finance and the Erosion of Capitalist Diversity', in C. Crouch and W. Streek (eds) *Political Economy of Modern Capitalism*, London: Sage.

Clarke, S. (1992) 'The Global Accumulation of Capital and the Periodisation of the Capitalist State Form', in W. Bonefeld, R. Gunn and K. Psychopedis (eds) *Open Marxism, Vol.I, Dialectics and History*, London: Pluto Press.

Cohen, B.J. (2008) 'After the Fall: East Asian Exchange Rates Since the Crisis', in A. MacIntyre, T.J. Pempel and J. Ravenhill (eds) *Crisis as Catalyst: Asia's Dynamic Political Economy*, Ithaca: Cornell University Press.

Eder, M. (2004) 'Populism As A Barrier To Integration With The EU: Rethinking The Copenhagen Criteria', in Mehmet Uğur and Nergis Canefe (eds) *Turkey's Europe: An Internal Perspective On EU-Turkey Relations*, London: Routledge, 49–74.

Erdem, N. (2007) 'A Hot Debate: Financial Crises in Turkey, Mexico and South Korea', in A.H. Köse, F. Şenses and E. Yeldan (eds) *Neoliberal Globalisation as New Imperialism*, New York: Nova Science Publishers, 129–51.

Evans, P. (1992) 'The State as Problem and Solution: Predation, Embedded Autonomy, and Structural Change', in Stephan Haggard and Robert Kaufman (eds) *The Politics of Economic Adjustment: International Constraints, Distributive Conflicts, and the State*, Princeton: Princeton University Press.

Frenkel, R. (2001) 'Reflections on Development Financing', *CEPAL Review*, 74, August.

Gamble, A. (2006) 'Two Faces of Neo-Liberalism', in Richard Robison (ed.) *The Neo-Liberal Revolution: Forging the Market State*, London: Palgrave, 20–35.

Grindle, M. (1991) 'The New Political Economy', in G. Meier (ed.) *Politics and Policy Making in Developing Countries: Perspectives on New Political Economy*, San Francisco: ICS Press.

Hale, W. (2006) 'Christian Democracy and the JDP: Parallels and Contrasts', in H. Yavuz (ed.) *The Emergence of a New Turkey: Democracy and the AK Parti*, Salt Lake City: The University of Utah Press.

Huntington, S. (1968) *Political Order in Changing Societies*, New Haven: Yale University Press.

IMF (2003) *Lessons from the Crisis in Argentina*, prepared by the Policy Development and Review Department, 8 October 2003. Online, available at: www.imf.org.

İnsel, A. (2003) 'The AKP and Normalizing Democracy in Turkey', *The South Atlantic Quarterly* 102: 2/3, spring/summer 2003.

İnsel, A. (2007) 'The Praetorian State and Its Owners'. Online, available at: www.birikimdergisi.com/birikim/article.aspx?mid=512&article=The%20Praetorian%20State%20and%20Its%20Owners.

Jessop, B. (2008) *State Power*, Cambridge: Polity.

Köse, A.H. and E. Yeldan (1998) 'Turkish Economy in the 1990s', *New Perspectives on Turkey*, 18, spring.

Krueger, A. and İ. Turan (1993) 'The Politics and Economics of Turkish Policy Reforms in the 1980s', in R. Bates and A. Krueger (eds) *Political and Economic Interactions in Economic Policy Reform*, Oxford: Blackwell.

Lafay, J. and J. Lecaillon (1993) *The Political Dimension of Economic Adjustment*, Paris: OECD.

Martin, J. (2008) 'Introduction', in J. Martin (ed.) *The Poulantzas Reader*, London: Verso.

Mortimore, M. and W. Peres (2001) 'Corporate Competitiveness in Latin America and the Caribbean', *CEPAL REVIEW*, 74, August.

Morton, A.D. (2007) 'Disputing the Geopolitics of the States System and Global Capitalism', *Cambridge Review of International Affairs*, 20: 4, 599–617.

Mosley, P., J. Harrigan and J. Toye (1991) *Aid and Power: The World Bank and Policy-based Lending*, Vols. I–II, London: Routledge.

OECD (2002) *OECD Reviews of Regulatory Reform, Regulatory Reform in Turkey Enhancing Market Openness Through Regulatory Reform*, Paris: OECD.

Öniş, Z. (1992) 'The East Asian Model Development and the Turkish Case: A Comparative Analysis', *METU Studies in Development*, 19: 4.

Öniş, Z. (2003) 'Domestic Politics versus Global Dynamics: Towards a Political Economy of the 2000 and 2001 Financial Crises in Turkey', in Z. Öniş and B. Rubin (eds) *The Turkish Economy in Crisis*, London: Frank Cass.

Öniş, Z. (2006a) 'Beyond the 2001 Financial Crisis: The Political Economy of the New Phase of Neo-Liberal Restructuring in Turkey', paper presented at International Studies Association, Annual Convention, San Diego, California, USA (March). Online, available at: http://portal.ku.edu.tr/~zonis/publications.htm.

Öniş, Z. (2006b) 'Globalisation and Party Transformation: Turkey's Justice and Development Party in Perspective', in Peter Burnell (ed.) *Globalising Democracy: Party Politics in Emerging Democracies*, London: Routledge.

Öniş, Z. and İ. Bayram (2008) 'Temporary Star or Emerging Tiger? Turkey's Recent Economic Performance in a Global Setting', *New Perspectives on Turkey*, 39, 47–84.

Palma, G. (2000) 'Three Routes to Financial Crises: The Need for Capital Controls', CEPA Working Paper series III, No. 18, New School for Social Research, New York.

Panitch, L. and S. Gindin (2008) 'The Current Crisis'. Online, available at: www.socialistproject.ca/bullet/bullet142.html.

Poulantzas, N. (1975) *Classes in Contemporary Capitalism*, London: New Left Books.

Rabasa, A. and S. Larrabee (2008) 'The Rise of Political Islam in Turkey', prepared for the Office of the Secretary of Defense, RAND, National Defense Research Institute, www.rand.org.

Robinson, W. (2002) 'Globalisation as a Macro-Structural-Historical Framework of Analysis: The Case of Central America', *New Political Economy*, 7: 2.

Rodrik, D. (2001) 'Why is There So Much Economic Insecurity in Latin America?', *CEPAL Review*, 73, April.

Rogoff, K., E. Prasad, S.-J. Wei and M. Ayhan Kose (2003) 'Effects of Financial Globalisation on Developing Countries: Some Empirical Evidence', IMF, 17 March 2003.

Ropp, S. (1998) 'Beyond Praetorianism: The Latin American Military in Transition', *Journal of Interamerican Studies and World Affairs*, 40: 1, 95–7.

Schmitter, P. and C. Schneider (2003) 'Conceptualising and Measuring the Liberalisation of Autocracy and the Consolidation of Democracy Across Regions of the World and From Different Points of Departure', paper presented to the Fourth Mediterranean Social and Political Research Meeting, European University Institute, Robert Schumann Centre for Advanced Studies, Florence, Montecatini-Terme, March 2003.

Taylor, L. (2005) 'Foreword', in BSB (2006) *Turkey and the IMF: Macroeconomic Policy, Patterns of Growth and Persistent Fragilities*, Penang, Malaysia: Third World Development Network.

Tünay, M. (1993) 'The Turkish New Right's Attempt at Hegemony', in Atila Eralp, M. Tünay and Birol Yeşilada (eds) *The Political and Socioeconomic Transformation of Turkey*, Westport: Praeger, 11–30.

Williamson, J. (1990) 'What Washington Means by Policy Reform', in J. Williamson (ed.), *Latin American Adjustment: How Much has Happened?* Washington, DC: Institute for International Economics.

World Bank (1987) *World Development Report*.

World Bank (1990) *Adjustment Lending Policies for Sustainable Growth*, World Bank Policy and Research Series, No. 14.

World Bank (1999) *Turkey: Economic Reforms, Living Standards and Social Welfare Study*, Vol. 1, April.

World Bank (2003) *Memorandum of the President to the Executive Directors on a Country Assistance Strategy of the World Bank Group for the Republic of Turkey*, 2 October, Report No. 26756 TU.

World Bank (2005a) *The World Bank in Turkey: 1993–2004*, An IEG Country Assistance Evaluation, World Bank, December.

World Bank (2005b) *Turkey Labor Market Study*, Washington, DC: The World Bank.

Uzgel, İ. (2003) 'Between Praetorianism And Democracy: The Role of the Military in Turkish Foreign Policy', *Turkish Yearbook of International Affairs*, 34, 177–211.

Yalman, G.L. (2001) 'The Turkish State and Bourgeoisie in Historical Perspective: A Relativist Paradigm or A Panoply of Hegemonic Strategies?', in N. Balkan and S. Savran (eds) *The Politics of Permanent Crisis: Class, State and Ideology in Turkey*, New York: Nova Science Publishers, 21–54.

Yalman, G.L. (2007) 'Rethinking the Nature of the Beast: The Turkish State and the Process of Europeanisation', in A.H. Köse, F. Şenses and E. Yeldan (eds) *Neoliberal Globalisation as New Imperialism*, New York: Nova Science Publishers, 225–43.

Yalman, G.L. (2009) *Transition to Neoliberalism: The Case of Turkey in the 1980s*, İstanbul Bilgi University Press.

Yeldan, E. (2002) 'On the IMF-Directed Disinflation Program in Turkey', in N. Balkan and S. Savran (eds) *The Ravages of Neoliberalism: Economy, Society and Gender in Turkey*, New York: Nova Science Publishers, 1–20.

Yeldan, E. (2006) 'Patterns of Adjustment under the Age of Finance: The Case of Turkey as a Peripheral Agent of New-Imperialism', paper prepared for the annual meetings of the Union for Radical Political Economy (URPE), Chicago, 5–7 January 2007.

9 Neoliberalism, industrial restructuring and labour

Lessons from the Delhi garment industry

Alessandra Mezzadri

The deep capitalist world crisis of the 1970s and the rise of neoliberal globalisation in the 1980s signalled the end of the labour-friendly regime (Silver and Arrighi 2000), which characterised the Keynesian era and was defined by a sort of international 'compromise' between capital and labour. In the developing countries, this shift determined the passage from 'the development project' to the 'globalisation project' (Bair 2005), which has relegated these countries to the role of 'full package suppliers' (Gibbon 2001) in global commodity chains.

Within the logic of neoliberal globalisation, developing countries compete according to their comparative advantage, namely cheap labour. The way in which this 'cheapness' is ensured is heavily based on the segmentation of labour markets on the basis of traditional social structures. Arguably, these structures pre-exist neoliberalism, and they are highly country-specific. With reference to India, which this chapter focuses on, Harriss-White (2003) has highlighted the fundamental role that structures such as caste, gender, space, religion and family labour play in the local accumulation process.

Looking at the case of the Delhi export-oriented garment sector, this chapter shows how, today, these structures are also acquiring broader regulatory functions. In fact, Indian garment exporters, who are subject to global competition, make use of the local social structures available to them in order to minimise labour costs and successfully participate in global production. In this way, such structures are further reinforced, and, arguably, *transnationalised*, as they acquire an even more significant role, not simply within the local economy, but also within the global economy. They contemporaneously mediate the process of working-class formation in the local economy as well as in neoliberal global production, imposing patterns of labour commodification and control which are highly diversified and which exploit the social profile of the workers. This chapter is based on fieldwork findings and observations gathered in India between October 2004 and July 2004. The methodology used is based on a combination of quantitative and qualitative research methods. Data presented come from the archive of the Apparel Export Promotion Council (AEPC), a sector-specific governmental agency with various regulatory and export-promotion functions. Qualitative accounts are based on interviews with exporters, subcontractors and other agents actively involved in the production process, and labour organisations supporting and organising garment workers (mainly the Centre for Education and Communication – CEC, and the Centre of Indian Trade Unions – CITU).

Goodbye labour friendliness, hello neoliberal globalisation

The rise of neoliberalism in the 1970s signalled the beginning of a deep economic restructuring, which impacted both developed and developing countries. In the context of the new neoliberal agenda, developing countries' industrialisation strategies changed dramatically. IS (Import Substitution) was abandoned in favour of Export Oriented Industrialisation (EOI). It was the end of the labour-friendly regime (Silver and Arrighi 2000). The new anti-labour stance manifested itself in developed and developing countries in different ways. In developed countries, the migration of manufacturing production towards poorer economies imposed new ways of discipline on expensive and troublesome 'northern' labour. In developing countries, labour defeat to capital was imposed as a pre-condition for successful economic development (see Breman 1995). In fact, cheap labour was re-conceptualised as the main comparative advantage of these countries.

These transformations reconfigured the international division of labour (Jenkins *et al.* 2002). In fact, in the context of the new transnational neoliberal production, developing countries became the production nodes of what Gereffi and Korzeniewicz (1994) called global commodity chains. The decentralisation of manufacturing production initially focused on assembly, but soon extended to the whole product cycle, to what became known as full-package supply (Gibbon 2001).

The transnationalisation of production signalled what Bair (2005) refers to as the end of the 'development project' and the birth of the 'globalisation project'. Production went global. However, this globalisation was far from being a natural or necessary evolution of the world capitalist system. Shaped by neoliberal policies, it was part and parcel of the new neoliberal political project (see Kiely 2005). It was a *neoliberal globalisation*. In the context of neoliberal globalisation, development was reconceptualised as successful integration into global markets.

The formation of global commodity chains determined a profound disarticulation between the governance of production and labour. In fact, if transnational corporations (TNCs) were in charge of the governance of production networks, the governance of labour was a different matter. Indeed, through global outsourcing, 'TNCs were able to cut labour costs and the costs of risks and investment' (Raikes *et al.* 2000: 12). However, 'global' governance could impose only one general diktat on labour: that of its 'cheapness'. Arguably, the ways in which this cheapness is realised, a very compelling area of enquiry, may vary considerably. The following sections discuss how this process unravels in the Delhi garment industry.

Delhi becomes a production node in global garment production

The garment industry was one of the first industries to go global. By the 1960s, well before the rise of neoliberalism, production started relocating to East Asia, especially in Taiwan, Hong Kong and South Korea. By the 1970s, the decentralisation of garment manufacturing to these economies was very significant (Jenkins *et al.* 2002). Garment export was a crucial component of the region's economic success, as it provided the foreign exchange necessary to fuel IS strategies.

In 1974, the birth of the Multi Fibre Arrangement (MFA) established quota ceilings to textile and garment exporters. These ceilings were apt to protect developed countries' domestic production, and to avoid that any country or region could develop a monopolistic power over textile or garment exports. Despite its protectionist aims, the MFA had the effect to expand the geographical reach of transnational garment production. In fact, buyers had to differentiate their outsourcing strategies 'working with' different countries in order to meet their production targets. In a way, this regulation directly sustained the neoliberal design, as it drew an increasing number of developing countries into the logic of EOI and into the global garment commodity chain.

As growth rates steadily increased, wages followed, eroding the region's initial comparative advantage in cheap labour. Soon, the global garment commodity chain moved again, in search of new sites of cheap(er) labour. In this second shift, it first reached South East Asia and Latin America, then China and South Asia (Gereffi and Ramaswamy 2000). By the 1980s, India started being incorporated into neoliberal global garment production (see Tables 9.1 and 9.2).

In India, the implementation of the MFA was managed through the AEPC, a government body in charge of quota allocation and registration. Created in the late 1970s, the council registered export turnover from all the centres engaging in garment export production in India. These centres are Delhi, Tiruppur,

Table 9.1 Share of ready-made garments in India's exports 1960–1 to 2000–1 (rupees, million)

Year/ value	Ready-made garments		Textiles		Manufacture goods		Total exports	
	Total	%	Total	%	Total	%	Total	%
1960–1	10	0.16	790	12.29	2,910	45.26	6430	100
1970–1	290	1.89	1,450	9.45	7,720	50.29	15,350	100
1980–1	5,500	8.20	9,330	13.90	37,470	55.83	67,110	100
1990–1	40,120	12.32	69,260	21.28	237,360	72.91	886,690	100
1994–5	103,050	11.6	199,450	22.5	646,830	72.90	886,690	100
2000–1	254,780	12.52	–	–	1,607,230	78.95	2,035,710	100

Source: adapted from Table 3.1 in Singh and Kaur Sapra (2007: 43); based on DGCI&S data cited in Economic Survey 2002–2003, Table 7.3, 7.4, Government of India, various issues.

Table 9.2 India's share in world exports, apparel and clothing accessories (US$ million)

Year	World	India	India's share (%)	Total export (world)	Percentage of garments of world export
1970	109	–	–	313,804	0.03
1975	308	–	–	876,094	0.04
1980	32,369	590	1.82	1,997,686	1.62
1985	38,718	887	2.29	1,930,849	2.01
1990	94,577	2,211	2.34	3,303,563	2.86
1995	160,535	4,124	2.57	4,946,096	3.25
1998	185,936	4,821	2.59	5,091,105	3.65
1999	185,746	5,229	2.82	5,522,372	3.36

Source: Singh and Kaur Sapra (2007: 44), Table 3.2; data from UNITC Year book, cited in Economic Survey 2002–2003, Government of India, Table 7.5.

Mumbai, Chennai, Bangalore, Calcutta, Ludhiana, Jaipur, Hyderabad and Cochin (AEPC 2004). In many of these centres, production generally clusters around a number of industrial areas, and is defined by an industrial fabric mainly composed of small and medium enterprises (SMEs) (Tewari 2008; interviews with the United Nations Industrial Development Organisation, UNIDO).

According to AEPC data, today Delhi is the first Indian export centre in terms of value exported from India, and the second in terms of quantity (number of garments exported).[1] An established tailoring centre during Mughal times (see Blake 1993), Delhi entered readymade garment export production in the 1960s.[2] It was in this period, well after independence, that India started being known in international markets. The boom of the hippy culture in the West was an important trigger for export production. Production increased considerably in the 1980s, when India was drawn into global garment production (see Table 9.1). Since the 1980s, Delhi managed to maintain its leading position in Indian export market.

In Delhi, garment production is spread across a number of areas. It used to cluster around Okhla, a commercial area inside the walled city, but soon was relocated to the outskirts of the city, in industrial areas which geographically belong to the neighbouring states of Haryana and Uttar Pradesh (UP). These areas are NOIDA (in UP), Gurgaon and Faridabad (in Haryana), which, together with Delhi city, form the National Capital Region (NCR). This fragmented industrial space is corresponded by a very fragmented organisation of production activities, and by a complex labour regime.

A highly decomposed organisation of production

Delhi specialises in the production of women's clothing. This type of production has two main features. First, it is characterised by very volatile product cycles, which change rapidly according to changes in fashion. Second, it is defined by a high number of ancillary activities. The main garmenting activities which generally take place inside one unit in Delhi are cutting, thread-cutting, stitching, checking and packing. Then, there are some processing activities, such as printing and washing, which would normally take place in specialised units. Few larger industrial set-ups may have washing plants inside their premises (interviews with AEPC-Delhi and with Delhi exporters). Ancillary activities, crucial in the production of women's clothing, are mainly designed to 'embellish' garments (interviews with Delhi exporters).

The supply chain is managed by the exporter, who has direct access to final markets. The exporters may be either manufacturer-exporters or merchant-exporters, according to AEPC classification (AEPC 2002). Manufacturer exporters have manufacturing capacity and their own industrial units, while merchants do not, and rely on small producers with no access to the export market. However, manufacturers do not necessarily have large production facilities. The majority of them also rely, like the merchants, on a number of small producers to whom they subcontract significant shares of the orders they receive from the global buyers. Subcontractors are very numerous in Delhi. They may provide the exporter with extra stitching capacity, in which case they are called fabricators, or they can specialise in other specific tasks, in which case they are generally called job-workers. Often, small producers may work both as fabricators and as job-workers. Through high levels of subcontracting, Delhi exporters manage to protect themselves from the high production risks due to the continuous fluctuations in export orders. In turn, the subcontractors deal with risk by diversifying their production and working for numerous exporters (interviews with Delhi exporters and subcontractors).

This fragmented production landscape is further complicated by the presence of ancillary activities, in particular those which define the 'embellishment network', crucial in the production of women's clothing. This network is composed by several embroidery activities and, in the Delhi context, it is not simply a forward linkage, but rather a crucial part of the product cycle. In fact, through the process of embroidery, the price of garments can increase considerably. For example, Lal (2004) reports that, in Okhla, non-embroidered low-end garments are sold to buyers at 73 rupees, while embroidered items are sold at 125.

There are three types of embroidery in Delhi: computerised embroidery, machine-embroidery and hand-embroidery. The first is not heavily practiced, and it is monopolised by a few capital-intensive units which have expensive machines called 'heads'. Some larger garment units might have these machines inside their premises, although generally this activity is contracted out to computerised embroidery units. Machine and hand-embroidery are more systematically integrated into the product cycle. They are managed by specialised agents called 'vendors', who organise the last segment of the production process for the exporter. Vendors generally specialise either in machine-embroidery or in hand-embroidery, as these are defined by different types of networks (interviews with Delhi exporters, vendors and proprietors of machine-embroidery units).

Machine-embroidery takes place in units in and around the main industrial areas of the NCR. The proprietors of the units own the machines and organise production, although they generally also exploit their own labour. The most common types of hand-embroidery needed by the industry are *adda-work* and *moti-work*, also known as 'beading'. *Adda-work* is a particularly intricate type of embroidery made on a type of handloom called *adda*. In the NCR, this activity takes place in a few units in and around the main industrial areas. However, these units only deal with 'urgent' orders or sampling. *Adda* is a scarce and very expensive skill in Delhi. It does not traditionally come from the capital city, but rather from the rural areas around Bareilly, a small town in UP. Here, *adda* is not a scarce skill and it is not expensive, as it is very commonly learnt and practiced in many villages. For this reason, as stressed by Delhi exporters and vendors, most of the production takes place in these villages. Delhi-based vendors have connections with a number of local sub-vendors in UP, whom they rely on to carry out orders. Finally, *moti-work*, or beading, takes place in homes scattered in and around Delhi's main industrial areas. It is a home-based activity, and it is considered very low-skill, at the bottom of the employment ladder (interviews with Delhi exporters, vendors and proprietors of machine-embroidery units).

A complex combination of multiple 'labours'

This highly fragmented organisation of production is paralleled by a complex labour regime, where different labours are connected to one another along the supply chain. The type of labour employed in the factories and that employed in the non-factory realm of production vary considerably.

Around 90 per cent of the labourforce employed in export and subcontracting units in Delhi is migratory. Initially, the industry used to employ workers coming from the caste of *Darzis*, a traditional tailoring caste in northern India (Alam 1992). However, the export boom created a shortage of labour. The industry had to find new reservoirs of labour, and this labour had to be cheap, so that Indian exporters could successfully compete in the global market. It was at this point that an army of migrant workers coming from UP and Bihar, among the poorest states in India, started being recruited. They do not seem to belong to any specific caste (see Krishnamoorthy 2004; Mezzadri 2008), although, as underlined by labour organisations, all garment workers belong to the 'castes of poverty'. The migrants are rarely directly employed by the garment producers (exporters or subcontractors). Generally, they are managed by labour contractors, called *thekedaars*. Delhi-based *thekedaars* recruit groups of workers through their contacts with local *thekedaars* in UP and Bihar. These groups of workers, or *toli*, arrive in Delhi and are placed in garment units under the supervision of the contractor (interviews with Delhi exporters, CITU-Delhi and CEC).

In this way, the management of labour becomes disarticulated from that of production. Exporters (as well as subcontractors) are lightened of the 'labour burden', which instead is managed by the labour contractor. Moreover, through this practice, known as 'in-contracting' and already described by Castells and Portes (1989) with reference to Latin America, it is possible to prevent the formalisation of labour relations even in apparently formal production contexts, such as export factories. In fact, the majority of factory workers, who respond to the *thekedaars*, are employed on a temporary or casual basis. The use of labour contractors allows exporters to expand their productive capacity without increasing their responsibility towards the labourforce. Interviews with exporters underline this point with particular emphasis. Significantly, when asked about their manufacturing capacity, exporters only mention the number of stitching machines they own. On the other hand, when asked about the number of workers they employ, they simply answer, as already highlighted by Chari (2004: 115) in his study of Tiruppur, that they 'own the machines, but not the work'.

Bihari and Uttar Pradeshi migrants generally come from a rural background (Krishnamoorthy 2004) and they tend to be first-generation industrial workers. They look for jobs in large urban centres to escape from the high poverty levels in their villages. In this way, rural poverty contributes to the expansion of what first Breman (1996) and then Davis (2006) define as the urban 'footloose proletariat', a trend stressed by both Rigg (2006) and Bernstein (2003, 2007). The geographical mobility and lack of industrial background of these workers are relevant assets for the *thekedaars* and, indirectly, for the Delhi exporter. These features of the workforce ensure both labour cost minimisation and minimal risks of unionisation. Exporters report that they further discourage unionisation through the spread of production capacity across multiple units, a practice which further reinforces and reproduces high levels of industrial fragmentation. Arguably, anti-unionisation tactics increased considerably since the 1970s, when India started crafting its own labour-unfriendly regime (Lerche, 2007). In fact, this regime is characterised by a rise in what Datt (2002) calls employers' militancy.[3]

The mobility cycle of migrant garment workers is 'fluid' and repetitive. Migrants do not settle in Delhi; rather, they stay only for nine to ten months. In April, at the beginning of lean season, they return to their villages. They remain there for around two to three months, then they move back to Delhi, and the cycle starts again. According to unions and labour organisations, this cycle is shaped by exporters' strategies for labour cost minimisation, as exporters fire workers when the lean season starts (interviews with Delhi exporters, CITU-Delhi and CEC). On the contrary, according to exporters and subcontractors, workers leave voluntarily because they want to return to their villages, for harvesting, festivals or weddings. Fieldwork findings do not allow a final conclusion on this issue. Indeed, it can at least be argued that the industry found an 'ideal' workforce, which not only well matches industrial (flexible) requirements, but which also reproduces the conditions for its own casualisation.

In contrast, the embellishment network is characterised by non-factory based activities. Here different types of non-factory labour are used. Each of these 'labours' guarantees the minimisation of cost in each of the segments of the network. Machine-embroidery units employ the same type of labour found in garment factories; i.e. UP and Bihari migrants. Delhi-based *adda-work* units, which, as mentioned previously, are only used for specific tasks, employ a high percentage of child labour. Working children, who can be as young as eight years old, are migrants from Bihar, who arrive in Delhi through local *thekedaars*.

They are all males and they work and live inside the units. This particularly exploitative form of child labour serves the purpose to minimise costs in a segment of production which otherwise would be extremely expensive for the exporter. In fact, these children are paid half the 'wage' of an adult worker per each piece embroidered; they 'make' *adda-work* become a less expensive skill in the metropolitan setting (interviews with vendors and owners of Delhi-based *adda-work* units).

The share of *adda-work* which takes place in the villages around Bareilly is carried out by a different type of labour. I visited one of these villages, which I will call D, together with the factory manager of one big Delhi-based exporting firm. In this village, sub-vendors distribute the work among local rural households. Generally, the husband organises the family unit distributing the work among the various family members, his wife and children (interviews held in the Village of D with household members and vendors). Households engage in *adda-work* six days a week, around ten to 12 hours per day. Sunday is their 'day off'. In this case, household labour, although still owning the means of production (the handlooms), can be defined as a disguised form of wage labour.[4] In fact, households are stably incorporated into the product cycle, and they are given work on a continuous basis. They are paid piece-rates and the exporter, by the way of the vendor, provides all the necessary inputs of production (mainly threads and beads). The use of household production is very cost-effective for the Delhi exporter. In this case, cost minimisation is not realised, as in Delhi, through the use of age-wage differentials, but rather through the exploitation of rural/urban and factory/household labour wage-differentials.

Moti-work is realised through a network of homeworkers. The vendor distributes the garments to different homes in and around industrial areas in the NCR. Beading, a low-skill activity which is at the bottom of the garment employment ladder, is considered a 'female' task. Women homeworkers generally work in groups. They may either work in their own home, or in the house of the contractor. Children, both boys and girls, generally help their mothers (interviews with Delhi vendors and homeworkers). The feminisation of labour in this production segment, further minimises the costs related to this low-skill activity. In fact, women are paid extremely low piece-rate wages. Therefore, in this case, labour cost minimisation can capitalise on gender differences.

In all production segments, both in factory and in non-factory settings, the minimisation of labour costs is realised through a tight social regulation of labour. Delhi exporters, by the way of a wide range of other production actors or specialised agents, can exploit various social institutions and structural differences, ranging from mobility, geographical provenience, age, rural–urban differentials or gender, in order to make and remake labour cheap. Through him, all these different institutions and differences are connected to and incorporated within the global garment commodity chain.

In India, the relevance of the social regulation of labour is widely acknowledged in the literature focusing on the local, informal economy. Harriss-White (2003), drawing from the Social Structure of Accumulation school (SSA) of

Kotz *et al.* (1994), argues that the Indian informal economy is regulated by a number of social institutions. These institutions pave accumulation patterns in the Indian informal economy, becoming India's 'social structures of accumulation'. In particular, Harriss-White stresses the relevance of institutions such as the local state, the structuring of the labouring classes, gender, religion, caste and space. These institutions govern what she calls the 'India of the 88%'; that is rural and small-town India. Other scholars, like Breman (1996), highlight the increasing relevance of mobility in sustaining accumulation patterns in South Asia.

Building on these studies, the case presented in this chapter allows a number of final considerations. First, Indian social structures also govern employment patterns in urban, metropolitan settings. With reference to the Delhi garment sector, given structures, such as caste, have partially lost their regulating role, due to the need to find new reservoirs of cheap labour to compete in global markets. Indeed, in this case, in factory settings, caste is substituted with mobility. The structure of the labouring classes is crossed by multiple lines of social segmentation, which subdivide the production space. This space is inhabited by different types of labour. Migratory, child and female labour are combined in complex solutions, and together they set the basis of the labour process in the industry.

As these institutions are proactively used to respond to the global imperative to provide cheap labour to neoliberal global garment production, their regulatory role overcomes the boundaries of the local or national economy, and it is projected into the neoliberal global arena. This is not a paradoxical outcome. In fact, there is an intrinsic compatibility between the functioning logic of neoliberal globalisation and the social regulation of labour. First, as neoliberal globalisation places a premium on global labour flexibility and labour deregulation, it opens up spaces for 'alternative' forms of regulation to 'fill the gap'. Second, it can be argued that while global outsourcing succeeds in disarticulating production and labour in the global arena, the 'local' social regulation of labour, through which local exporters make and remake labour cheap for global production, succeeds in disarticulating production and labour in the local arena, and in pricing such labour even before it reaches labour markets. Patterns of commodification and discipline of labour start in the private sphere of the individuals, exploiting the social characteristics of these individuals. In a study on migrant workers in Lebanon, Chalcraft (2007) highlights the 'particularism' of the process of commodification of the labour power of these workers, and underlines the crucial role which social identity plays in this process.

In the case presented here, the particularism of the process of commodification of labour acquires a profound complexity. Multiple groups of individuals are called to perform a variety of tasks, and each group is commodified in a different way, based on their social profile. Each of these groups is paid a price which is somehow perceived as corresponding to such a profile. It is a particularistic as well as a *discriminatory* process of commodification, which seems much more intrusive. In fact, it entails the commodification of given social features of the workers *before* they actually become workers. Through the subsumption of the informal economy into the logic of neoliberal production, this discriminatory process of commodification of labour and the local structures of power which define it are strengthened, reinforced and *transnationalised*. They mediate the process of working-class formation not only in the local, but also in the global arena.

Conclusion

The rise of neoliberalism signalled the end of the labour-friendly regime, in both developed and developing countries. As troublesome northern labour was disciplined through the decentralisation of manufacturing production abroad, the subjugation of southern labour to capital was set a pre-condition to development, as this (cheap) labour was re-conceptualised as developing countries' comparative advantage. The instantiation of this regime had severe repercussions on the international division of labour and on the industrial trajectories of developing countries.

The intensification of the process of transationalisation of production under neoliberalism determined the shift from the 'development project' to the 'globalisation project'. In the context of this globalisation, which is specifically neoliberal, developing countries rapidly moved from IS to EOI, becoming production nodes in what today are well known as GCCs. Global governance imposes a simple specific diktat on southern labour: its 'cheapness'. However, the ways in which this 'cheapness' is realised is the compelling question to address.

This chapter focused on the Indian garment sector, and specifically on the Delhi industrial area. India became incorporated into neoliberal global garment production in the 1980s, after that garment production left East Asia, which was the first 'global' manufacturing site. Delhi, today, is one of the leading export centres in India, both in terms of quantity and value. This industrial area, which specialises in the production of women's clothing, is characterised by the interlocking of multiple production spaces and complex organisational solutions apt to maximise flexibility, crucial to compete in markets subject to the volatility of shifting consumers' taste. Organisational flexibility is matched by peculiar patterns of labour flexibility. The product cycle is decomposed in different production spaces, which are inhabited by different labours. These labours are highly socially regulated, in ways which guarantee cheap labour to the exporter and, therefore, to global buyers. Social regulation fragments the labourforce across different lines of differentiation, such as mobility, age, geographical provenance and gender.

The relevance of given social institutions in regulating Indian informal economy is widely acknowledged in the literature on Indian labour markets. In particular, Harriss-White argues that given social institutions work as social structures of accumulation in rural and small-town India, while Breman stresses the increasing role played by mobility in accumulation patterns in South Asia. In the context of the case analysed here, these social institutions are proactively used to make and remake labour cheap and subjugate it to the logic of neoliberal global garment production. By the way of these institutions, labour cheapness is realised by pricing labour before it reaches labour markets. Therefore, it can be argued that such institutions mediate a process of commodification of labour which starts in the private sphere of individuals. This process is 'particularistic' as well as discriminatory, as it implies a pre-determination of wages and tasks. Both wages and tasks are not allocated by the market, but rather by structures of oppression and power. It is a deeper and more intrusive process of commodification of labour, as it extends to given social features of individuals. It could be challenged only by challenging, at once, all those resilient structures of power it is based on.

As the Indian informal economy is subsumed into neoliberal global production, the regulatory role of given 'local' institutions or structures overcomes local or national boundaries, and goes through a process of *transnationalisation*. These institutions and structures acquire new, broader regulatory roles within the neoliberal capitalist architecture. In particular, as already the migration of manufacturing production from developed to developing countries, they serve the purpose to secure labour value while obscuring the multiple and complex ways in which this process takes place.

Notes

1 Quantity here refers to the total pieces exported. According to AEPC latest estimates, in 2003, Delhi's quantity and value shares of total Indian garment export were, respectively, 28.3 per cent and 37.56 per cent.
2 Until the 1960s, garment export was virtually non-existent in the whole subcontinent. See Appelbaum (2005).
3 The rise of this militancy is confirmed by changing patterns in industrial disputes. Since the 1970s, lockouts started outnumbering strikes. See Datt (2002).
4 Other studies raise the issue of disguised wage labour in rural labour markets in developing countries; see, for instance, Sender *et al.* (2006).

References

AEPC (2002) *Directory of Apparel Exporters*, New Delhi: Apparel Export Promotion Council.
AEPC (2004) *Handbook of Export Statistics*, data from 1983–2003, various issues, New Delhi: Apparel Export Promotion Council.
Alam, G. (1992) *Industrial Districts and Technological Change: a Study of The Garment Industry in Delhi*, Mimeo, New Delhi: Centre for Technological Studies
Appelbaum, R.P. (2005) 'TNCs and the Removal of Textile and Clothing Quotas', in *Global and International Studies Program*, paper 38, University of California, Santa Barbara, New York and Geneva: UNCTAD.
Bair, J. (2005) 'Global Capitalism and Commodity Chains: Looking Backward, Going Forward', *Competition and Change*, 9(2), pp. 163–80.
Bernstein, H. (2003) 'Farewell to the Peasantry', *Transformation*, 52. Online, available at: www.transformation.ukzn.ac.za/archive/tran052/trans052002.pdf.
Bernstein, H. (2007) 'Capital and Labour from Centre to Margins' – keynote address for

conference on 'Living on the Margins, Vulnerability, Exclusion and the State in the Informal Economy', Cape Town, 26–28 March 2007. Online, available at: www.povertyfrontiers.org/ev_en.php?ID=1953_201&ID2=DO_TOPIC.

Blake, S. (1993) 'Shahjahanabad: the Sovereign City in Mughal India 1639–1739', *Cambridge South Asian Studies*, Cambridge: Cambridge University Press.

Breman, J. (1995) 'Labour, Get Lost: A Late Capitalist Manifesto', *Economic and Political Weekly*, 30(37), pp. 2294–300.

Breman, J. (1996) *Footloose Labour: Working in India's Informal Economy*, Cambridge: Cambridge University Press.

Castells, M. and Portes, A. (1989) 'World Underneath: the Origins, Dynamics and Effects of the Informal Economy', in A. Portes, M. Castells and L.A. Benton, *The Informal Economy: Studies in Advanced and Less Developed Countries*, Baltimore: Johns Hopkins University Press, pp. 11–37.

Chalcraft J. (2007) 'Labour in the Levant', *New Left Review*, 45, pp. 27–47.

Chari, S. (2004) *Fraternal Capital: Peasant-Workers, Self-Made Men, and Globalization in Provincial India*, New Delhi: Permanent Black.

Datt, R. (2002) 'Industrial Relations-the Menacing Growth of the Phenomenon of Lockouts', in R.K. Sen (ed.), *Indian Labour in the Post-Liberalisation Period*, K.P. Kolkata: Bagchi & Company.

Davis, M. (2006) *Planet of Slums*, London: Verso.

Gereffi, G. and Korzeniewicz, M. (1994) *Commodity Chains and Global Capitalism*, Westport: Praeger.

Gereffi, G. and Ramaswamy, K.V. (2000) 'India's Apparel Exports: the Challenge of Global Markets', *Developing Economies*, 28(2), pp. 186–210.

Gibbon, P. (2001) 'Globalisation, Present-Day Capitalism, Commodity Chains', in J. Degnbol-Martinussen and L.S. Lauridsen (eds), *Changing Global and Regional Conditions for Development in the Third World*, Occasional Paper 21, Graduate School, International Development Studies, Roskilde University 2001, pp. 21–32.

Harriss-White, B. (2003) *India Working-Essays on Society and Economics*, Cambridge: Cambridge University Press.

Jenkins, R., Pearson, R. and Seyfang, G. (2002) *Corporate Responsibility and Labor Rights-Codes of Conduct in the Global Economy*, London: Earthscan.

Kiely, R. (2005) *The Clash of Globalizations-Neo-Liberalism the Third Way and Anti-Globalisation*, Leiden: Brill.

Kotz, D.M., McDonough, T. and Reich, M. (1994) *Social Structures of Accumulation: the Political Economy of Growth and Crisis*, Cambridge: Cambridge University Press.

Krishnamoorthy, S. (2004) *Structure of the Garment Industry and Labor Rights in India – the Post MFA Context*, New Delhi: Centre for Education and Communication.

Lal, T. (2004) *Diagnostic Study, Report & Action Plan for the Ready Made Garment Cluster*; New Delhi, Government of India, SISI Okhla, Cluster Development Executive section.

Lerche, J. (2007) 'A Global Alliance against Forced Labour? Unfree Labour, Neo-liberal Globalisation and the International Labour Organisation', *Journal of Agrarian Change*, 7(4), pp. 425–52.

Mezzadri, A. (2008) 'The Rise of Neoliberal Globalisation and the New Old Social Regulation of Labour: a Case of Delhi Garment Sector', *The Indian Journal of Labour Economics*, 51(4), pp. 603–18.

Raikes, P., Friis Larsen, M. and Ponte, S. (2000) *Global Commodity Chain Analysis and the French Filière Approach: Comparison and Critique*, Working Paper, Centre for Development Research, Copenhagen, Denmark.

Rigg, J. (2006) 'Land, Farming, Livelihoods, and Poverty: Rethinking the Links in the Rural South', *World Development*, 34(1), pp. 180–202.

Sender, J., Oya, C. and Cramer, C. (2006) 'Women Working for Wages: Putting Flesh on the Bones of a Rural Labour Market Survey in Mozambique', *Journal of Southern African Studies*, 32(2), pp. 313–33.

Silver, B.J. and Arrighi, G. (2000) 'Workers North and South', in L. Panitch and C. Leys (eds), *Socialist Register 2001*, London: Merlin Press, pp. 51–74.

Singh, N. and Kaur Sapra, M. (2007) 'Liberalisation in Trade and Finance: India's Garment Sector', in B. Harriss-White and A. Sinha (eds), *Trade Liberalisation and India's Informal Economy*, New Delhi: Oxford University Press, Chapter 3, pp. 42–127.

Tewari, M. (2008) 'Varieties of Global Integration: Navigating Institutional Legacies and Global Networks in India's Garment Industry', *Competition & Change*, 12(1), pp. 49–67.

10 The developmental state and the neoliberal transition in South Korea

Hae-Yung Song

The rapid economic development that took place in the post-war period in South Korea (hereafter 'Korea') has often been identified with a distinctive type of state, the developmental state. Numerous analyses have been conducted on the Korean state, and academics and policy-makers alike have exploited exhaustively the term 'developmental state' since Chalmers Johnson first coined it in the early 1980s referring to the Japanese case. Contrary to the wide usage of the term, and despite the fact that this is a heavily documented field, the statist assumptions of the developmental state analysis have more often been taken for granted than inquired into and problematised. Current discussions on the transition of the Korean state towards neoliberalism have hardly advanced from, and are still conditioned by, the statist presuppositions attached to the developmental state. The aim of this chapter is to address the theoretical flaws inherent in the statist understanding of the developmental state, and how they condition the analysis of its transformation.

The developmental state is characterised by Chalmers Johnson (1982, 1987, 1995), Alice Amsden (1989, 1994) and Robert Wade (1990, 1992, 1998a, 1998b) as one that stands above society and narrow interest groups and, especially, the capitalist class. According to this view, the developmental state, being in possession of the discretionary power to allocate financial resources, was able to direct and discipline enterprises so that they would invest in strategic sectors under a long-term developmental and industrial plan. These propositions have been contrasted with those of market fundamentalists (e.g. Bhagwati 1978; Krueger 1978; World Bank 1993), who understand the rapid economic growth of Korea as the outcome of free market or market-conforming policies.

However, understanding the developmental state in terms of an opposition between the state and the market, that is, whether the state *or* the market brought about rapid growth, necessarily confines the analysis of its transformation within the same dichotomous framework. If the developmental state is defined in terms of the degree to which it intervened in the economy and controlled capital for national development, its transformation is, naturally, seen primarily in relation to whether the state still exercises this power over capital and how heavily it directs development. Consequently, it is normally concluded that either the developmental state has survived, and maintained its commanding role over the capitalists (Lee 2001, 2002, 2006; Weiss 2005) or, alternatively, that it has metamorphosed into a regulatory (neoliberal) state because market rules now take precedence over state discretion (Jayasuriya 2005; Pirie 2005, 2008; Woo-Cumings 1997, 1999).

The methodological assumptions underpinning the state–market dichotomy also traverse the internal–external dichotomy. As the developmental state, and state–market relations, are examined in the national framework, the financial crisis of 1997–8, when the neoliberal reforms accelerated, was largely perceived as having been caused by external pressures (Wade 1998a, 1998b; Wade and Veneroso 1998; Gowan 1999; Harvey 2003). Alternatively, the crisis has been blamed on elite policy choices, although there are diverging views over whether these choices have been either rational and successful (Mathews 1998; Pirie 2005, 2008), or failures (Chang 1998; Chang and Yoo 1999).

Most Marxist accounts, that should be sensitive to the class dimensions of capitalism, hardly transcend statism when assessing the developmental state. For instance, Robert Brenner attributes the rapid growth of the East Asian economies to their developmental states and the close national networks between states, firms and banks (Brenner 1998: 150). In his critique of US financial imperialism, Peter Gowan maintains that US imperialism compels the development models of Japan and the East Asian countries to converge towards neoliberalism. In this transformation, he claims, 'the pattern of Japanese capitalist expansion has been different in the eighties and nineties simply because Japanese capitalism has been far more genuinely productive as a national capitalist system than the capitalism of the Atlantic world' (Gowan 1999: 127). David Harvey distinguishes between different kinds of capitalist development. He does not raise the issue of the developmental state directly, but his understanding of state-led development can be drawn from his conceptualisation of the 'new imperialism'. His distinction of US imperialism between 'hegemony-based imperialism' (1945–70) and 'neo-liberal imperialism' (1970–2000) is linked to his basic contrast between capital accumulation through 'expanded reproduction' and 'accumulation by dispossession'. The first period is characterised by accumulation of capital through expanded reproduction, when 'profits were reinvested in growth as well as in new technologies, fixed capital, and extensive infrastructural improvements' (Harvey 2003: 57). In contrast, neoliberal imperialism corresponds to the era of financial volatility and speculation detached from production, turning to a violently predatory mode of capital accumulation that is 'accumulation by dispossession' (ibid.).

In these analyses on the transformation of the developmental state, the notion that development is autonomous from social actors is based upon dichotomous understandings of the state–market and internal–external relations. These have become the touchstone of assessments of neoliberalism in Korea. Neoliberalism is contrasted with what supposedly characterises the preceding period, that is, the high-growth manufacturing-based development model led by the developmental state. One of the consequences of conceptualising the neoliberal transformation in this way is to further juxtapose the state against the market and the internal against the external. In this case, neoliberalism is defined as the market taking over the state, and the external domain overriding internal (developmental) priorities. In particular, critical approaches, including the contemporary Marxist discussions outlined above, tend to identify neoliberalism with a shift from nationally-oriented and manufacturing-centred development towards finance-led development. Within this framework, the more neoliberalism is criticised, the more the developmental state appears to represent a mode of development that is 'more national' and 'less contradictory' than the neoliberal alternative.

Discussing the encroachment of neoliberalism in terms of the market overriding the state, and the external taking over the internal, follows from taking for granted the statist assumptions underpinning the concept of the developmental state, instead of relating them to *capitalism* and the *capitalist* state. With *capitalist* development remaining unproblematised as an encompassing force that reorganises in a particular fashion production and social relations, including politics, the state becomes an unquestioned category. It is seen as an entity external to, and interacting with, the economy. It also tends to be understood in individualistic terms, in reference to elite groups or policy-makers negotiating with other agents, such as business groups pursuing their own interests in equal terms with other (interest-)groups. The state is perceived in managerial and technical rather than social-relational terms. In brief, the capitalist content of development is taken for granted, and the question of the specifically capitalist character of the state is evaded. Social relations are reduced to the interactions between atomised units, and varieties of capitalism are categorised depending on the extent to which the state intervenes in the economy.

Form of the capitalist state and the developmental state

If statism follows from taking capitalism for granted, an alternative approach to the Korean developmental state and its transformation requires bringing to the fore the questions of *capitalist* development and the *capitalist* state. However, problematising the capitalist state entails more than emphasising its capital-serving characteristics, such as oppressing labour in the period of rapid industrialisation, favouring the capitalist class and maintaining the capitalist mode of production. This way of assessing the capitalist state is limited to a critique of the class *content* of the state, merely reiterating that the capitalist state represents the interests of the capitalist class, and serves them (Chibber 2003, 2004), or that it supports the exploitation of labour (Cammack 2007; Deyo 1987).

This view only offers a partial critique of the capitalist state: it understands the state as being neutral *ex ante*, while happening to have a capitalist-serving content, either because its apparatus is directly occupied by the capitalist (ruling) class, or because it structurally maintains the capitalist mode of production. This typifies a functionalist and instrumentalist position, which was articulated by Marxist scholars in the late 1960s (such as in the Miliband–Poulantzas and instrumental–structuralist debates), and subsequently refuted.[1] This approach suggests that the nature of the state would change according to the group in charge of the state. Furthermore, the emphasis on the function of the capitalist state assumes that the state can be separated from the economy: implicitly, the state can serve the interests of *non*-capitalists and *non*-capitalist modes of production. The class content-oriented analysis of the capitalist state is unable to grasp the particularity and historicity of the capitalist state, a political form separate from the economy, arising from the capitalist mode of production which, in turn, is a historically specific form of social domination. The shortcomings of the content-oriented critique of the state have also become apparent in analyses of the transformation of the developmental state. Either the unchanged capitalist character of the Korean state is not inquired into, since democratisation and labour activism tempered its authoritarian façade, or the transformation of the developmental state is explained in individualistic terms, such as the notion that the state was captured by the capitalist class (Chibber 2004).

An approach that aims to provide an alternative to statism as well as to content-limited critiques of the capitalist state must inquire not only into the class content but also the form of the state, and the separation between the state and the market, i.e. why the capitalist state appears to be separate from the economic domain. Evgeny Pashukanis raised the question of the form of the capitalist state as early as the 1920s, asking:

> Why does class rule not remain what it is, the factual subjugation of one section of the population by the other? Why does it assume the form of official state rule, or – which is the same thing – why does the machinery of state coercion not come into being as the private machinery of the ruling class; why does it detach itself from the ruling class and take on the form of an impersonal apparatus of public power, separate from society?
>
> (Pashukanis 1989: 139)

The form-analysis allows us to assess the capitalist state in historically determinate terms, in relation to the capitalist mode of production and the capitalist mode of social domination. The apparent separation of the state from society and the immediate process of class exploitation derive from the way in which surplus value is extracted and exploitation takes place in capitalism. In this mode of production, the relation between the exploiters and the exploited is based on equivalent commodity exchanges between seemingly equal and independent individuals. In capitalism, class domination does not take the form of the direct and personal subjugation of the exploited, which characterises pre-capitalist social relations. In capitalism, social or class domination takes place by economic means (market compulsion), as opposed to non- or extra-economic means. This gives rise to a particular mode of existence of the political and the economic. The capitalist state assumes its form as detached from the immediate processes of surplus value extraction and class exploitation, as a quasi-objective and impersonal power.

Understood in this way, the apparent separation between the economic and the political is an aspect of the historically specific form of existence of capitalist social relations. The fact that the capitalist state is quasi-independent from societal and economic processes gives rise to the notion of state autonomy: it begets the seemingly autonomous state, and introduces a distinction between the political elites (including the professional politicians) and the (economically) dominant capitalist class. The form-analysis of the capitalist state suggests that the historically specific form of the state that exists as an alienable entity from the economic arena of direct exploitation is typical of the capitalist mode of class domination, which is exercised not through the economically dominant class directly, but through the formal rules embodied in the state.

The developmental state should be located within this general understanding of the capitalist state. The Korean developmental state is a particular form of capitalist state that emerged in the context of economic catching-up. The question, then, is what contradictions the developmental state embodies, first, as a capitalist state in general and, second, as a specific type of state arising in a social formation of late capitalist development. Assessing the developmental state and its transformation at the levels of the general and the concrete offers two significant advantages. On the one hand, this understanding of the form of the state renders irrelevant debates about the dominance of state or the market. It allows us to assess the state as a political form of social relations in capitalism, and to see capitalist social relations as 'separation in unity', or as a totality. On the other hand, it allows us to capture the specificity of the developmental state, which appears to stand above capital by commanding individual capitalists in the interest of national development. In fact, this state plays the role of capitalist rationality in historical conditions in which capitalist social and production relations did not emerge gradually within a bounded national space, but were reinforced politically from above and externally by imperialist forces in the context of late development.

The overt features of the developmental state, such as its autonomy to pursue national developmental goals independently of specific class interests, which statist views often take as given, are due to the positioning and timing of a particular social formation undergoing capitalist development. What is taken by the statist views as 'class neutrality' and 'autonomy' as distinctive features of the developmental state become the ways in which the contradictions of the developmental state appear in the context of late capitalist development.

Conceptualising the developmental state as a type of state within the global system of capitalism is crucial to assessing its transformation beyond the statist framework. This interpretation denies *national* development. Instead, the rise of the developmental state should be explained in relation to the global dynamics of capitalism. The Korean capitalist transition and the rapid industrialisation of the country were, to a large extent, initiated by Japanese colonialism and the capitalist development of the metropolis which, itself, was a late-developing country within the global system of capitalism. The landlord–tenant–farmer relationship, that was artificially reinforced during the first half of the colonial period (between the 1920s and the early 1930s), and the suppression of the Korean bourgeoisie by the Japanese imperialist state, point to the fact that Korean class configurations can be examined only in conjunction with the development of capitalism in Japan.

By the same token, the rapid economic growth in Korea in the mid-1960s was limited by the US security imperative to contain communism in the region during the Cold War. Korea was offered generous aid by the United States in the 1950s, and granted privileged private and state loans, especially by Japan, under the US–Japan–Korea post-war alignment. While the Cold War provided the conditions in which Korean economic development took off, the type of development in the country was qualitatively different from that in the developed countries. Owing to the country's low level of capital accumulation and basic state of technology, commerce became the main source of revenue for Korean capital, for example, buying US aid goods cheaply and selling them dearly in the domestic market. Even after industrial production started to develop, in the 1960s, profitability was primarily secured from cheap labour and long working hours and a heavily gendered division of labour.

This analysis suggests that the rise of the authoritarian state was essentially a prerequisite to rapid industrialisation in Korea. The oppressive labour regime of the developmental state was *not* external to the rapid growth of the Korean economy. It was, instead, inherent to the position of the Korean economy and the type of production in which it was specialising. In other words, the repressive form of the developmental state can be explained largely by how and when Korean development took place in the global system of capitalism, rather than being determined primarily by the 'autonomous' policy choices of the developmental state.

Looking at the developmental state as a type of the capitalist state means that its nature and characteristics must be understood in class terms. The Korean developmental state emerged in a context in which there was no endogenous capitalist class, as it had been deliberately kept in check by the Japanese colonial state, which also inhibited the transformation of the landlord class itself into a class of capitalists. After the liberation from Japan, in 1945, the defeat of the left before and during the civil (Korean) war eliminated all paths to development other than capitalism. The war also opened up the possibility of state-led development. After the war, the state dominated society in the absence of social and class forces strong enough to challenge it. The state was strengthened further by the urgent need to deliver capitalism in the face of the spread of communism across Asia. In these circumstances, the capitalist class was fashioned by the state through the privatisation of properties seized from the Japanese colonialists and, until then, vested upon the state. The Korean state, under the guidance of the US occupation army, virtually gave away these properties to a small number of former managers and collaborators with the Japanese, while denying collective forms of property and self-management of production facilities by the workers. In this context, the newborn Korean state became a centralised modern state, helped by the possession of coercive force and anti-communist (nationalist) ideology.

The way in which the repossessed properties were disposed had clear class implications, functioning as primitive accumulation by transferring social wealth to a small number of capitalists who would, eventually, turn them into conglomerates (*chaebols*). The oppression of social dissent in the country was intensified by the subsequent military regimes, which forcefully demobilised opposing class and social forces. Consequently, the 'autonomy' of the state from society and from class interests, which is conventionally seen as distinctive features of the Korean developmental state, does not suggest its immunity from broader social pressures but, instead, is a reflection of the specific class configuration in Korea, as well as the continuing class conflicts in the country. Furthermore, the Japanese and US interventions also had a clear class orientation. This suggests that the external domain (including the influence of imperialism) should be understood as a dynamic concept related to class and social conflicts, instead of a rigid structure imposed from the outside upon a separate 'national' domain.

The transition of the developmental state and neoliberalism

Having set out a conceptual and historical framework to assess the developmental state beyond the conventional statist framework, the neoliberal transformation of the Korean developmental state should be understood neither as a reflection of a move from a national to global economy, nor as being triggered by separate external (or internal) forces. This section shows that the methodological framework of state–market and internal–external dichotomies is insufficient to assess the neoliberal restructuring of the Korean state after the crisis of 1997–8. It highlights the fact that the neoliberal transition in Korea is associated with a new modality of class and social domination, as the outcome of a complex interplay between new material and social forces, which are both global and domestic.

One of the distinctive features of neoliberalism in Korea is the simultaneity of the processes of democratisation (political liberalisation) and economic liberalisation. This suggests the need to investigate the content of democracy and the reasons why democracy had the effect of facilitating economic liberalisation. Due to the strong legacy of authoritarianism of the developmental state, and the highly personalised relationships between state elites and the *chaebols* (which were often termed 'crony capitalism'), the immediate challenge to the developmental state came from democratic social forces. With the rise of the liberals as a dominant force vis-à-vis the traditional military elites and radical social forces in the process of democratisation, in the 1980s, democratisation meant, in this context, separating the state from the economy and severing the personal links between the state elites and the large capitalists.

Historically Korean capital had grown, since its inception, in the form of monopolies based on state favouritism. Naturally, the public aspiration for democracy went hand in hand with antipathy towards the *chaebols*. The demands for 'rational' and 'objective' state–capital relations, which provided the core content of the campaign for democratisation in Korea, gathered further momentum after the financial crisis of 1997–8. This crisis called into question the model of Korean development, and brought into light the personalised relations between the state and the *chaebols*. A consensus emerged among the liberals and the democratic social forces that the economic crisis was largely due to heavy borrowing and reckless expansion by the *chaebols*, which had been allowed by the state because of the lack of democracy. In these circumstances, further economic liberalisation and distancing the state from the economy were equated with democratisation. They constituted the core content of the restructuring of the state after the crisis.

Moreover, when granting rescue loans to the Korean government in order to bail out debt-ridden banks and *chaebols*, the IMF demanded a comprehensive reform of the major sectors of the economy as well as the government; restructuring and eliminating non-performing banks and bad loans; expansion of commercialisation (marketisation) of the banking business; developing the capital market; liberalisation of the securities market to foreigners and of foreign investment in the domestic financial sector (Bank of Korea 1997). It also required the Korean government 'to eliminate inter-subsidiary loan guarantees, lower debt-to-equity ratios and improve transparency' (Cumings 1998: 63). The agenda of the IMF was, to a large extent, commensurate with that of the Korean government led by Kim Dae-Jung, a former democratisation activist who came to power amid the financial crisis. The fact that the institutional characteristics of Korean capitalism amplified the severity of the crisis also allowed the neoliberal remedies proposed by the IMF to be received with less resistance, at least among the left-liberals who became a hegemonic force domestically since the crisis. This created the situation in which the neoliberal advocates of the IMF, the left-liberals and the democratic social forces converged around a single reform programme.[2]

The neoliberal restructuring after the crisis not only contradicts assessments based on the dichotomy between internal and external forces, but suggests that the transformation of the developmental state cannot be grasped under the perspective of whether and how much the state intervenes on the market. For example, the Korean state introduced a market-regulating mechanism through banking and financial regulatory agencies, such as the Financial Supervisory Commission and the Bank of Korea Act, granting it more independence from political influence. At the same time, the state intervened heavily in the restructuring of *chaebols* and banks, and sponsored small and medium-sized firms specialising in high technology. The restructuring of non-performing banks and firms involved the recapitalisation of potentially viable ones by huge injections of public funds, and their sale to foreign and other (larger) domestic firms. Moreover, the overlapping investments and the overcapacity among the top five *chaebols* was resolved by taking over their debts and bad loans with public funds, and offering them fresh loans mediated by the state ('the Big Deal').

The apparent contradictions between what the Korean state claims to pursue (the free market mechanism) and the way it intervened in the restructuring process led the contemporary debates on the Korean state to either claim that the developmental state continues to exist (Weiss and Lee) or that it had shifted towards neoliberalism (Pirie). However the tension between state intervention and market-led reforms appears perplexing only if the state and the market are assumed to be separate entities playing a zero-sum game. The only way to resolve the apparent contradictions of the developmental state and its transformation is to bring into the question the *capitalist* nature of the state, understanding it both in terms of its class content and its form of existence.

First, the post-crisis restructuring has clear class implications. Despite the fact that Korean workers recorded extremely long working hours and the lowest level of welfare in the period of rapid industrialisation, the IMF included in the rescue loan agreement 'anti-labour' or 'labour flexibility' conditionalities.[3] However, Korean officials *asked* the IMF to include anti-labour provisions in the reform package (Cumings 1998: 54). This implies that there are few conflicting interests between the 'internal' and the 'external', or between the state and the market as such. As much as Korean capital, the foreign capitals that were to take over Korean firms and banks had an interest in lax labour laws and regulations. While there is a unified interest of capital against labour, the state is not a blameless victim of external pressures.

The Korean government moved promptly to contain the strength of labour after the Great Struggle in 1987, and reintroduce the anti-labour legislation withdrawn by the Kim Young-Sam administration in the face of the 1996 general strike. The democratic government led by the left-liberal Kim Dae-Jung, unlike the previous military administrations, introduced tripartite talks with labour and enterprises for the first time in Korean history, but this was primarily in order to gain concessions from the workers. Numerous examples illustrate continuing assaults against labour and the deteriorating living standards in the country, including an increasing share of non-protected contractual labour and widening disparities between rich and poor.[4] While foreign capital bought up banks and firms that had been saved from bankruptcy by public funds at fire-sale prices, Korean capital, especially the *chaebols*, were forced to restructure and rationalise their operations with the help of fresh credit channelled by the state. Since the financial crisis, foreign ownership in the banking sector and in major corporations has increased, and the concentration of capital has become even more pronounced.[5]

Conclusion

The transformation of the developmental state is neither a transition from an interventionist to a non-interventionist state, nor from the national to the global. The Korean neoliberal state is a capitalist state, no less than the developmental state that preceded it, and that had a clear interest in subordinating labour to capital accumulation. At the same time, the transition to neoliberalism has been facilitated by democratisation which, in turn, further releases capital from the barriers to accumulation in Korea.

The rise of the neoliberal state makes the relations between the state and the economic domain, and state–capital relations in particular, appear to be more objective and distant. What is required in a class analysis of the capitalist state is not merely to explore its functional role and class content, but to understand the way in which the state appears and the form it takes as separate or alienated from the economic, which is related to a specific mode of social domination. The mode of existence of the political in capitalism, as separate from the immediate process of production and exploitation, allows us to capture the transformation of the Korean developmental state in line with the processes of democratisation and neoliberal restructuring.

These economic reforms were meant to rationalise the operations and internal structures of the *chaebols*, transforming the role of the state into a neutral party, freed from personal and crony relations with individual capitalist interests. Democratisation facilitated this shift in the relations between state and capital, state and society and capital and labour, and transformed the ways in which social and class domination are attained. If the apparent separation between the state and the economy is the form taken by social relations in capitalism, democratisation in Korea brought about not the detachment of the state from capital, but a shift in the mode of class domination towards a form more conducive to the 'normality' in capitalism, in which there are more 'objective' relations between state and capital and state and society. This shift, or the neoliberal transition, transformed – within the framework of the capitalist mode of production – both state and capital, along with their relationship. It did not, however, reverse their relations of domi-nation, since the domination of a separate 'state' over 'capital' (or 'the economy') never existed in the first place and, at least from the perspective of the Marxist form-analysis inspired by Pashukanis, cannot logically exist.

Notes

1 For a detailed instrumentalist-structuralist discussion on state autonomy, see Barrow (1993) For a critique of Miliband and Poulantzas, see Holloway and Picciotto (1978). In an endeavour to construct a materialist theory of the capitalist state, Holloway and Picciotto reject the division between political and economic categories and argue, instead, that 'the task is not to develop "political concepts" to complement the set of "economic concepts", but to develop the concepts of capital in the critique not only of the economic but also of the political form of social relations' (Holloway and Picciotto 1978: 4). With the renewed interest in Marx's *Capital* in the late 1960s, which initiated the 'state derivation debate', Holloway and Picciotto (ibid.) claim that the contribution of Marx's critique of political economy is not to analyse the 'economic' level, but to offer a materialist critique of political economy, i.e. of bourgeois attempts to analyse the economy in isolation from the class relations of exploitation on which it is based.

2 For example, many critics of the *chaebols* welcomed IMF demands for rationalisation and transparency in accounting rules, i.e. the prohibition of widow-dressing settlements and prudential measures in the financial sectors (Kim 2002). IMF economists also com-plained that IMF policies were criticised more by outsiders. Another illustration of this paradoxical marriage was that, while foreign ownership of the commercial banks was extended by the banking reforms, the takeover of commercial banks by the *chaebols* was not allowed. This was not only because of external pressure. It was also feared that the banks would be misused for the self-financing of *chaebols*, as had happened with the merchant banks before the crisis.

3 There is an abundance of data indicating the poor working conditions of the Korean workers in the period of rapid industrialisation, which compare unfavourably even with countries that underwent a similar path of development. The annual paid holidays in Korea were 10.3 days in 1989, while in Japan in 1978 it reached 15.3 days and, in Taiwan, 10.3 days in 1987. Only 1 per cent of Korean workers worked five days a week, as opposed to 29.5 per cent of the Japanese workers. In 1989, the total annual working hours in Korea were 2,590, while they were 2,522 in Japan, 2,214 in Singapore and 2,423 in Taiwan. In contrast, annual working hours were only 1,683 in France, 1,598 in Germany and 1,948 in the US. The rate of work-related deaths was 0.18 per cent in Korea and 0.13 per cent in Taiwan. This is 7–9 times higher than in Sweden and the United States (Shin 1999: 48).

4 As there had been no welfare system in place in Korea (the country's 'developmental welfare regime' included the lowest level of expenditures among OECD members), the increase in poverty and employment instability after the crisis had more serious social consequences than in developed countries. Korea is defined as an upper middle-income economy by the World Bank. The average ratio of government welfare spending among these countries was 24.9 per cent in 1972 and 20.6 per cent in 1983. In Korea, it was only 5.8 per cent and 5.9 per cent. This was lower than in low-income countries (7.3 and 5.8 per cent) (World Bank 1986: 222–3, quoted in Sonn 2006: 231). In 1998, the United States and the UK spent 20 per cent of GDP on social welfare. In Korea, before Kim Dae-Jung, in 1997, the figure was 6.5 per cent, rising to 8.7 per cent in 2001 (Sonn 2006: 251). The ratio of low-paid employment, earning less than two-thirds of average income, increased from 22.9 per cent in 2001 to 25.9 per cent in 2005. This is the highest level in the OECD; in the United States it is only 18.1 per cent (Lee 2005: 56).

5 The democratisation of the relations between business and the state, which was one of the arguments for liberalisation, actually strengthened the interests of large-scale capital. Most underperforming banks and *chaebols*, that were previously financed by state-guaranteed debt (which underlines a key problem of the developmental state model) were nationalised amid the crisis and rescued by huge injections of public funds, reaching US$200 billion. They were subsequently sold to foreign firms on extremely favourable terms. Three out of eight commercial banks are currently foreign-owned, and four out of the remaining five have large foreign holdings. In 2005, the ratio of foreign market share in banking is 21.8 per cent, higher than in Mexico (20 per cent). The liberalisation of financial markets to foreign investors and the shift to a market-based financial system created a new financing mechanism in which firms primarily raise investment funds issuing shares. However, this financial reform benefits the *chaebols*, because only large firms can raise sufficient capital on the stock market since domestic and foreign investment is concentrated on these firms. In Korea, 5.3 per cent of shareholders possess 82.2 per cent of the shares. These are mainly foreign investors and *chaebols* (Lee 2005: 50–1).

References

Amsden, A. (1989) *Asia's Next Giant: South Korea and Late Industrialization*. New York: Oxford University Press.

Amsden, A. (1994) 'Why Isn't the Whole World Experimenting with the East Asia Model to Develop? Review of the East Asian Miracle', *World Development*, 22 (4), pp. 627–33.

Bank of Korea (1997) *Letter of Intent to the Government of Korea*. Online, available at: www.imf.org/external/np/loi/122497.htm.

Barrow, C.W. (1993) *Critical Theories of the State: Marxist, Neo-Marxist, Post-Marxist*. Wisconsin: The University of Wisconsin Press.

Bhagwati, J. (1978) *Foreign Trade Regimes and Economic Development: the Anatomy and Consequences of Exchange Control*. Cambridge: NBER/Balinger.

Brenner, R. (1998) 'Uneven Development and the Long Downturn: the Advanced Capitalist Economies: from Boom to Stagnation, 1950–1998', *New Left Review*, no. 229.

Cammack, P. (2007) 'Class Politics, Competitiveness and the Developmental State', Papers in the Politics of Global Competitiveness, no. 4. Manchester Metropolitan University.

Chang, H.-J. (1998) 'Korea: The Misunderstood Crisis', *World Development*, 26 (8), pp. 1555–61.

Chang, H.-J. and C.-G. Yoo (1999) 'The Triumph of the Rentiers? The 1997 Korean Crisis in a Historical Perspective'. Paper presented at the Workshops on the World Financial Authority, organized by the Centre for Economic Policy Analysis, New School University, New York, USA.

Chibber, V. (2003) *Locked in Place: State-Building and Late Industrialization in India*. Princeton: Princeton University Press.

Chibber, V. (2004) 'Reviving the Developmental State? The Myth of the "National Bourgeoisie"', *Socialist Register 2005*, pp. 144–65.

Cumings, B. (1998) 'The Korean Crisis and the End of "Late" Development', *New Left Review*, 231, pp. 43–72.

Deyo, F. (1987) 'Coalitions, Institutions, and Linkages Sequencing – Toward a Strategic Capacity Model of East Asian Development', in Deyo, F. (ed.), *The Political Economy of New Asian Industrialism*. Ithaca: Cornell University Press.

Gowan, P. (1999) *Global Gamble: Washington's Faustian Bid for World Dominance*. London and New York: Verso.

Harvey, D. (2003) *The New Imperialism*. Oxford: Oxford University Press.

Holloway, J. and S. Picciotto (1978) 'Introduction: Toward a Materialist Theory of the State', in Holloway, J. and S. Picciotto (eds), *State and Capital: a Marxist Debate*. London: Edward Arnold.

Jayasuriya, K. (2005) 'Beyond Institutional Fetishism: From Developmental to the Regulatory State', *New Political Economy*, 10 (3), pp. 381–7.

Johnson, C. (1982) *MITI and The Japanese Miracle: the Growth of Industrial Policy, 1925–1975*. Stanford: Stanford University Press.

Johnson, C. (1987) 'Political Institutions and Economic Performance: the Government-Business Relationship in Japan, South Korea, and Taiwan', in Deyo, F.C. (ed.), *The Political Economy of the New Asian Industrialism*. Ithaca: Cornell University Press.

Johnson, C. (1995) *Japan: Who Governs: The Rise of the Developmental State*. New York and London: Norton.

Kim, K.-W. (2002) *Is Chaebol Reform Over*. Seoul: Hanul (in Korean).

Krueger, A. (1978) *Foreign Trade Regimes and Economic Development: Liberalisation Attempts and Consequences*. Cambridge: NBER/Balinger.

Lee, B.-C. (2005) 'Jayuhwa, Yangkŭkhwa Sidaewa Much'aekim Jabonjuŭi' (Irresponsible Capitalism in the Era of Liberation and Polarization: An Alternative of Social Integrative Civic Economy), *The Journal of Asiatic Studies*, 48 (3), pp. 43–71 (in Korean).

Lee, Y.-H. (2001) 'Limits of Kim Dae-Jung's Neoliberal Reforms', *Sasang* (Thoughts), 49, pp. 103–23 (in Korean).

Lee, Y.-H. (2002) 'Financial Reform and the Transformation of the State in Korea', *Hankuksawhehak* (Korea Sociology Journal), 35 (1), pp. 59–88 (in Korean).

Lee, Y.-H. (2006) 'Democratic Deepening and Its Impact on the Changes in the Nature of the Regulatory State: The Korean Case', *Shinasea* (New Asia), 13 (2), pp. 26–54 (in Korean).

Mathews, J.A. (1998) 'Fashioning a New Korean Model out of the Crisis: the Rebuilding of Institutional Capabilities', *Cambridge Journal of Economics*, 22, pp. 747–59.

Pashukanis, B.E. (1989) *Law and Marxism: A General Theory*. Worcester: Pluto Press.

Pirie, I. (2005) 'The New Korean State', *New Political Economy*, 1 (1), pp. 27–44.

Pirie, I. (2008) *The Korean Developmental State, From Dirigisme to Neo-Liberalism*. Oxford: Routledge.

Shin, K.-Y. (1999) *Industrialization and Democratization in East Asia*. Seoul: Moonhakgwajiseongsa (in Korean).

Sonn, H.-C. (2006) *Haebang 60nyŏnŭi Hankuk Jungch'i* (60 Years of Korean Politics since National Liberation). Seoul: Imagine (in Korean).

Wade, R. (1990) *Governing the Market: Economic Theory and the Role of Government in East Asian Industrialization*. Princeton: Princeton University Press.

Wade, R. (1992) 'East Asia's Economic Success: Conflicting Perspectives, Partial Insights, Shaky Evidence', *World Politics*, 44 (2), pp. 270–320.

Wade, R. (1998a) 'The Asian Debt-and-Development Crisis of 1997–?: Causes and Consequences', *World Development*, 26 (8), pp. 1535–53.

Wade, R. (1998b) 'From "Miracle" to "Cronyism": Explaining the Great Asian Slump', *Cambridge Journal of Economics*, 22 (6), pp. 693–706.

Wade, R. and F. Veneroso (1998) 'The Asian Crisis: The High Debt Model Versus the Wall Street-Treasury-IMF Complex', *New Left Review*, 228, pp. 3–24.

Weiss, L. (2005) 'The State-augmenting Effects of Globalisation', *New Political Economy*, 10 (3), pp. 345–53.

Woo-Cumings, M. (1997) 'Slouching towards the Market: South Korea', in Loriaux, M. (ed.), *Capital Ungoverned: Liberalising Finance in Interventionist State*. New York: Cornell University Press.

Woo-Cumings, M. (1999) 'The State, Democracy, and the Reform of the Corporate Sector in Korea', in Pempel, J.T. (ed.), *The Politics of Asian Economic Crisis*. New York: Cornell University Press.

World Bank (1993) *The East Asian Miracle*. World Bank Policy Research Report, Oxford University Press.

11 Korean left debates on alternatives to neoliberalism[1]

Seongjin Jeong

In 2007, discourses on the alternatives available to the Korean economy were pouring out, commemorating the tenth anniversary of the 1997 economic crisis as well as the twentieth anniversary of the Great Democratic Struggle of 1987. However, it was mainly because the Korean economy, trapped in a decade-long period of reduced growth and deepening social polarization, was urgently seeking alternatives to the neoliberal policy framework that had been enforced since 1997. Indeed, exploiting the dismal state of the economy, Lee Myung-bak, a conservative CEO, won the latest presidential election with the slogan of 'Saving the Economy'. However, the conservatives seem to have no alternative except going back to the outdated Park Chung-Hee-style state-led capitalism, or resorting to an all-out neoliberal big bang through the Korea–United States Free Trade Agreement.

Meanwhile, nearly a dozen alternatives to neoliberalism have been proposed from the progressive camps. This chapter critically examines them from a Marxist standpoint.

First, it presents an overview of the recent transformation of Korean capitalism. Then, it examines the so-called 'financialization' thesis, which currently dominates the discussion of Korean progressives. In addition, it argues that the economic policy of the current Lee Myung-bak government is nothing but the combination of an outdated version of Park Chung-Hee's model of state capitalism, with the neoliberal big bang. It also examines Ha-Joon Chang's 'Democratic Welfare State Model' as well as the Keynesian 'Strategy for Social Solidarity'. Finally, it concludes by confirming the relevance of Marxian socialist alternatives in Korea.

Overview of the transformation of Korean capitalism

As discussed in Jeong (1997), the statist regime of accumulation that had sustained the 30-year-long boom since the 1960s began to malfunction in the 1980s and crumbled with the 1987 Workers' Great Struggle, resulting in the falling rates of profit and the long downswing in the 1990s. Having produced 'miraculous' growth, by the late 1980s the statist accumulation regime was running into its limits. The 1997 economic crisis was not a thunderbolt from the blue but, instead, the inevitable consequence of the demise of the old statist accumulation regime without its replacement by a new one, and despite the attempts by the hegemonic bloc to restructure the Korean economy along neoliberal lines since the 1980s. Indeed, the rate of profit of the non-farm business sector, measured by the ratio of pre-tax profits to net fixed capital stock, fell from approximately 12–16 per cent over the period 1970–86 to just 5.1 per cent (the lowest level since 1970) in 1996, the year before the 1997 crisis (see Figure 11.1).

The recent development of capitalism in Korea since the beginning of the statist accumulation regime can be divided into three periods: its heyday, between 1961 and 1987; the transition period, between 1987 and 1997; and the period since 1997, when neoliberalism has prevailed. Shin and Chang (2003) and Weiss (2003) have argued that the developmental state, rather than the market fundamentalist minimal neoliberal state, has continued to function on the grounds that the Kim Dae-jung government resorted to Keynesian state intervention, such as the injection of as much as 150 trillion Korean won of public money for the restructuring of the financial sector in order to escape from the 1997 economic crisis.[2] However, what matters is not the degree of the intervention of the state but its nature. The Korean government has intervened in the economy in order to enforce on the economic actors nothing other than neoliberal market principles, such as the competitiveness discourses or so-called global standards.

The essential role of the neoliberal state resides in establishing market institutions and enforcing market discipline. It must also be remembered that the recovery hinged upon the intensified exploitation of working people, rather than government intervention. However, it is hard to argue that the new neoliberal regime of accumulation has become firmly established in Korea after the 1997 economic crisis. All-out neoliberal restructuring after the crisis has mainly led to

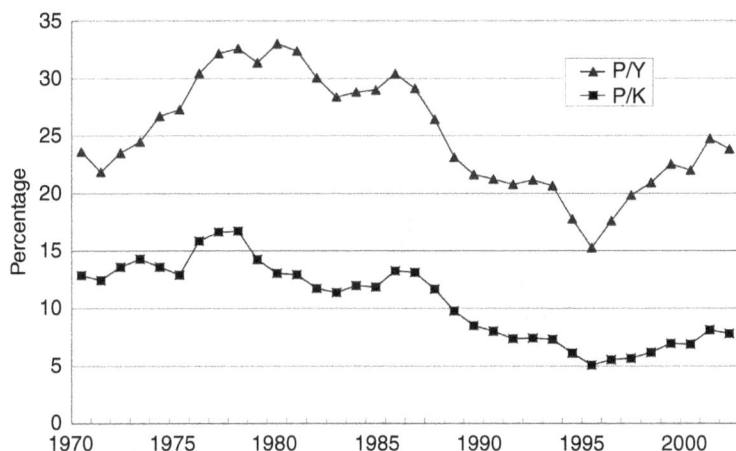

Figure 11.1 Profitability of non-farm business sector in Korea, 1970–2003 (source: Jeong 2007 with update).

Notes
1 P/Y (profit share): ratio of profits to value added
2 P/K (rate of profit): ratio of profits to net fixed capital stock

lower growth rates and increased inequality, without succeeding in establishing a new accumulation regime such as a 'finance-led regime of accumulation' or a 'knowledge-based economy'. Indeed, the so-called democratic governments of Kim Dae-jung and Roh Moo-hyun failed to establish a new stable accumulation regime despite the ten-year long neoliberal restructuring since the 1997 crisis, as was epitomized by President Lee Myung-bak's presidential campaign catch-phrases in 2007, such as 'Lost Decade', or 'Saving the Economy', despite their ideological and exaggerated tone.

Establishment of a new finance-led accumulation regime after the 1997 economic crisis?

Korean progressives, regardless of whether they are 'developmental statists' or Keynesians, generally adopt the thesis of financialization or the transition to a 'finance-led accumulation regime' when they characterize twenty-first century capitalism and the Korean economy after the 1997 economic crisis. For them, a fundamental contradiction of today's capitalism is that between production and finance. Only speculative financial capital is to blame. They assume that industrial capital is progressive, while financial capital is a reactionary parasite. In this context, Keynesians and developmental statists, among them Ha-Joon Chang, argue for the resurrection of industrial policy in order to support the development of industrial capital.

However, simply regulating financial capital cannot prevent the explosion of the contradictions of capitalism that are inherent in the exploitative system of accumulation based on industrial capital. Keynesian statists also believe that the post-crisis neoliberal restructuring is leading to the consolidation of a new finance-led accumulation regime in Korea. Since this 'financialization' not only triggered the crisis but was also responsible for the current economic difficulties in the country, these scholars also call for policies designed to reinvigorate statism. I reject this characterization of the restructuring process and the associated reformist Keynesian statist policy recommendations.

According to Crotty (2002), 'financialization' is generally defined by the following trends: the hegemony of financial capital over industrial capital, the dominance of direct finance through equity and bonds over indirect finance through banks and the related rise of the principle of 'shareholder capitalism', the increasing debts of non-financial corporations, the growing importance of financial assets over tangible assets for non-financial corporations, and the securitization of household financial assets. While there appears to be some empirical support for these trends in the United States and France, the same is not the case for Korea. For example, the ratio of financial assets to tangible assets in the manufacturing sector rose from approximately 40 per cent in the 1970s to 65 per cent in the 1980s, but remained at that level through most of the 1990s and even decreased slightly since 1997. Moreover, although Korean non-financial corporations have always been highly indebted, their total liabilities have become *lighter* rather than heavier since the 1997 economic crisis. Indeed, the ratio of total liabilities of non-financial corporations to GDP fell from 194 per cent in 1998 to 174 per cent in 2005. Looking just at the manufacturing sector, the debt to equity ratio decreased from 396.3 per cent in 1997 to 123.4 per cent in 2003, while the ratio of equity to total assets more than doubled over the same period, from 20.2 per cent to 44.8 per cent (Bank of Korea, *Financial Statement Analysis*).

Moreover, there is little to indicate that Korea is undergoing a securitization of household assets. In fact, financial assets of Korean households are overwhelmingly composed of bank deposits, and the share of bank deposits in total financial assets has *increased* from 42.8 per cent in 1975 to 58.4 per cent in 2005. Conversely, the share of equities in total household financial assets has decreased from 17.2 per cent in 1975 to 5 per cent in 2005. There is also little reason to believe that non-financial corporations have fundamentally altered their methods of finance away from bank loans and towards direct issuance of equity. Although direct finance, especially stock issuance, did increase rapidly after the 1997 economic crisis, its share in the total finance of non-financial corporations reached only 38.4 per cent in 2003; this was lower than the share of indirect finance, which was 41.6 per cent (Bank of Korea, *Flow of Funds*). Loans by financial institutions still compose the largest part of the liabilities of non-financial corporations (32.2 per cent in 2005), although the share of stocks increased after the crisis, from 11.6 per cent in 1998 to 20.6 per cent in 2005.

In addition, the ratio of financial outflows – that is, the sum of interest, dividends and rent relative to the operating profits of non-financial corporations – has remained stable (at 60 per cent) since the 1980s. Although it skyrocketed to 138.8 per cent in 1998, it soon fell back to 37.5 per cent in 2005. Interest rates have also remained low in the post-crisis period. After soaring to 28 per cent in early 1998, the call rate of the Bank of Korea steadily fell to as low as 3.5 per cent in mid-2004.

Finally, in the so-called Korean 'high-debt model', the financial profitability of non-financial corporations has generally been *lower* than real profitability due to continuous financial outflows, especially in the form of interest payments. In other words, contrary to the 'financialization' thesis, the drain of profits from the real sector to the financial sector of the economy has been an intrinsic and continuous tendency in the Korean economy. In short, in their desire to champion Korea's past statism, Keynesians mistakenly transformed an exceptional and transitory phenomenon into a structural and long-term trend.

What the Korean economy has experienced since the 1997 crisis is not 'financialization' but a deepening dependence on transnational flows of financial capital. Many progressive economists who accept the 'financialization' hypothesis often attempt to find supporting evidence in every country in the world since the 1990s. What is missing in their theorization is an understanding of the current neoliberal globalization as a project of US imperialism. For them, globalization is just financial globalization. However, 'financialization' in the centre could not be reproduced in the same form in the periphery, owing to the hierarchical structure and the polarizing tendencies inherent to the structure of the imperialist world economy. 'Financialization' in the centre usually requires the financial dependence of the periphery on the centre in order to exist. Unlike industrialization, 'financialization' is intrinsically a 'zero-sum game'. Indeed, the evidence of deepening financial dependence in Korea since the 1997 crisis could be found in the following data:

1 rapid increase of foreigners' share in the market value of outstanding equities in Korean corporations;
2 rapid increase of foreign direct investment; and
3 rapid increase in the outflow of value.

For example, the outflow of value from Korea, estimated as the sum of royalties, interest and dividends, increased from a stable level around US$4 billion until 1994, to US$15.8 billion in 2005 (Bank of Korea, *Balance of Payments*).

'Saving the economy'?

In December 2007, Lee Myung-bak, former CEO of Hyundai Group, was elected President of Korea with the slogan 'Saving the Economy'. However, this slogan is highly questionable. Indeed, the category of 'economy', as the object to be saved, suggests some sort of trans-class '(national) economy', which is simply an ideological construct. It is impossible for such a category to materialize in actuality in a capitalist class society. The so-called '(national) economy' cannot but be reduced to the 'capitalist economy' or the 'workers' economy' in a capitalist society characterized by the antagonism between two classes.

In the history of capitalism, the real process behind the ideology of 'Saving the Economy' has always been the saving of capitalist profitability by intensifying the exploitation of the working class. In Korea, a capitalist could recover profitability only by victimizing the workers after the 1997 crisis. As is shown in Figure 11.1, when the rate of profit of the non-farm business sector in Korea began to recover after 1997, the rise in the profit share (P/Y) or, alternatively, the rate of exploitation, explains the recovery almost entirely. Indeed, the profit share increased from 15.3 per cent in 1996 to 23.8 per cent in 2003. This implies that the neoliberal restructuring after 1997 represents nothing more than the restoration of capitalist profitability through the intensified exploitation of the working class.

The Kim Dae-jung and Roh Moo-hyun administrations tried to camouflage their pro-chaebol stance through the gestural regulation of chaebols and the introduction of social safety nets. In contrast, current President Lee Myung-bak openly advocates pro-chaebol policies, including the abolition of the principle of separation of ownership between financial and non-financial institutions, and the abolition of investment limits by local conglomerates.

Lee Myung-bak's slogan of 'Saving the Economy' is not just an ideology serving the chaebols' interests; it is, itself, a false statement. If the phrase 'Saving the Economy' makes sense, the Korean economy should be in a state of crisis or stagnation. However, this is simply not true. According to the World

Bank (2007), the average rate of growth of GDP in Korea during 2003–5 was 3.9 per cent, which was 1.4 percentage points higher than the OECD average for same period, 2.5 per cent.

The real challenge for the Lee Myung-bak administration is not saving the allegedly moribund economy from itself, but saving it from the abyss of the evolving world economic crisis. However, the government has already failed this test. Indeed, there is nothing new in Lee Myung-bak's economic policies, not to speak of his lack of understanding of the need to renew the accumulation regime. As Lee Myung-bak tries to throw away the policies of the previous Kim Dae-jung and Roh Moo-hyun administrations as 'left-oriented', including even their attempts to reform the outdated accumulation regime, what is left to Lee is only going back to Park Chung-Hee's style of state-led, pro-chaebol, anti-labour, quantitative-centred accumulation regime. It looks as if Lee Myung-bak ignores even what the 1997 crisis demonstrated clearly: Park Chung-Hee-style statism, which he so cherishes, has been gone for a very long time.

Since the primary contradiction of Korean capitalism lies in the over-accumulation of capital, epitomized by a falling rate of profit, Lee Myung-bak's drive to increase investment by lifting the regulations constraining the operations of the chaebols will aggravate over-investment, making the coming crisis even deeper. If Lee Myung-bak bulldozes pro-chaebol investment promotion policies, like building the Great Canal, it will result in unprecedented over-investment and an enormous real estate bubble that will ultimately burst. Facing the coming crisis, the Lee Myung-bak administration will again resort to the ideology of 'Saving the Economy', and attempt to impose additional sacrifices on the working class. However, they will not be deceived again by the ideology of 'Saving the Economy', and are likely to resist the capitalist offensive to recover profitability through the intensification of the exploitation.

Building a progressive accumulation regime in Korea

Progressive alternatives to Korean capitalism, since the 1980s, can be grouped into three positions:

1   the 'Democratic Welfare State Model', proposed by Ha-Joon Chang and some economists in the Alternative Policy Forum and the National Liberation (NL) faction of the Democratic Labor Party (DLP);[3]
2   the 'Strategy for Social Solidarity', which stresses 'growth with equity', 'dismantling the chaebol system' and redistribution of income *within* the working class, especially from organized regular workers to irregular workers, and is proposed by the Peoples' Democracy (PD) faction of the DLP; and
3   Anti-Capitalist Socialist Alternatives.

The theoretical and political origins of the Korean progressive alternatives listed above can be traced back to the left debates during the 1980s, on the nature of the Korean social formation. If the first position, the Democratic Welfare State Model, is the continuation of the NL tendency, the Strategy for Social Solidarity, can be viewed as an emasculated version of the PD tendency in the 1980s. The difference between them is that, in the 1980s, the NL and PD were in competition to be the 'real' revolutionary socialists within the same Stalinist framework. In contrast, today, the NL and PD openly claim that they are ex-socialists and pursue different versions of reformism. Additionally, unlike in the 1980s, revolutionary Marxist currents now exist as an independent third position among the Korean progressive camp. However, the first two versions of reformism remain dominant within this group. In contrast, the revolutionary socialist alternatives are still a minority among the progressive currents.

Limit of the national reformistic alternative: Ha-Joon Chang

Ha-Joon Chang is the main representative of the Democratic Welfare State Model.[4] Although Chang has contributed greatly to debunking the neoliberal myth of market fundamentalism, his politics are not anti-capitalist: he seeks piecemeal reforms within the framework of capitalism. Indeed, he is an admirer of the Nordic type of capitalism, especially the Swedish model. He also believes that the chaebol system has great merit because of its superior economic efficiency and growth performance. He wishes to build a Swedish social welfare state based upon a social compact with the chaebols in Korea. As he puts national interests ahead of class interests, his position can be classified as 'progressive competitiveness' (Albo 1997), or a 'national-developmentalist approach' (Ercan and Oguz 2007).

Chang understands neoliberalism in terms of three dichotomies: market vs. state, finance capital vs. industrial capital and foreign capital vs. national capital. What remains missing is the fundamental antagonism in capitalism, which is the contradiction between capital and labour. Chang equates neoliberalism with the dominance of the principle of shareholder capitalism. For Chang, virtually all the problems of the Korean economy are due to neoliberalism. He also argues that the main cause of the low growth of the Korean economy is low investment, which he attributes to the neoliberal restructuring after the 1997 economic crisis.

However, Chang's understanding of neoliberalism is flawed. First, Chang theorizes neoliberalism as an actually existing socio-economic system. However, neoliberalism in Korea should be treated primarily as a new strategy of domination of the capitalist class. Above all, it should be conceptualized in terms of class relations, more specifically, a capitalist offensive to recover profitability through the intensification of the exploitation of the workers.

Chang also privileges external pressures, especially those of foreign capital after the 1997 economic crisis, as the main driver for the transition to neoliberalism in Korea, while downplaying the role of domestic class relations. Chang also emphasizes the conflict between the chaebols and neoliberalism. However, the relation between them cannot be described as a contradiction in the precise sense of the word but, rather, as a kind of symbiosis, regardless of the chaebols' persistent complaints about the expanding influence of foreign capital in Korea. Indeed, the chaebols have been the main drivers of the transition to neoliberalism in Korea since the 1980s. The origins of neoliberalism in Korea are primarily domestic. Indeed, they can be traced back to the 1980s, when the Cheon Doo-hwan administration began to pursue the goal of a 'business-led economy' at the request of the chaebols. The main actor behind the Korea–United States Free Trade Agreement, which is currently waiting for ratification, was also the chaebols, especially the Samsung Group, as well as the Roh Moo-hyun government. US imperialism and transnational finance capital have only assisted these processes. The symbiosis of the chaebols with neoliberalism was eventually vindicated in the policies of the Lee Myung-bak administration, which is attempting to resurrect and refurbish the Park Chung-Hee regime, especially its chaebol system, and combine it with the neoliberal logic of the CEO currently occupying the presidential palace.

The thesis of transition to a finance-led accumulation regime, which Chang also shares, is problematic, as is discussed above. Recently, industrial capital has succeeded in becoming more independent from finance by radically reducing its bank debts. Indeed, some of the biggest chaebols have now become powerful enough to dominate finance capital, and they have succeeded in abolishing the separation of finance from industrial capital, as well as scrapping the limit on chaebol investment into their own affiliates.

Contrary to Chang's assertion that the chaebol system was weakened after the 1997 crisis, under the combined pressures of neoliberal restructuring and foreign capital inflows, the chaebols concentrated further their economic power. Indeed, many Koreans now call the country the 'Republic of Samsung' or even the 'Kingdom of Samsung'. It turns out that the neoliberal logic of 'shareholder capitalism' did not represent a hindrance to the chaebols' accumulation of capital – quite the contrary.

Chang even argues for the acceptance of the chaebol managers' illegal bequests of management rights to their children, asserting that this is necessary in order to defend national capital against the attack of foreign capital, and to enhance economic efficiency. Chang opposes the idea of dismantling the chaebols, the main slogan of the PD faction of the DLP, on the grounds that it will destroy the economic efficiency that is alleged necessary for the so-called 'second-stage catching-up' (Shin and Chang 2005: 428). Chang's pro-chaebol position seems to have nothing to do with progressive policies of any kind.

Ha-Joon Chang also argues that there is no future for Korean capitalism without a social compact, or a social compromise between the main social actors. In order to strike a social compact in Korea, he suggests a 'big deal' between the government and the chaebols, with the government offering the chaebols guarantees about the succession of their management rights to their children, in exchange for increased chaebol investment in building a welfare state.

This imagined social compact would provide the basis for a Swedish-type 'stakeholder capitalism' in Korea. Chang calls this ideal state the 'democratic welfare state model'. This model seems to combine an East Asian developmental state model with a Swedish welfare state model. However, how chaebols could legitimately participate in this 'stakeholder capitalism' when most of them do not even observe the rights of other major stakeholders, such as minority share-holders and labour unions, is not clear. It is also inconsistent for Chang to try to ratify the chaebols' bequest of management rights to their offspring while, at the same time, arguing for a 'stakeholder capitalism'. Without the participation of key stakeholders in the management of chaebols, including the labour unions and local communities, 'stakeholder capitalism' is merely a façade. The realiza-tion of Chang's ideal of building a 'democratic welfare state' based upon a social compact would requires the dismantling of the chaebol system, especially the suspension of the illegal monopoly of management rights by chaebol families, which goes against Chang's proposed policies.

Moreover, Chang's model of a social compact is fundamentally different from the Swedish model in that it does not recognize the organized workers as key part-ners in the social compact. Chang includes, instead, the so-called 'common people'. However, since the organized workers are one of the most important social forces in Korea since the 1987 Great Workers' Struggle, any proposal for a social compact without their inclusion is simply unrealistic. Indeed, the social compact and the welfare state in Europe, especially the Swedish model, were the product of the historically unprecedented surge of mass revolts after the 1917 October Revolution. Any attempt to extrapolate or benchmark the Swedish model outside of its historical context of class power relations is just a pipe dream.

Contradictions of the Keynesian alternative: the 'strategy for social solidarity'

A recent key phrase of the international progressive movement is 'socialism for the twenty-first century'. Nevertheless, most Korean progressives have yet to escape from the ideology of TINA. What they are now seeking is simply a 'progressive' or 'less evil' variant of capitalism. Although there can be fierce disagreements within this camp, as is evidenced by the recent spin-off of a PD faction from the NL-dominant DLP, the common thread that binds them together is their opposition to neoliberalism, the recognition of the supposed inevitability of the market, and their adherence to some sort of reformed capitalism. They also accept the basic principles of Keynesian economics.

Indeed, Keynesian catchphrases such as the 'euthanasia of the rentier', the 'socialization of investment', the 'Tobin Tax', 'growth through redistribution', 'progressive competitiveness', 'capitalism with a human face', and so on, are fashionable for many Korean progressives. Some of them advocate the necessity of Keynesianism simply because Korea has skipped the stage of Keynesianism and leapt directly from developmental statism to neoliberalism. Keynesian eco-nomics, denigrated as a variant of bourgeois economics during the heyday of 'revolutionary' discourse in the 1980s, is now seen as the feasible progressive alternative to neoliberalism. Of course, this exemplifies how devastating to Korean progressives was the ideological impact of the demise of the USSR.

Despite their differences at the level of detail, all Korean Keynesians emphasize the role of the state, the need to regulate the market and the logic of competitiveness. They also seem to have a close affinity with neoliberalism in that they do not negate the importance of 'competitiveness', 'growth' or 'efficiency', which neoliberalism worships. The difference between Korean Keynesians and neoliberals lies only in the *method* of enhancing competitiveness. While the neoliberals seek to strengthen competitiveness through cutting wages, deregulation and market liberalization (the so-called 'low road strategy'), the Korean Keynesians argue for increased competitiveness through enhancing the skill of workers and innovation (the so-called 'high road strategy'). Indeed, the self-proclaimed 'left neoliberal', Roh Moo-hyun, also frequently used Keynesian rhetoric, including 'social capital' and 'social investment state'. In Roh's rhetoric, 'left neoliberalism' unwittingly reflects the convergence between neoliberalism and Keynesianism in practice.

The dominant ideological discourse on a world scale has recently shifted from neoliberal market fundamentalism (the 'Washington Consensus') to 'social liberalism' (Roh Moo-hyun's 'left neoliberalism') or the 'post-Washington Consensus'. The implication for progressives is obvious. It will be self-defeating for them to continue to frame their strategy within the dichotomy of market vs. state, or neoliberalism vs. Keynesianism (or 'anti-neoliberalism'), when the dominant ideological discourse of the global ruling class has *shifted* towards the convergence between neoliberalism and Keynesianism. Sticking to the artificial dichotomy of neoliberalism vs. anti-neoliberalism (Keynsianism) will not be just anachronistic but also disarming. Korean progressives need to transcend the dichotomy between the market (neoliberalism) and the state (Keynesianism or anti-neoliberalism), in order to develop a socialist perspective.

In this respect, it is a serious mistake for Korean progressives, especially the PD faction of the DLP, to be incorporated into the same ideology as Lee Myung-bak's 'Saving the Economy', and advocate Keynesian solutions, including *intra-class* redistributive growth policies and the 'Strategy for Social Solidarity', especially concessions by organized regular workers to irregular workers. This is recipe for deepening social polarization in Korea. Although it is true that the irregular workers have borne the brunt of the sacrifices since 1997, the essence of the neoliberal restructuring is *inter-class* polarization, or the recovery of capitalist profitability through the intensification of the exploitation of the working class as a whole.

The so-called 'Strategy for Social Solidarity' turns away from the primary contradiction between capital and labour to privilege intra-class polarization, especially the contradiction between regular workers and irregular workers, and the contradiction between the chaebols and small and medium enterprises, which are secondary. It is hard to find any evidence that the organized regular workers took advantage of the suffering of irregular workers. It is the capitalist class as a whole that has benefited from the super-exploitation of the irregular workers, aggravating social polarization in Korea. Therefore, concessions by regular workers would not increase the wages or employment levels of the irregular workers but would, instead, reduce the total wage bill of the working class as a whole. This will accelerate the over-accumulation of capital and worsen the under-consumption crisis, in contrast with the Keynesian expectations of the 'Strategy for Social Solidarity'.

Conclusion

If the long Korean boom of 1961–87 was due to the country's statist regime of accumulation, the downturn after the 1990s was due to the malfunctioning of this regime, and the 1997 crisis was the combined result of the malfunctioning of the statist accumulation regime and the failures of the rush towards neoliberalism. Neoliberalism was introduced in Korea as the response to the malfunctioning of the statist regime, and established after the 1997 crisis under the combined pressure of IMF structural adjustment and neoliberal administrations.

This chapter has argued that neoliberalism has been unable to build its own regime of accumulation after the 1997 crisis, establishing a so-called 'finance-led accumulation regime' or a 'knowledge-based economy'. It has only succeeded in deepening the low growth trajectory of the economy, increasing socio-economic polarization and furthering denationalization. Recent experiences also show the limitations and contradictions of attempts to build a progressive regime of accumulation in Korea, such as national developmentalist statist or the Keynesian 'egalitarian' regime of accumulation. Korean progressives trying to break with the neoliberal trap of low growth and polarization should break, first, with these twin versions of reformism, and renew the project of transcending the capitalist system based on the Marxian socialism that they discarded after the fall of Communism. That is the surest way to rebuild the progressive movement, which is currently in retreat after their defeat in the presidential election, and to win over the working people who are now challenging Lee Myung-bak's ultra-neoliberal, pro-chaebol, anti-labour and polarizing policies.

Notes

1 I am thankful to Alfredo Saad-Filho's encouragement and help writing this chapter. This work was partly supported by Korea Research Foundation Grant (KRF-2007–411-J04601).
2 Shin and Chang (2005: 413) argue that 'the quick recovery of the Korean economy was actually caused by the reversal of the IMF macroeconomic policy, i.e. an aggressive Keynesian macroeconomic package'. Yoo (2006: 221) has also emphasized 'the role of the government sector' during the recovery period after the 1997 crisis.
3 The DLP is the only progressive parliamentary party backed by major organizations of mass movements, especially the Korean Confederation of Trade Unions (KCTU), and currently has five seats in the National Congress. It is a sort of loose coalition of several factions, of which NL is the majority.
4 Chang's Democratic Welfare State Model is clearly articulated in Chang (2007), on which I will concentrate. In what follows, all references are to Chang (2007), unless indicated otherwise.

References

Albo, G. (1997) 'A World Market of Opportunities? Capitalist Obstacles and Left Economic Policy', *The Socialist Register*.

Chang, H. (2007) 'Twenty Years After Democratization, Economic Democracy, and the Great Social Cmpromise', Pressian Lecuture, 22 August, www.pressian.com (in Korean).

Crotty, J. (2002) 'The Effects of Increased Product Market Competition and Changes in Financial Markets on the Performance of Nonfinancial Corporations in the Neoliberal Era', *PERI Working Paper series*, No. 44.

Ercan, F. and Oguz, S. (2007) 'Rethinking Anti-Neoliberal Strategies Through the Perspective of Value Theory: Insights from the Turkish Case', *Science & Society*, Vol. 71, No. 2.

Jeong, S. (1997) 'The Social Structure of Accumulation in South Korea: Upgrading or Crumbling?', *Review of Radical Political Economics*, Vol. 29, No. 4.

Jeong, S. (2007) 'Trend of Marxian Ratios in Korea: 1970–2003', in Hart-Landsberg, M., Jeong, S. and Westra, R. (eds), *Marxist Perspectives on South Korea in the Global Economy*, Aldershot: Ashgate.

Shin, J. and Chang, H. (2003) *Restructuring Korea Inc.*, London: RoutledgeCurzon.

Shin, J. and Chang, H. (2005) 'Economic Reform after the Financial Crisis: a Critical Assessment of Institutional Transition and Transition Costs in South Korea', *Review of International Political Economy*, Vol. 12, No. 3.

Weiss, L. (ed.) (2003) *States in the Global Economy*, Cambridge: Cambridge University Press.

World Bank (2007) *World Development Indicators*, CD-ROM.

Yoo, Jong-Il (2006) 'The Long and Winding Road to Liberalization: The South Korean Experience', in Taylor, L. (ed.), *External Liberalization in Asia, Post-Socialist Europe and Brazil*, Oxford: Oxford University Press.

12 China and the quest for alternatives to neoliberalism

Dic Lo and Yu Zhang

Viewed from the perspective of globalisation, China's experience of economic transformation over the past three decades appears to be anomalous – indeed paradoxical. The sustained rapid growth of the Chinese economy has been in sharp contrast to the prolonged stagnation in most parts of the non-Western world. The mixed economic system that has persisted despite market reforms further contradicts the orthodox doctrines of globalisation, i.e. the doctrines of market fundamentalism commonly known as the Washington Consensus.

There is of course no shortage of proponents of the Washington Consensus attempting to interpret the Chinese experience in a way that is consistent with the orthodox doctrines. There is a recurring proposition which states that China's economic system has been a mix of market-conforming and market-supplanting elements, that its developmental achievements have been ascribable to the conforming elements whilst its accumulated problems are due to the supplanting elements, and that the problems have tended to outweigh the achievements as the country's economic transition proceeds from the allegedly 'easy' phase to the 'difficult' phase (*The Economist* 1998; IMF 2000; OECD 2005; World Bank 2002). Essentially, this proposition is based on the belief that economic development as dictated by principles of the market, and the actual working of the world market in reality, is somehow natural or easy. This is the notion of the 'natural path of development', the ultimate promise of globalisation.

This interpretation of the Chinese experience has been shared by many in the critical, anti-globalisation scholarship. There is a widely-held view in this camp that, rather than fundamentally deviating from principles of the market, China has actually followed through a capitalist transformation. Indeed, it is posited that China has been following the extreme form of capitalist transformation, namely neoliberalisation. What distinguishes these critical scholars from the orthodoxy is in terms of assessment. They have often argued that China's seemingly phenomenal developmental performance has been mainly based on the 'super-exploitation' of Chinese labour (and the natural environment), as well as on 'under-cutting' the world working class as a whole (Hart-Landsberg and Burkett 2004; Harvey 2005; Walker and Buck 2007). Essentially, the fact that these writers unequivocally deny that China's sustained rapid economic growth is a real process of development appears to reflect the belief that capitalism can never deliver development anywhere, any time, on a world-significant scale. This belief can be called the 'natural path of under-development'.

This chapter takes on the orthodox, market-fundamentalist discourse on China, while also attempting to engage with the critical scholarship. Specifically, it seeks to construct an alternative account of China's economic transformation, based on the following two-fold proposition. First, China's economic transformation has been mainly based on productivity growth, and is thus to a significant extent a *real* development. Second, development has been achieved mainly through a process of 'governing the market' by a set of structural-institutional factors that are China-specific, but can be of general importance for late developing countries. Based on this proposition, this chapter will also attempt to explore the future prospects for China's economic transformation and draw some lessons for late development.

The dynamics and conditions of Chinese economic growth

China's sustained rapid economic growth since the late 1970s is a world-phenomenal event, not only in terms of the rate of growth but also in terms of its structural-institutional attributes. This process has three important attributes: first, industrialisation has persistently been the immediate driving force of economic growth; second, there was clearly a switch in the early 1990s from labour-intensive growth to capital-deepening growth and; third, the growth path switched from consumption-led to investment-led between the two halves of the reform era. The analysis of the dynamics and conditions of these three attributes is key to the understanding of China's overall economic transformation.

There should be no mistake that the immediate dynamics behind Chinese economic growth over the reform era is a process of rapid industrialisation. Between 1978 and 2007, the average annual growth rate of real GDP and per-worker real GDP was 9.8 per cent and 7.5 per cent, respectively. In the same period, the average annual real growth rates of industrial value added and per-worker industrial value added were 11.6 per cent and 9.2 per cent, respectively. Both the output and labour productivity growth rates of industry substantially exceed those of the economy as a whole, on average by around two percentage points each year.

The transition from labour-intensive growth to capital-deepening growth is also clearly evident. As can be seen from Table 12.1, between 1978 and 1992 economic growth, along with rapid productivity improvement, was associated with the fast expansion of labour employment. The average annual growth rate of employment actually exceeded that of the labourforce. Productivity growth accelerated further after 1992, along with the slowdown in employment expansion: employment growth has lagged behind that of the labourforce, on average by almost one percentage point per annum.

The transition from consumption-led to investment-led growth is equally apparent. Figure 12.1 charts the composition of Chinese GDP by expenditures. It can be seen that, among China's aggregate expenditures, consumption accounted

Table 12.1 Average annual growth rates (%) of China's real GDP, employment and labourforce

	(a) Real GDP	(b) Employment	(c) Labourforce	(a)-(b)	(b)-(c)
1978–2007	9.82	2.27	2.30	7.55	−0.03
1978–92	9.39	3.63	3.60	5.76	0.03
1992–2007	10.16	1.02	1.10	9.15	−0.08

Sources: National Bureau of Statistics, *China Statistical Yearbook 2008.*

for a substantially larger share in the first half of the reform era than in the second half, on average by more than ten percentage points. The opposite was basically true for the share of investment in aggregate expenditures. It is only since 2005 that the third component, net exports, has accounted for a significant – and rapidly rising – share of aggregate expenditures.

To analyse these attributes of Chinese economic growth requires a theoretical perspective of transformational growth – that is, seeing growth as a process of change rather than simply as a process of expansion. Succinctly, the analysis needs to clarify the structural-institutional arrangements that underlie the growth process (the productivity regime), and the condition that facilitates the working of these arrangements (the demand regime). It is the interaction between these two aspects that determines a particular economic growth path, such as those

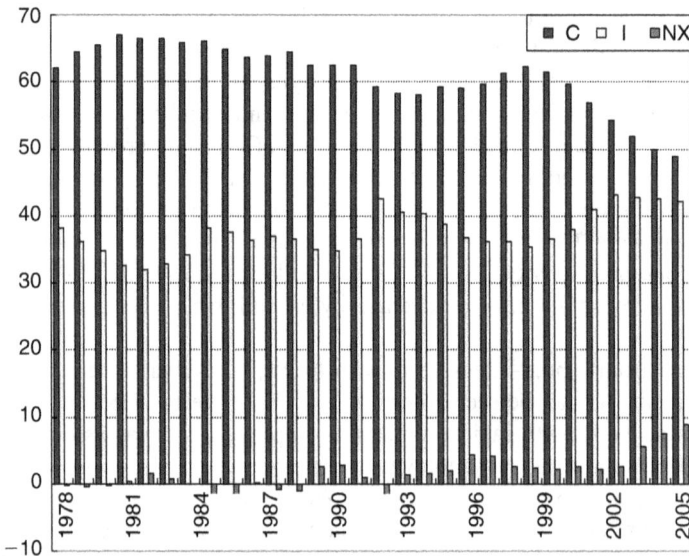

Figure 12.1 Composition of GDP by expenditures (%) (sources: China State Statistical Bureau, *China Statistical Yearbook*, various issues).

Note
C = final consumption; I = investment; NX = net export of goods and services.

that prevailed in China in the two sub-periods of the reform era (for a review and synthesis of the relevant theories, see Lo and Smyth 2004).

A prominent feature of Chinese industrialisation throughout the reform era is a process of structural change within the industrial sector itself: the rapid expansion of the share of heavy manufacturing in total industrial output, along with the relative shrinking of extractive industries and light industries processing farm products. A closer look at the evolution of the composition industrial output further reveals that it is the broad machinery sector, i.e. the sector encompassing all mechanical and electronics industry, that has had the biggest gain in output share (Lo 2006). This seems unusual, for it is a well-known feature of Soviet-type centrally planned economies that the machinery sector plays a leading role in the economy. In the case of China, by 1980, this sector had already expanded to the extent of accounting for up to one-quarter of the total output of Chinese industry. Does the further expansion of this sector in the reform era signify a continuation of the Soviet-type Feldman-Mahalanobis model of economic growth – that is, a growth path that is based on 'producing investment goods for producing investment goods'? In view of the aforementioned three attributes of China's economic growth process, the answer appears to be 'no' for the first half of the reform era and probably 'yes' for the second half.

In the first half of the reform era, the massive expansion of the machinery sector (and light industries processing non-farm products) was associated with a phenomenal development that was felt by the entire Chinese population: the 'consumption revolution' through the explosive growth of a wide range of consumer durables, ranging from electrical and electronic home appliances in the 1980s to mobile phones, personal computers and the like in the 1990s. These products are not investment goods, but they belong to the mechanical and electronics industry. It was the explosive growth of these new consumer durables that accounted for the expansion of the machinery sector in the 1978–92 period. And the machinery sector was the main driving force behind the growth of Chinese industry as a whole, as well as the transfer of productivity gains from industry to the rest of the economy via changes in relative prices and other mechanisms.

In terms of technical and economic characteristics, the new consumer durables belong to mass production industries that are characterised by rapid technological change, extensive backward and forward linkages and high income elasticity of demand. The explosive growth of the output of these industries in the first half of the reform era was sustained by the existence of mass consumption in the domestic market. More generally, it may be argued that China's rapid economic growth in the period 1978–92 was based on the following nexus of causal relationships: consumption induced investment and thereby the overall expansion of demand, thus making it possible to absorb labour transfer from agriculture and to improve industrial productivity via dynamic increasing returns. There was a virtuous circle between consumption and production, and between the expansion of industry and overall economic growth.

The nexus of causal relationships underpinning China's economic growth during the first half of the reform era, described above, presupposes a necessary condition: a relatively egalitarian pattern of income distribution supporting mass consumption, thereby inducing investment and overall demand expansion. Income distribution, in this context, includes both monetary and non-monetary incomes, particularly for urban residents in the first half of the reform era. The degree of egalitarianism is thus difficult to be gauged by conventional measures of income distribution such as the Gini index. Perhaps much more appropriate measures would be social development indicators such as life expectancy at birth, the infant mortality rate and the adult illiteracy rate. It is well known that, in these measures, China's performance in the late 1970s was very close to the average of all middle-income economies in the world, even though it was a low-income economy. By the early years of the twenty-first century, China's performance in these social development indicators remained very close to the average of all middle-income economies (despite a significant deterioration in distribution and the collapse of several aspects of social welfare provision). Overall, it would be appropriate to assert that, for the main part of the reform era, China's pattern of income distribution tended to be egalitarian by international standards – although it is also true that egalitarianism tended to wither as the market reforms advanced further.

It was precisely the worsening of the pattern of income distribution under the market reforms that led to the fundamental shift of China's growth path in the early 1990s. The leading role of consumption was taken over by investment in sustaining economic growth on the demand side. And the contribution of labour transfer to economic growth – that is, the improvement in allocative efficiency as a source of productivity growth – has tended to weaken. What has been of increasing importance is dynamic increasing returns within industry. Conceptually, in the relevant theoretical literature, there is a well-developed proposition which states that the sustainability on the demand side of a growth path based on 'producing investment goods for producing investment goods' is determined by the pace of product innovations. It is through product innovations that the variety of investment goods could continuously expand and the saturation of demand for the output mix of the economy would not set in (Lo and Li 2006). The sources, and pace, of product innovations in Chinese economic growth particularly since the early 1990s is an important issue requiring further study. Nevertheless, one point seems clear: in addition to domestic generation, a very important source of product innovations is from continuous, large-scale imports of foreign technology. It is in this particular respect that external dynamics have played a crucial role in China's economic transformation.

Gradual marketisation, neoliberalisation and the quest for alternatives

The logical starting point in the nexus of causal relationships underpinning China's economic transformation in the first half of the reform era, as depicted in the preceding section, is the existence of an egalitarian pattern of income distribution. This pattern of income distribution has been, in turn, based on China's specific political economy. For a major part of the reform era, and especially in the first half, the economy has been dominated by public ownership, and within the publicly-owned sector egalitarianism in distribution has been the norm. In 1992, state-owned and collectively-owned enterprises combined to account for 86 per cent of the output of Chinese industry as a whole. By the turn of the century, their share remained at 64 per cent.

All these notwithstanding, it is not true that China has always shunned the policy doctrines of the Washington Consensus throughout the reform era. There was a high tide of neoliberalisation in China in the mid-1990s. This mainly took the form of the 1993–5 financial liberalisation and the 1995–7 enterprise downsizing drive. There were also policy measures adopted during this period for working towards the targets of liberalising external finance and balancing the state budget by the turn of the century.

The 1995–7 downsizing drive in state (and collective) enterprises had especially far-reaching implications. This drive was initiated by the state leadership with the goal of transforming large and medium enterprises into modern corporations and small-scale enterprises into shareholding cooperatives. It was subsequently seized upon by local authorities to simply sell off state assets while unilaterally abandoning the state's obligation towards workers' job security (and transferring the liabilities of these enterprises onto the state banks and, ultimately, to central government). Consequently, unemployment surged, consumption expansion slowed down and investment growth stagnated. Together with the worsening external environment caused by the 1997–8 East Asian crisis, these reforms plunged China into deflation and a steadily worsening financial performance of enterprises in the closing years of the century.

Against this background, there was a fundamental policy reversal in 1998. The Chinese state leadership adopted four main types of anti-crisis policies between 1998 and 2002. First, it launched several Keynesian fiscal packages for expanding investment, which were financed by debt issuing on an unprecedented scale. Second, it implemented a range of welfare policies aimed at reversing the stagnation of consumption growth. Third, it adopted policies to revitalise the state sector in order to improve the financial position of the state-owned enterprises and the balance sheet of the state banks. Fourth, it adopted a cautious approach to the reform of the external transactions. In particular, the liberalisation of the capital account of the balance of payments was, effectively, shelved. As an anti-crisis strategy, these policies embody the idea of helping enterprises, as well as the government, to 'grow out of debt'. The robust growth of the Chinese economy in the crisis-prone years of 1998–2002, as well as the substantial decrease in the indebtedness of the state, state banks and state-owned enterprises (as a proportion of GDP) indicate that the adoption of these policies was justified.

Meanwhile, albeit intended to be short-term anti-crisis measures, these policies turned out to be consistent with the long-term social and economic development strategy of China's state leadership in the new century. This strategy, known as 'constructing a harmonious society', emphasises the need to reverse the trend of increasing social polarisation under the market reforms. A central aspect of social polarisation to be dealt with is the declining trend of labour compensation as a share of national income. Although the economic growth process has not been mainly based on cheap labour or 'super-exploitation' (as indicated above with reference to Table 12.1), it is true that labour compensation has experienced very sluggish growth in the main part of the reform era. This is evident in Figure 12.2, which shows the fact that, up until the turn of the century, the growth of the real urban wage rate (the formal sector of the Chinese economy) lagged far behind the growth of per capita real GDP. The reversal in recent years reflects the deliberate efforts of the state to improve the workers' compensation. These include enhancing the protection of labour rights, working towards the target of establishing collective bargaining in all enterprises, enforcing the stipulation of setting up unions in all enterprises, and introducing a new employment contract law – all breaking with the previous laissez-faire approach towards labour employment.

These labour rights-enhancing policies are consistent with the prevailing capital-deepening path of economic growth and, thus, they appear to have a solid material underpinning. The same applies to the broader policies for income

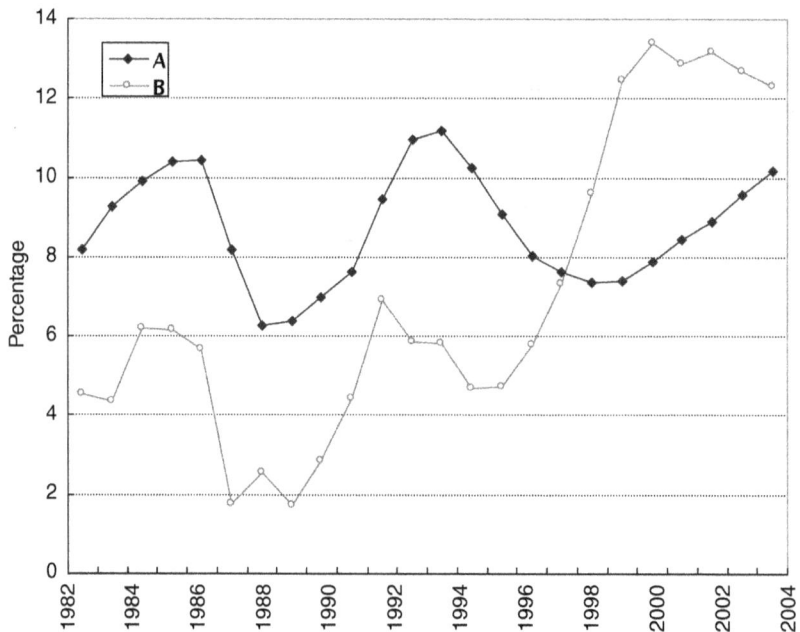

Figure 12.2 Annual growth rate of per capita real GDP and real urban wage rate (five-year moving average, %) (source: National Bureau of Statistics, *China Statistical Yearbook 2008*).

Note
A = per capita real GDP; B = urban real wage rate.

redistribution, social welfare provision, as well as the attempts to reconstruct a government-funded healthcare system for the population as a whole, including the rural population. Nevertheless, given that China has by now already deeply integrated itself into the world market, it will be a challenge of unprecedented scale to move against the currents of globalisation in the pursuit of 'constructing a harmonious society'.

The impact of China's transformation on globalisation

Central to the contemporary process of 'globalisation' has been a process of financialisation, that is, the rapidly rising predominance of speculative financial activities in the world economy. As Robert Wade (2006) has observed, financialisation implies a tendency of financial interests to dissociate themselves from real investment and the productive process in general. There is, thus, an intrinsic contradiction within financialisation: the speculative pursuit of profitability tends to crowd out productive activities, thus undermining the sources of aggregate profitability. Financialisation is intrinsically unsustainable.

But financialisation has actually been sustained, at least until recently. The reason, as David Harvey (2005) has argued, is mainly because of the cheapening of productive inputs worldwide. It is in this connection that national and international policies associated with neoliberalism can be seen as essential to the current round of globalisation. These policies facilitate the cheapening of productive inputs, labour in particular, and their incorporation into global capitalism. Institutionally, as Harvey has further argued, financialisation necessarily requires flexible production: logical to the rising mobility of capital is the inclination towards minimising fixed investment and maximising profits through the extraction of absolute surplus value. A central tenet of neoliberalism is precisely to create flexible institutions in the form of the casualisation of employment, which is made possible by the creation of an 'unlimited supply of labour' and the elimination of arrangements that could undermine the flexible working of the labour market, such as unionisation and legislative protection of labour. This appears to be what has actually occurred to date.

Nevertheless, this neoliberal tenet is not inevitable, even in the sense of underpinning the kind of flexible production needed for competing in the world market. In line with the literature on techno-economic paradigms (Lo and Smyth 2004), it could be posited that the behavioural flexibility of the productive system could arise from two different, contrasting types of institutional arrangements. One consists in casualisation, that is, 'flexible institutions, flexible behaviour', which is based on the principles of the detailed division of labour and deskilling of labour. The other arrangement is rigid, or long-term-oriented institutions, constructed on the basis of the social division of labour – that is, 'rigid institutions, flexible behaviour', where behavioural flexibility arises from collective learning and horizontal coordination. Theoretically, there is no a priori reason to claim that one of these arrangements is intrinsically more competitive than the other. In reality, however, the triumph of neoliberalism, in conjunction with the drive to financialisation, has resulted in the predominance of the 'flexible institutions, flexible behaviour' model across the world. This has been so despite the observation that the historical record of the alternative 'rigid institutions, flexible behaviour' model embodies a much higher degree of solidarity, egalitarianism and social justice, and the argument that this alternative model is less prone to produce systemic demand deficiency that could undermine economic growth (Dore 2002).

In this context, China's development experience and policy efforts since the turn of the century deserve special attention. It could be asserted that a main aspect of globalisation is the expansion of the world labour market associated with the incorporation of China into the international economic system. According to the International Monetary Fund (2007), weighing countries' labourforce by their export-to-GDP ratio, the effective global labour supply quadrupled between 1980 and 2005, with East Asia contributing about half of the increase. And, during this period, there has been an accelerating trend of relocation of industry and jobs to China from the rest of East Asia. As of year-end 2005, China's share of the world total of workers producing for the global market reached 25 per cent. Because of its significant and rising position in the world economy, China's attempt to construct an alternative model of development is bound to make a systemic impact on the future of globalisation. As noted, the worldwide cheapening of labour over the past quarter-century and particularly since the early 1990s has been, in a very significant measure, associated with the incorporation of China's relatively low-wage labourforce into the world market. Now that there have emerged strong state and societal efforts in China to resist the cheapening drive, some fundamental adjustments in world development are likely to occur. Whatever the precise nature of these adjustments, the hegemony of neoliberalism is likely to be less complete in the future than in the previous quarter-century. Real development worldwide has a stake in the success or otherwise of China's attempt to construct an alternative to neoliberalism.

Conclusion

The Chinese experience of economic transformation over the past three decades offers important lessons for late development under globalisation. In hindsight, the country appears to have undergone a transition from labour-intensive industrialisation and economic growth to an alternative, capital-deepening path. In both phases, the developmental achievements cannot be reduced to the orthodox policy doctrines of globalisation – that is, the market fundamentalism of the Washington Consensus, or to neoliberalism. In particular, the capital-deepening growth path has emerged and persisted in connection with a range of structural-institutional factors that are market-supplanting in nature. It is the interaction between these factors and the prevailing growth path that appears to constitute a promising, alternative model of late development.

Put differently, since the turn of the century China's state and society have focused their efforts on 'constructing a harmonious society'. These efforts represent a quest for a model of development that deviates fundamentally from neoliberalism. In particular, state development policies and institutional reforms in recent years have tended to target labour compensation-enhancing economic growth, rather than growth based on 'cheap labour'. This chapter argues that the new development model does represent a more feasible and desirable pursuit than neoliberalism. The chapter concludes with a discussion on the impact of this new Chinese development model on the future direction of globalisation.

References

Dore, Ronald (2002) 'Stock Market Capitalism and its Diffusion', *New Political Economy*, 7 (1): 115–27.

The Economist (1998) 24–30 October, pp. 15–16 and pp. 23–8.

Hart-Landsberg, M. and P. Burkett (2004) *China and Socialism: Market Reforms and Class Struggle*, a special issue of *Monthly Review*, July–August 2004.

Harvey, D. (2005) *A Brief History of Neoliberalism*. Oxford: Oxford University Press.

IMF (2000) *World Economic Outlook*, October, Washington, DC: The International Monetary Fund.

—— (2007) *World Economic Outlook*, April, Washington, DC: International Monetary Fund.

Lo, D. (2006) 'Making Sense of China's Economic Transformation', Economics Department working paper no. 148, SOAS, University of London. Online, available at: www.soas.ac.uk/economics/research/workingpapers.

Lo, D. and G. Li (2006) 'China's Economic Growth, 1978–2005: Structural Change and Institutional Attributes', Economics Department working paper no. 150, SOAS, University of London. Online, available at: www.soas.ac.uk/economics/research/working-papers.

Lo, D. and R. Smyth (2004) 'Towards a Re-interpretation of the Economics of Feasible Socialism', *Cambridge Journal of Economics*, 28 (6): 791–808.

OECD (2005) *Economic Survey of China 2005*, Paris: Organisation for Economic Co-operation and Development, September. Online, available at: www.oecd.org/document /21/0,2340,en_2649_201185_35331797_1_1_1_1,00.html.

Wade, R. (2006) 'Choking the South', *New Left Review*, no. 38: 115–27.

Walker, R. and D. Buck (2007) 'The Chinese Road: Cities in the Transition to Capitalism', *New Left Review*, no. 46: 39–66.

World Bank (2002) *Transition – The First Ten Years: Analysis and Lessons for Eastern Europe and the Former Soviet Union*, Washington, DC: The World Bank.

13 Globalisation, neoliberalism, labour, with reference to South Africa

Henry Bernstein

It is capitalist accumulation itself that constantly produces ... a relatively redundant working population, i.e. a population which is superfluous to capital's average requirements for its own valorisation, and is therefore a surplus population.

(Marx 1976: 782)

The global informal working class ... is about one billion strong, making it the fastest-growing, and most unprecedented, social class on earth.

(Davis 2006: 178)

Unemployment is always hard to measure in labour markets in which 'jobs' are not what most people do most of the time.

(Standing *et al.* 1996: 124)

What I do is not work as such; it is just to keep me going as I wait for employment. If I could get employed, I could let go of this activity and work. I am looking for work.

(Street vendor quoted in Ceruti 2007b: 24)

In this chapter I use 'globalisation' as convenient shorthand for the current phase of the restructuring of capital and its conditions of accumulation, manifested in new forms of the international centralisation and concentration, as well as mobility (and 'financialisation'), of capital. I distinguish globalisation from neoliberalism as a political and ideological project to support and promote the restructuring of capital and its modalities of accumulation. And I use the term 'classes of labour' to refer to 'the growing numbers ... who now depend – directly *and indirectly* – on the sale of their labour power for their own daily reproduction' (Panitch and Leys 2001: ix; my emphasis).

Back to Marx: the reserve army of labour

The indispensable theorisation of capitalism in general terms (the capitalist mode of production) remains Marx's *Capital*, and for present purposes, specifically Vol. 1, Ch. 25, 'The General Law of Capitalist Accumulation', section 3 'The progressive production of a relative surplus population or industrial reserve army'.

First,

> it is capitalist accumulation itself that constantly produces ... a relatively redundant working population, i.e. a population which is superfluous to capital's average requirements for its own valorisation, and is therefore a surplus population ... The fact that the means of production and the productivity of labour increase more rapidly than the productive population expresses itself ... in the inverse form that the working population always increases more rapidly than the valorisation requirement of capital.
>
> (Marx 1976: 782, 798)

In turn, the relative surplus population or industrial reserve army of labour is 'the background against which the law of the demand and supply of labour does its work' in relation to wage levels (ibid.: 792).

Second, the size and composition of the industrial reserve army of labour fluctuates; it expands and contracts with the periodic alternations of the accumulation cycles of capital and the demand for labour power they generate, that is, their structures of employment (ibid.: 790).

Third, Marx sketches different forms of the relative surplus population that he termed 'floating', 'latent', 'stagnant' and 'pauperism'. Of these, for example, he remarks that the 'stagnant' component is part of the active labour army but 'with extremely irregular employment', providing capital with 'an inexhaustible reservoir of disposable labour-power' with maximum hours and minimum wages, especially in 'special branches of capitalist exploitation' like 'domestic industry' (ibid.: 796). This has a contemporary ring to it, and indeed there are few social forms and practices of exploitation in the past histories of capitalist development that can not be found somewhere today. 'Domestic industry' may appear 'archaic' yet, as we know, it is incorporated in some of the 'cutting edge' organisational forms of contemporary large-scale capital (global commodity chains, varieties of outworking, and so on). In short, such incorporation provides specific examples of the combined and uneven development of capitalism on a world scale.

Finally, I quote Marx on pauperism ('chronic poverty' in today's policy parlance), which includes

> the demoralised, the ragged and those unable to work, chiefly people who succumb to their incapacity for adaptation, an incapacity which results from the division of labour; people who have lived beyond the worker's average life-span; and the victims of industry, whose number increases with the growth of dangerous machinery, of mines, chemical works etc., the mutilated, the sickly, the widows, etc. Pauperism is the hospital of the active labour-army and the dead weight of the industrial reserve army.
>
> (Ibid.: 797)

Forward from Marx: globalisation, neoliberalism, labour

Marx's observations resonate powerfully in the twenty-first century world of globalising capitalism. Of course, there are important issues today that Marx did not consider (or not in any systematic fashion). This is hardly surprising given the momentous historical distance between what he observed and analysed over three or four decades in nineteenth-century England and the world of global capitalism now. That distance is inscribed in the formation, cycles and mutations of the world economy since his time, and their links with the histories of colonial imperialism and their legacies; with the developmentalism of the newly independent countries of Africa and Asia (and their Latin American counterparts) in the context of the 'long boom'/'golden age' of the world economy in the 1950s and 1960s; and with the subsequent crisis of accumulation that terminated the 'golden age' and catalysed both contemporary globalisation and the hegemonic ambitions of the neoliberal project.

The crucial decade of this momentous shift was the 1970s. As Beverly Silver and Giovanni Arrighi put it (2000: 56): 'The deep capitalist crisis of the 1970s was first and foremost a reflection of the inability of world capitalism as instituted under US hegemony to deliver on the promises of a Global New Deal.' This led to

> a liquidation of the labour-friendly and development-friendly international regime of the preceding thirty years in favour of a capital-friendly regime … Under the new regime, the crisis of capitalism quickly turned into a crisis of organised labour and of the welfare state in rich countries, and of the crisis of Communism and of the developmental state in poorer countries.

Like others, Silver and Arrighi also remark that this new 'capital-friendly regime (is) reminiscent of late nineteenth- and early-twentieth century *laissez-faire* capitalism' (ibid.: 56), which perhaps highlights the contemporary resonances of Marx (who died in 1883) and of Lenin who extended Marx's economic analysis, precisely between the late 1890s and 1910s. Marx would not be surprised that the size of the reserve army of labour, as 'surplus' to the current valorisation requirements of capital, has increased as a result of globalisation; nor that this is driven by a major crisis of accumulation and subsequent restructuring of capital; nor, as we observe virtually everywhere today and especially in the 'global South', that the boundaries between the active and reserve armies of labour become ever more fluid, together with a shrinking 'core' of relatively secure wage employment in the former, and a growing component of the latter that is 'informalised' (and pauperised).

Neoliberal ideology promotes deregulation as the expansion of freedom. This is certainly true for capital as deregulation means removing controls on its mobility and operations, including its modes of recruitment and deployment of labour – so-called labour market flexibilisation. It also means, in effect, reducing its contributions to the social income of the workers employed by particular capitals and to the social reproduction fund generally through taxation and government spending on social provision: the redistributive 'transfers' abhorred by neoliberalism. At the same time, of course, the outright or creeping privatisation of public goods represents a massive new frontier for investment and profit by transnational capital in water, energy supply, telecommunications, transport systems, health services, pensions and so on.

On the part of labour, deregulation means a loss of freedom, of its hard-won rights in labour markets, in opportunities and terms of employment, and in claims on publicly provided social income that supplement wages in various ways, to various degrees – or that 'compensate' for the lack of wages, to a greater or lesser extent. Once more Marx is apposite here: pauperisation, he says, 'forms part of the *faux frais* ["incidental expenses", HB] of capitalist production: but capital usually knows how to transfer these from its own shoulders to those of the working class and the petty bourgeoisie' (1976: 797).

If all this results in growing income insecurity as well as employment insecurity and the downward pressures on reproduction exerted by the erosion of social provision for those in 'standard' wage employment – who are shrinking as a proportion of classes of labour in the South, as noted, and in some instances in absolute terms as well – it has even more serious consequences for the growing numbers of the reserve army or 'informalised' classes of labour (for trends of growing employment and income insecurity across the major regions of the world, see Standing 1999; ILO 2004).

According to the CIA's *World Factbook* of 2002, 'By the late 1990s a staggering one billion workers representing one-third of the world's labour force, most of them in the South, were either unemployed or underemployed'. I take the quotation from Mike Davis, who restates it in his own way: 'The global informal working class ... is about one billion strong, making it the fastest-growing, and most unprecedented, social class on earth' (2006: 199, 178). Two immediate qualifications are in order, however. One is that the notion of un- or under-employment is misleading. As everyone knows, 'informal' workers have to work (and 'hustle') extremely hard to be able to eat. The second qualification is that 'the global informal working class' is inevitably highly differentiated in various ways (as Davis among others shows). Here are five (hypo)theses that bear on the differentiation of classes of labour.

1   In the words of Silver and Arrighi once more (2000: 54):

the so-called North-South divide continues to constitute ... the main obstacle to the formation of a homogeneous world proletarian condition. In spite of the relocation of industrial activities from North to South typical of the current crisis, conditions of working-class formation remain thoroughly dependent on the huge and still widening gap that separates the wealth, status and power of a relatively small number of Western countries from those of the countries that contain the vast majority of the world's population.

2   Beyond this, there are important variations between different regions and countries of the 'South', not least in terms of the extent and forms of activity of the reserve army of labour, as well as of its internal differentiation, including in the informal economy. The relative size and weight, and importantly the composition, of the informal economy vary significantly with historically specific patterns of capitalist development – a matter of, *inter alia*, their structures, forms and circuits of production, distribution and consumption, and how they are articulated (Meagher 1995, for sub-Saharan Africa; Breman 1996 and Harriss-White 2003 for India; Carr and Chen 2002, for export production using informalised labour in certain branches in Asia and Latin America). And, as Davis (2006: 181) observes:

Part of the informal proletariat, to be sure, is a stealth workforce for the formal economy.... Likewise, there is probably more of a continuum than an abrupt divide between the increasingly casualized world of formal employment and the depths of the informal sector.

3   Classes of labour in the 'South' have to pursue their reproduction through insecure and oppressive – and typically increasingly scarce – wage employment and/or a range of likewise precarious small-scale and insecure 'informal sector' ('survival') activity, including farming in some instances; in effect, various and complex *combinations* of employment and self-employment. Additionally, many pursue their means of reproduction across different sites of the social division of labour: urban and rural, agricultural and non-agricultural, as well as wage employment and self-employment – the 'footloose labour' that Jan Breman's studies of south Gujarat document and analyse in such a compelling manner (Breman 1996). The social locations and identities that classes of labour inhabit, combine and move between, make for ever more fluid boundaries where the masses of 'surplus' labour, the 'informal working class' and formal and informal economies intersect. In short, there is no 'homogeneous proletarian condition' within the 'South', other than that essential condition: the need to secure reproduction needs (survival) through the sale of labour power (direct and indirect). Beyond this, the ways in which this is done defy inherited assumptions of fixed (and uniform) notions of 'worker', 'peasant', 'trader', 'urban', 'rural', 'employed' and 'self-employed'.

4   While concepts of 'self-employment' are highly problematic, often including those who are 'wage workers in thin disguise' (Harriss-White and Gooptu 2000: 96, also 91, 93), the prevalence of petty commodity production, in all its extraordinary diversity of activities and forms, makes its own particular contribution to what I term the fragmentation of classes of labour. In capitalism petty production is a contradictory combination of the class places of capital and labour, hence of exploitation: of 'self' and commonly of others too. This is why the informal economy is a domain of 'relentless micro-capitalism': 'Petty exploitation (endlessly franchised) is its essence,

and there is growing inequality *within* the informal sector as well as between it and the formal sector' (Davis 2006: 181).

5   The 'myriad ... networks of exploitation' of the informal economy (ibid.) are permeated by 'social regulation' in Barbara Harriss-White's use of the term (2003/4), that is to say, social differences/divisions of a typically hier-archical, oppressive and exclusionary nature, of which gender is the most ubiquitous and which often also include race and ethnicity, religion and caste. These are not social differences/divisions that necessarily originate in capitalism, nor are they necessarily in 'the interests of capital', a notion which usually signals a functionalist approach. There is a crucial difference between thinking that whatever exists in the world of capitalism does so because it serves the 'interests of capital' (in general), and thinking that what exists manifests the always contradictory dynamics of capitalist social relations (including the unintended consequences of particular strategies of accumulation, both economic and political). Of course, there are innumera-ble instances past and present of capitals consciously constructing, exploit-ing and manipulating divisions of gender and race, religion and caste. In short, the structural sources of exploitation and inequality inherent in all capitalist production (petty and grand, informal and formal) combine with other forms of social inequality and oppression to create divisions within classes of labour. Such divisions are often indicators of the boundaries between the active and reserve armies of labour, and of the distribution of social categories of labour between formal and informal employment and between relatively better and worse prospects within each.

What future does 'the informal proletariat', in whole or in large part, have within current, or foreseeable, patterns of capitalist accumulation? Jan Breman's answer (2003: 13) is that

A point of no return is reached when a reserve army of labour waiting to be incorporated into the labour process becomes stigmatised as a permanently redundant mass, an excessive burden that cannot be included now or in the future, in economy and society. This metamorphosis is ... the real crisis of world capitalism.

And Mike Davis (2006: 178, 202) concludes that 'the majority of the ... labour-ing poor are truly and radically homeless in the contemporary international economy', that they confront 'terminal marginality within global capitalism'. Or, as Arrighi and Moore (2001: 75) put it, in less apocalyptic terms:

The underlying contradiction of a world capitalist system that promotes the formation of a world proletariat but cannot accommodate a generalized living wage (that is, the most basic of reproduction costs), far from being solved, has become more acute than ever.

What might contest or qualify such views? First, there are various arguments that the normal dynamics of capitalist accumulation can generate sufficient new employment, both formal and informal, to resolve or at least relieve this 'real crisis of world capitalism' as 'a permanently redundant mass' of labour that confronts 'terminal marginality'. One type of argument claims the authority of Marx: capitalism has not yet completed its 'historic mission' and remains 'the only game in town' (Kitching 2001; Desai 2002), with all the pain that its dialectic of destruction and creation entails (Sender and Pincus 2006), and even if its forward march requires extensive and effective state intervention to discipline capital and direct its patterns of investment (in effect, the 'developmental state' once more). In this last respect, it clearly diverges from the neoliberal version of globalisation as uniquely capable of both generating growth within the world economy and overcoming poverty, as long as free markets prevail. This version of globalisation may be hegemonic, but its ideological robustness and plausibility are also under increasing strain from the contradictions that increasingly confront it.

Here it is well to remember that the economic and social power of capital, rooted in commodity relations, has to be secured through its political and ideological rule (a necessary condition of accumulation). How the rule of capital is constituted and exercised, adapted and reproduced – and what political possibilities this may disclose – is better interrogated without assuming any simple instrumentality or coherence in how it seeks to justify its moral order, or assuming that it is equipped with any guarantees of effectiveness in how it perceives, anticipates, assesses, confronts and tries to contain its social contradictions and their effects.

This is illustrated, *inter alia*, by variations in state restructuring as a result of globalisation and neoliberalism, and in the role of governments: whether, why and how they promote, resist or try to negotiate processes that advance the freedoms of capital and suppress the prospects and rights of labour, or are complicit with or otherwise helpless in face of the forces that do. For example, Sandbrook *et al.* (2007) analyse what they term social-democratic regimes in the 'South' that, in important ways, have managed to defend social provision against the hegemony of neoliberalism from the 1980s, in Kerala, Costa Rica, Mauritius and Chile (since 1990). Whether any of them might be considered 'developmental states' in terms of economic development and accumulation is another matter.

South Africa

Is South Africa (just) another case of neoliberalism in practice, as Harvey (2005), among others, suggests? There is little doubt that ANC (African National Congress) governments have pursued fairly orthodox economic policies from the beginning: their embrace of openness to the world economy (removal of capital controls, trade liberalisation, concern or obsession with global competitiveness, and so on) and pursuit of monetary stabilisation and fiscal conservatism (*inter alios* Habib and Padayachee 2000). In certain, if not all, respects, South Africa thus fits well with the general picture of neoliberal globalisation (Saad-Filho and Johnston 2005). At the same time, these processes are necessarily uneven, which requires explanation not only by how the dynamic of global accumulation (and the dominant role in it of finance capital) is mediated by the structures of particular economies, especially in the South, but also by variations in 'the political authority exercised by ruling classes and capitalist states' (Colas 2005: 70). Indeed, it is necessary to consider whether, how and how much, the latter functions to shape the ways that the former, the dynamic of global accumulation, is mediated in different countries and experienced by different classes within them, not least in terms of pressures 'from below' and more and less coherent and effective responses to them.

For South Africa, it is well to heed Bill Freund's advice to avoid 'simply looking at the present as apartheid *manqué*' and ANC governments since 1994 as 'neoliberal lapdog' (2007: 661–2). Freund rightly directs attention to consideration of the complex 'political settlement' and its volatile trajectory since the end of apartheid, that includes BEE (black economic empowerment) and assessing recent (and admittedly implausible) government claims to be a developmental state. He also highlights massive social change, similarly emphasised by Karl von Holdt who argues the inadequacy of the standard 'double transition' view – political transition to democracy and economic transition to a more globalised economy – and the need to add a third transition, that to a post-colonial society: 'a deeper and broader process of social transformation: a multitude of struggles, compromises and pacts better understood as a process of internal decolonisation and reconstruction of society' (2003: 3).

In South Africa, 'core' employment has grown since 1994, above all in services – in part the effect of the rapid growth of the black middle class, but also, for example, of the extension of retail distribution to black rural areas as well as metropolitan townships (du Toit and Neves 2007). However, it is a shrinking proportion of the working-age population, about 40 per cent of whom are unemployed on the 'broad definition' (Altman 2007). The very high rates of those 'on the margins of the labour force' who have never had a job, and the associated high rates of unemployment of young Africans, especially young women, and of long-term unemployment, that Standing *et al.* (1996) reported for the mid-1990s, persisted some ten years later. Nor have the extreme income inequality and poverty rates of the end of the apartheid period diminished; in fact, inequality has increased albeit 'deracialised' in the upper deciles of income distribution (Hoogeveen and Özler 2006) and the numbers in poverty have increased (May and Meth 2007).

There is much discussion of casualisation and informalisation in South Africa, and claims that it is increasing (e.g. Bodibe 2006: 56–63; von Holdt and Webster 2005) although precise data on trends are elusive. On a connected issue, that of the 'working poor', Altman (2007: 22) defined them as those with wages of less than R2,500 a month in 2004, close to the threshold for payment of income tax at that time, and concluded that they amounted to 65 per cent of those (officially) employed, including 'the majority of machine operators and craft related occupations' in manufacturing (ibid.: 25). Valodia *et al.* (2006) calculated the numbers of the working poor by different monthly wage cut-offs, but do not comment on the trend suggested by their data that both the proportions and numbers of low paid workers, on the various earnings benchmarks they use, declined quite steeply between 1999 and 2004. Of course, this decline may register more the movement of low-paid workers (in low-skill jobs) to forms of casual employment and 'survival' activity that are less easily captured by the government's Labour Force Survey (LFS), and/or into unemployment, as von Holdt and Webster (2005) maintain. LFS data give 'informal economy' employment as about 17 per cent of total recorded employment outside both commercial and 'subsistence' agriculture in 2004 (calculated from Table 2 in May and Meth 2007: 278), which can be compared with ILO data suggesting informal employment as 48 per cent of non-agricultural employment in North Africa, 72 per cent in sub-Saharan Africa as a whole, 51 per cent in Latin America and 65 per cent in Asia (Valodia *et al.* 2006: 111).

This contrast is associated with South Africa's unusually high levels of 'open' unemployment of around 40 per cent. Seekings and Nattrass (2005) suggest that South Africa's historical growth path precluded the scale of labour absorption in small-scale farming and informal sector activity that is evident in some other regions of the 'South'; the relatively small size of the 'informal economy' in South Africa is 'not well understood', according to May and Meth (2007: 277). It seems to me that, apart from the problem of under-counting, the following contribute to its explanation, certainly as far as more productive branches of 'informal economy' are concerned: under apartheid South Africa developed an unusually highly centralised and concentrated structure of capital, with relatively little outsourcing to small engineering and other workshops in, for example, components production, and little small-scale manufacturing more generally; the entry of non-whites was severely limited by apartheid regulations and practices concerning their residence and activities; and the lack of artisan training that, in many other countries, enabled skilled workers to set up as independent operators.

Nonetheless, the political settlement that marked the transition from apartheid to a democratic political regime had some distinctive features, including, first, a series of progressive labour laws although, as always, their implementation and effects often fall short (sometimes far short) of their provisions (Theron 2005; Benjamin 2006). Of particular resonance, symbolically at least, was the recent extension of minimum-wage legislation to agricultural and domestic workers. Second, COSATU (Congress of South African Trade Unions) – the principal trade union confederation and formal 'ally' of the ANC and SACP (Communist Party) – sits with government and employers in NEDLAC (National Economic Development and Labour Council) although its influence on macroeconomic policy appears extremely limited. Third, South Africa has a system of social grants (universal old-age pensions, disability grants) which were instituted under apartheid and have been extended since 1994 (including the introduction of means-tested child support grants), although in 2002 the government rejected proposals to institute a Basic Income Grant of R100 a month in favour of generating employment creation through public works (Standing *et al.* 1996: 469–79, provide a sceptical discussion of public works as a policy to expand employment; see also Samson 2007 on recent South African experience). Finally, Leibbrandt *et al.* (2006) suggest that improved access to publicly provided goods and services since 1994 has mitigated poverty defined on income criteria alone.

Do workers, and especially those living on the margins, constitute actually or potentially dangerous classes – and increasingly so as globalisation intensifies their crises of reproduction? The responses of capital and state are commonly some or other mixture of repression and amelioration. The latter includes the panaceas or 'win-win' scenarios intrinsic to 'development' discourse and policy (Bernstein 2007), whose current neoliberal prescriptions might be tempered – or even sacrificed in some circumstances – to protect the fundamental underlying commitment to global accumulation. On the other side of the equation of class forces, some of the issues concerning the political sociology of collective action by (fragmented) classes of labour – a methodological Pandora's box (or can of worms?) – are indicated by Harriss-White and Gooptu (2000) and Davis (2006), among those on whom I draw heavily. Their comments reflect the recognition by Mahmood Mamdani (1996: 219, 272) that 'translating social facts into political ones' – especially when 'the many ways in which power fragment(s) the circumstances and experiences of the oppressed' are so pervasive an aspect of the 'social facts' – is always contingent and unpredictable. This sets an explosive device under any simplistic notions of movement from the first to the second term of the Hegelian couplet class-in-itself (structural location, conditions of social existence, objective interests) and class-for-itself (consciousness of class interests, collective action to pursue them), in effect from the socio-economic to the political, above all when this movement is conceived as 'natural' and obstructed only by the machinations of capitalists and bourgeois (or petty bourgeois) politicians, by the practices of policemen and priests or imams. The issue is (re)stated thus by Barbara Harris-White and Nandini Gooptu (2000: 89): that 'struggle over class' precedes and is a condition of 'struggle between classes'. In their magisterial 'mapping (of) India's world of unorganised labour', they explore how 'struggles over class' by the working poor are inflected (and restricted) by gender, caste and other social differences/divisions noted above and that permeate the labour regimes of different branches of production and types of enterprises. They suggest that the overwhelming majority of Indian classes of labour 'is still engaged in the first struggle (over class) while capital ... is engaged in the second' (class offensives against labour).

In South Africa the understanding of 'resistance' revolves around longstanding debates about the nature and role of trade unions in the struggle against apartheid and since, the emergence and (varied) fortunes of 'new' social movements (e.g. Ballard *et al.* 2006), the relations between them, and the forms of organisation and political practice able to (re)construct a 'common identity in a now heavily segmented workforce' (Ceruti 2007a: 17) – and which, it can be argued, entails going beyond the inherited positions of industrial unionism (Webster 2005; Appolis 2007).

If responsibly assessing the potential, extent and character of 'mass resist-ance' as a force contesting, modifying and maybe even defeating the ravages of neoliberalism, how does 'mass resistance' connect with 'policy'? Intense debates in South Africa, as elsewhere, revolve around what kinds of reforms are simul-taneously desirable (in terms of growth and welfare outcomes) and possible (in terms of 'realism'), to move towards a better version of capitalism, and the scope, role and capacity of state action in advancing this project. This is what the term 'policy', in South Africa as elsewhere, typically signifies in the reflections of, and exchanges between, progressive economists (and others): the revival or reinvention of a social democratic programme that is able to effectively chal-lenge neoliberal policies in contemporary conditions of globalisation.

The only full study of the South African labour market since the end of apartheid to focus on 'the big issues' (Altman and Valodia 2006), conducted by three pro-gressive economists for the ILO at the invitation of the Presidential Labour Market Commission, sought to influence South Africa's first democratic government, hence had to accept its commitment to a capitalist, and indeed globally oriented, growth path ('realism'). As a consequence, I presume, its macroeconomic analysis and pre-scriptions had almost nothing to say about regulating, and indeed disciplining, capital, nor about 'incentivising' investment, although it took the opportunity to criticise conventional stabilisation and labour market policies. It focused rather on labour market governance, and proposed a system of 'regulated flexibility'

> in which usually, and increasingly, labour relations and labour market trans-actions take place with acceptable costs to those concerned and with accept-able allowance for economic equity and distributive justice, both in the 'open' labour market where transactions between workers and managers take place, and in workplaces where explicit and implicit bargaining deter-mine efficiency and distributional outcomes ... [for it] to function in increas-ingly flexible labour markets, in which the underlying tendencies are labour market insecurity (mass unemployment) and income insecurity (high rates of poverty, a residual system of social protection and severe inequality), representative security is more important than anything else.
>
> (Standing *et al.* 1996: 130–1, my emphasis)

In ILO parlance 'representative security' means 'an adequately strong "voice"' on the part of labour 'to ensure that distributive justice is pursued consistently', in this instance in the interests of a specific trade-off:

> Strong local unions offer the prospect of an 'historic compromise' between capital and labour – an agreement to democratise the workplace and local labour market in return for a sustained commitment to raise profitability and productivity within the firm and community, and an agreement to promote functional flexibility (job insecurity) in return for the prospect of improved employment growth.
>
> (Ibid.: 496)

That was their hope in a particular political moment. It has not been realised, and any progress towards fuller employment in 'decent work', to use another ILO concept, surely requires the political spaces for more progressive policy measure that only effective mass struggles can provide.

References

Altman, M. (2007) *Low Wage Work in South Africa*. Pretoria: Human Sciences Research Council.

Altman, M. and I. Valodia (eds) (2006) *Transformation* 60, special issue on the South African Labour Market.

Appolis, J. (2007) 'Can Unions Organise the Unemployed? GIWUSA Gives it a Bash', *South African Labour Bulletin* 30 (5), pp. 40–2.

Arrighi, G. and J.W. Moore (2001) 'Capitalist Development in World Historical Perspective', in R. Albritton, M. Itoh, R. Westra and A. Zuege (eds), *Phases of Capitalist Development. Booms, Crises and Globalizations*. London: Palgrave, pp. 56–75

Ballard, R., A. Habib and I. Valodia (eds) (2006) *Voices of Protest. Social Movements in Post-Apartheid South Africa*. Scotsville: University of KwaZulu-Natal Press.

Benjamin, P. (2006) 'Beyond "Lean" Social Democracy: Labour Law and the Challenge of Social Protection', in M. Altman and I. Valodia (eds), *Transformation* 60, special issue on the South African Labour Market.

Bernstein, H. (2007) 'The Antinomies of Development Studies', *Journal für Entwicklungspolitik* 23 (2), pp. 12–27.

Bodibe, O. (ed.) (2006) *The Extent and Effects of Casualisation in Southern Africa*. Johannesburg: NALEDI.

Breman, J. (1996) *Footloose Labour. Working in India's Informal Economy*. Cambridge: Cambridge University Press.

Breman, J. (2003) *The Labouring Poor in India. Patterns of Exploitation, Subordination, and Exclusion*. New Delhi: Oxford University Press.

Carr, M. and M.A. Chen (2002) *Globalization and the Informal Economy: How Global Trade and Investment Impact on the Working Poor*, Employment Sector 2002/1, Geneva: ILO.

Ceruti, C. (2007a) 'Class in Soweto', *South African Labour Bulletin* 31 (1), pp. 8–11.

Ceruti, C. (2007b) 'Divisions and Dependencies Among Working and Workless', *South African Labour Bulletin* 31 (2), pp. 22–4.

Colas, A. (2005) 'Neoliberalism, Globalisation and International Relations', in A. Saad-Filho and D. Johnston (eds), *Neoliberalism. A Critical Reader*. London: Pluto Press, pp. 70–9.

Davis, M. (2006) *Planet of Slums*. London: Verso.

Desai, M. (2002) *Marx's Revenge. The Resurgence of Capitalism and the Death of Statist Socialism*. London: Verso.

du Toit, A. and D. Neves (2007) 'In Search of South Africa's Second Economy. Chronic Poverty, Vulnerability and Adverse Incorporation in Mt Frere and Khayelitsha'. Paper for conference on 'Living on the Margins', Cape Town, 26–8 March 2007.

Freund, B. (2007) 'South Africa: the End of Apartheid and the Emergence of the "BEE elite"', *Review of African Political Economy* 114, pp. 661–78.

Habib, A. and V. Padayachee (2000) 'Economic Policy and Power Relations in South Africa's Transition to Democracy', *World Development* 28 (2), pp. 245–63.

Harriss-White, B. (2003) *India Working. Essays on Society and Economy.* Cambridge: Cambridge University Press.

Harriss-White, B. (2003/4) 'Inequality at Work in the Informal Economy: Key Issues and Illustrations', *International Labour Review* 142 (4), pp. 459–70.

Harriss-White, B. and N. Gooptu (2000) 'Mapping India's World of Unorganized Labour', in L. Panitch and C. Leys (eds), *The Socialist Register 2001.* London: Merlin Press, pp. 89–118.

Harvey, D. (2005) *A Brief History of Neoliberalism.* Oxford: Oxford University Press.

Hoogeveen, J.G. and B. Özler (2006) 'Poverty and Inequality in Post-apartheid South Africa', in H. Bhorat and R. Kanbur (eds), *Poverty and Policy in Post-apartheid South Africa.* Cape Town: HSRC Press, pp. 59–94.

ILO (2004) *Economic Security for a Better World.* Geneva: ILO.

Kitching, G. (2001) *Seeking Social Justice through Globalization.* University Park: Pennsylvania State University Press.

Leibbrandt, M., L. Poswell, P. Naidoo and M. Welch (2006) 'Measuring Recent Changes in South African Inequality and Poverty Using 1996 and 2001 Census Data', in H. Bhorat and R. Kanbur (eds), *Poverty and Policy in Post-apartheid South Africa.* Cape Town: HSRC Press, pp. 95–142.

Mamdani, M. (1996) *Citizen and Subject. Contemporary Africa and the Legacy of Late Colonialism.* Cape Town: David Philip.

Marx, K. (1976/1967) *Capital,* Vol. 1. Harmondsworth: Penguin.

May, J. and C. Meth (2007) 'Dualism or Underdevelopment in South Africa: What does a Quantitative Assessment of Poverty, Inequality and Employment Reveal?', *Development Southern Africa* 24 (2), pp. 271–87.

Meagher, K. (1995) 'Crisis, Informalization and the Urban Informal Sector in Sub-Saharan Africa', *Development and Change* 26, pp. 259–84.

Panitch, L. and C. Leys (2000) 'Preface', in L. Panitch and C. Leys (eds), *The Socialist Register 2001.* London: Merlin Press, pp. vii–xi.

Saad-Filho, A. and D. Johnston (eds) (2005) *Neoliberalism. A Critical Reader.* London: Pluto Press.

Samson, M. (2007) 'When Public Works Programmes Create "Second Economy" Conditions', in P. Bond (ed.), *Transcending Two Economies – Renewed Debates in South African Political Economy,* special issue of *Africanus* 37 (2), pp. 244–56.

Sandbrook, R., M. Edelman, P. Heller and J. Teichman (2007) *Social Democracy in the Global Periphery: Origins, Challenges, Prospects.* Cambridge: Cambridge University Press.

Seekings, J. and N. Nattrass (2005) *Class, Race and Inequality in South Africa.* New Haven: Yale University Press.

Sender, J. and J.R. Pincus (2006) 'Capitalism and Development', in D. Clark (ed.), *The Elgar Companion to Development Studies.* Cheltenham: Edward Elgar, pp. 45–9.

Silver, B.J. and G. Arrighi (2000) 'Workers North and South', in L. Panitch and C. Leys (eds), *The Socialist Register 2001.* London: Merlin Press, pp. 53–66.

Standing, G. (1999) *Global Labour Flexibility. Seeking Distributive Justice.* London: Macmillan.

Standing, G., J. Sender and J. Weeks (1996) *Restructuring the Labour Market. The South African Challenge.* Geneva: ILO.

Theron, J. (2005) 'Employment Is Not What It Used To Be: the Nature and Impact of Work Restructuring in South Africa', in E. Webster and K. von Holdt (eds), *Beyond the Apartheid Workplace.* Scotsville: University of KwaZulu-Natal Press, pp. 293–316.

Valodia, I., L. Lebani, C. Skinner and R. Devey (2006) 'Low-waged and Informal Employment in South Africa', *Transformation* 60, pp. 90–126.

Von Holdt, K. (2003) *Transition from Below. Forging Trade Unionism and Workplace Change in South Africa*. Scotsville: University of KwaZulu-Natal Press.

Von Holdt, K. and E. Webster (2005) 'Work, Restructuring and the Crisis of Social Reproduction: A Southern Perspective', in *Beyond the Apartheid Workplace*. Scotsville: University of KwaZulu-Natal Press.

Webster, E. (2005) 'Trade Unions and the Challenge of the Informalisation of Work', in *State of the Nation 2005*. Cape Town: HSRC Press, pp. 3–40.

14 Social class and politics in Brazil

From Cardoso to Lula

Armando Boito

This chapter examines recent political developments in Brazil and the neoliberal model at the root of these processes. It departs from most texts on this subject by focusing on the role of class interests and politics under neoliberalism. Unsurprisingly, the dominant theoretical currents generally overlook social class when analysing contemporary Brazilian politics, presenting the national political process as a dispute between political parties, fickle waves of opinion and political personalities (Sallum Jr. 2008). Those scholars who consider social classes do so in terms of a binary opposition between the bourgeoisie and the working class, each conceived of as a monolithic bloc (Arcary 2008). However, in order to have a realistic and suitably complex picture of national politics it is insufficient to consider these elementary class labels. It is also essential to examine the class segments and layers that subdivide these basic classes, and the intermediary classes within Brazilian society so that we can finally map the interests, ideologies, convergences and conflicts emerging out of this complexity to the current political process, its main actors and key events.

The neoliberal power bloc

A suitable way to conceptualize the relationship between the bourgeoisie and other social classes and state politics is through the notion of power blocs.This concept takes into consideration both the general interest of the bourgeois class in safeguarding capitalism, and the specific interests of its segments. Generally, this power bloc finds itself under the hegemony of one of its segments – the segment whose specific interests are prioritized by the policies of the state to the detriment of the interests of other segments (Poulantzas 1968: 199–273).

In order to examine the power bloc under neoliberalism it should, first, be understood that political hegemony has been wielded by large domestic and international capital. Since the 1990s, the social policies and the political economy of the Brazilian state have attended preferentially the interests of international investors and those of national banks and investment funds, subordinating to them the interests of the other segments of the bourgeoisie (Saes 2001). Second, the political economy and the power bloc have entered a new phase, starting somewhat awkwardly during Fernando Henrique Cardoso's second term

(1998–2002), and consolidating gradually during the subsequent Lula administration. Essentially, there is a new order in the power bloc that has allowed for a better integration of the large domestic industrial and agrarian bourgeoisie into the hegemonic politics of financial capital.[1] This integration essentially takes place through aggressive government policies promoting export growth in order to finance the country's balance of payments and supporting national and international capital through tax and interest rate policies. An important component of this new setup is the Lula administration's foreign policy, which has focused heavily on opening up external markets to Brazilian agricultural products.

In order to understand the complex relationships between neoliberal policies and the various segments of the bourgeoisie, and to assess the significance of the shift described above, it is necessary dissect these policies into its three component parts. This, in turn, will make it clear that the financial bourgeoisie is the hegemonic segment of the power bloc because only this segment is vested in all aspects of neoliberal policy-making (Boito 2002).

The first aspect of neoliberalism that attends to the combined interests of the domestic bourgeoisie and imperialism is the deregulation of the labour market, leading to real wage cuts and the reduction or suppression of social rights. All capitalist enterprises, large or small, commercial, industrial or agricultural, national or foreign, benefit to some degree, directly or indirectly, from this cost reduction. There has been no significant shift with respect to this element of neoliberalism. The Lula administration has either retained or intensified the policies inherited from Cardoso: the lack of wage indexation; the cuts in education and health funding through cracks in the legislation that helped to bypass the constitutional requirement of a certain minimum percentage expenditure in these areas; and the policy of privatizing healthcare and education. In addition to these conservative policies, the Lula administration introduced new ones, including a reform of public pensions depriving the public-sector workers of some of their rights and supporting the growth of the pension funds, and reforms of labour law and trade union legislation reinforcing state control of the unions while, simultaneously, eliminating workers' rights. These policies have played a fundamental role in securing the support of all relevant segments of the Brazilian bourgeoisie to the neoliberal programme.

The second key aspect of the neoliberal model, privatization, is not as broadly supported. It has marginalized small and medium-sized capital in order to privilege domestic monopolies and imperialism (Saes 2001). During the privatization auctions under the Collor, Itamar and Cardoso administrations, it was mainly large Brazilian corporations in banking, industry and construction that tended to take over the large state-owned enterprises (SOEs). Once the energy sector had been privatized, foreign capital also began to invest significantly in the purchase of state assets, a process that peaked with the privatization of telecoms, when Portuguese and Spanish capital played a prominent role. The norms of the privatization process barred small investors from the auctions. During the Lula administration, auctions of SOEs lost importance, although there are still several large firms in the hands of the state.

The third aspect is even more exclusionary, marginalizing not only small and medium-sized capital but also most large capitals: the policies of free trade and deregulated markets. These policies did away with trade protection and with protectionist exchange-rate policies which were widely used during the developmentalist period (Diniz and Boschi 2008). These policy reforms generated heated discussions within the Brazilian bourgeoisie during the 1990s, because the reforms tend to privilege the banking segment of monopolistic capital and imperialist capital to the detriment of the domestic industrial bourgeoisie.

The liberalization policies associated with high interest rates and monetary stability reaches out to foreign investors and large domestic banks. A selected group of 25 Brazilian banks today controls 81 per cent of national banking activity. Throughout the Cardoso and Lula administrations, profitability in the banking sector has equalled or surpassed that of the industrial sector (Boito 2006). In this context, monetary stability is imperative to protect capital flows from uncertainties and losses due to sudden or dramatic shifts in the exchange rate and in relative prices. Likewise, high interest rates benefit the banking industry in two ways. First, being more liquid than the productive sector, it holds most of the public debt. Second, the central bank's high interest rate policy favours banking because it supports their freedom to set interest rates across the economy.

The manufacturing sector, including large and powerful industrial groups based in São Paulo, was generally adversely affected by these policies. High interest rates increased production costs, and the impact of trade liberalization, although somewhat contradictory, was mostly to erode the market share of local producers. During the 1990s, the Federação das Indústrias do Estado de São Paulo (Federation of Industries of the State of São Paulo, FIESP) waged several campaigns against these policies, which it presented as an 'exaggeration of neoliberal governance'. In May 1996, a year marked by industry activism against trade liberalization and high interest rates, FIESP and the Confederação Nacional da Indústria (National Confederation of Industry, CNI) organized a large national demonstration in Brasília, and the FIESP board unanimously approved a resolution in support of a workers' general strike against unemployment led by Central Única dos Trabalhadores (Trade Unions' Congress, CUT) and Força Sindical (Trade Union Power, FS), in June (Boito 1999: 62–5). This surprising position by the largest corporate entity of industrial capital is suggestive of the highly complex and contradictory relationship between the industrial bourgeoisie and neoliberal policies in Brazil. In general, however, industrial capital has sought to transfer the costs of the neoliberal policies imposed by the banks and impearialism to the popular classes. During Cardoso's two terms in office, FIESP often requested further privatization and cuts in social and labour rights as a sort of 'compensation' for interest rate hikes and growing external competition (Boito 1999: 66–7).

A new articulation of the power bloc

The Lula administration shifted the government's approach on the third element of neoliberal politics, in contrast with Cardoso's second term, in order to expand the bourgeois base of support to neoliberalism without revoking the hegemony of financial capital. On the one hand, the administration maintained financial capital control of economic policy but, on the other hand, it attempted to improve the space of domestic capital within the neoliberal model.

Economic policy during Cardoso's first term was based on trade and market liberalization combined with a stable and overvalued exchange rate, which was of interest to financial capital. The weaknesses of these policies were revealed during the 1994–5 Mexican crisis and the Brazilian exchange rate crisis of 1999. The ensuing pressure by the industrial bourgeoisie led the Cardoso administration to carve out a new combination of policies. Prior to the sharp devaluation of Brazilian real, the Cardoso administration prolonged the life of its cheap dollar policies for three months, in order to give speculative capital time to purchase relatively low-priced foreign currency and exit the country without great losses. It was only after US$30–40 billion had safely left that Gustavo Franco was removed from the presidency of the central bank, and the real was allowed to crash. The devaluation of the currenty offered the first singificant incentive for export growth in many years. Far from being incompatible with the hegemony of financial capital, this policy represented, under the new post-crisis circumstances, a demand for the reproduction of the power of imperialism and national finance. It sought to replace the dollar reserves without which financial capital would be threatened.

At this point, the Brazilian economy started on a race to the dollar. Under the neoliberal model, these dollars could be obtained only through export growth, given the reduction of foreign capital inflows after 2000, and the country's large external debt. The international commodity boom helped the Lula administration to implement this new policy. The pursuit of dollars through exports has revived what the *latifundistas* of the Old (pre-1930) Republic called 'Brazil's agricultural vocation'. The government has promoted export agribusiness heavily, and focused on exports of manufactures with low technological content. This policy strategy has confirmed the view of the critics of the neoliberal political economy, which argued that neoliberalism engendered deindustrialization in Latin America, leading to the reduction of the share of manufactures in GDP and changing the profile of industry, with the decline of the relatively sophisticated sectors and the corresponding rise of sectors processing raw materials (mining, paper, food products and so on).[2] As a result of this regressive specialization, many industrial sectors had their production chains disrupted by import liberalization, and now suffer trade deficits.

Since obtaining dollars had become the government's policy priority, it was necessary to prioritize export monoculture. The Cardoso administration initiated international contacts with Southern countries, in order to build up pressure on the imperialist nations to lower their agricultural subsidies, prohibitive tariffs and other obstacles to agricultural imports from peripheral states. In the same fashion, Lula articulated the Group of 22 (G-22), an alliance of grain-exporting countries, to pursue the same goals. The impact of privileging agricultural exports, just as during the Cardoso administration, is compounded by the abandonment of the promotion of high-technology industries, control of foreign investment, and other policies that could free the Brazilian economy from impe-rialism. Both in the World Trade Organization (WTO) and in Mercosur negotia-tions with the European Union, the Lula administration systematically adopted a policy of offering concessions to foreign investors, expanding their presence in the Brazilian market, in order to secure agricultural export growth. Lula accepts the international division of labour but wants every opportunity to obtain as much as possible as an exporter of raw materials and the low-technology manu-factured goods that this trade structure reserves for Brazil.

These policies can create trade conflicts with rival sectors in the imperialist countries, and it requires financial capital to make concessions to the internal bourgeoisie. Production for export requires, among other things, complementary investment, a compatible exchange rate, and export loans by the Banco Nacional de Desenvolvimento Econômico e Social (National Bank of Economic and Social Development, BNDES). However, as long as the traditional neoliberal collection of policies persists – high interest rates, bank autonomy to set the interest rates charged from borrowers, an inflated primary fiscal surplus to remu-nerate foreign and domestic holders of Treasury bills, and free capital flows, any incentive for the bourgeoisie to produce and export will be subordinated to the pursuit of dollars and higher fiscal surpluses.

Thus, we have in Brazil a politically hegemonic sector including large domestic and foreign financial capital, and a politically subordinated sector made up of the industrial bourgeoisie focusing on exports. The Brazilian state, repre-senting imperialism and finance, has redirected industrial production and placed renewed importance on agricultural exports, which consolidated further the power bloc around the neoliberal model. The political consequence of this arrangement has been to boost the hegemonic position of financial capital within the power bloc, and subordinating export-led industrial and agricultural bourgeoisie.[3]

The working classes and the new ideological phase of neoliberalism

Not all workers maintain the same relationship with state policies and the ruling class. The peasantry, the middle class, the workers, and the various sectors within these groups have specific relations with neoliberalism. A large part of the popular classes resists neoliberalism, but some segments may ally themselves with bourgeois segments in the power bloc, and others may be part of a support class motivated by complex ideological illusions which help to sustain neoliberal politics even though they are injured by it.[4] The ensuing relationships between the power bloc and the (heterogeneous) popular classes constitute a complex class structure that should be examined further for a better understanding of neo-liberal politics in Brazil.

Despite its multifaceted but generally anti-popular nature, neoliberalism has had a significant ideological impact on various segments of the working classes.

Brazilian critical thinking has resisted examining this hypothesis seriously, although widespread disappointment with Lula's conservatism has eroded this resistance (Petras 1996). The ideological impact of neoliberalism has enabled the reforms to obtain a diffuse support among the working classes, as was clearly demonstrated by the pensions reforms under both Cardoso and Lula. It seems that neoliberalism has secured a new ideological hegemony in Brazil. When speaking of the power bloc, 'hegemony' applies to the control of the political economy by financial capital. When speaking of working classes, the term refers to the ideological dominance of a given class segment insofar as this dominance extends to form a 'majority consensus' in society as a whole.[5] The popular impact of neoliberalism in Brazil does not mean that the nation has developed a 'popular enthusiasm for the market'. In fact, there is a widespread unease about the country's economic and social situation. However, the neoliberal economic model is not generally identified by the popular classes as the main cause of their current economic difficulties. Many workers see no alternative to this model, and accept it passively; others believe that the situation may improve if further reforms can be implemented – yet another pension-fund reform to do away with the remaining 'privileges' of small groups of workers, additional 'flexibility' in the labour laws in order to create more jobs, and so on.

An important source of support for neoliberalism outside the bourgeoisie is the upper middle-class, which itself is an ally of the bourgeoisie and imperialism. Social welfare, especially in its more advanced forms, is of no concern to them. More egalitarian and generalized social rights and public services represent a loss of income to them, due to the required taxation, and therefore a loss of relative social and economic status. Even though Brazil was never a welfare state, the upper middle-class has found the neoliberal critique of social rights attractive (Boito 2003).

Neoliberalism has also neutralized or attracted the working class and the popular sectors, although it does not correspond to their interests. The neoliberal project offers no gains for the working classes, and their support may be due to ideological illusions, political neutralization, or negative adherence. Thus, an unstable regressive hegemony can become consolidated because multiple sectors converge around it, despite their heterogeneity, in order to sustain neoliberalism. Lula's administration has also brought about important changes in the relations between the working classes and the state, which has also boosted support for neoliberalism.

The labour elite and the new corporatism

Many workers enjoying relatively high wages and with significant capacity for collective action, such as those employed in automobile assembly and the oil industry, have been neutralized by neoliberalism. They are represented mainly by the Articulação Sindical (Trade Union Alliance, AS), which is the hegemonic current within CUT, and linked to the current controlling Lula's Workers' Party (PT). At least 100 AS members hold top-level positions in the federal administration, including several positions in Lula's cabinet. These top-ranking union members in the administration had a significant ideological and political impact on workers.

These 'new unionists' imagine themselves to be part of the state power structure, and expect that Lula, as the 'unionist president', will manage a neoliberal model with rapid economic growth and job creation, rather than expecting a rupture with the neoliberal capitalist model. These workers have accepted some neoliberal privatizations, and believe that their powers of organization can be used to achieve improved conditions for themselves. This strategy was originally developed during the Collor and Cardoso administrations, and it is essential in order to understand the 'turn' of the PT under Lula.

In 1990, the AS started to shift its strategy in light of the changes brought about by Fernando Collor's victory in the presidential elections and the subsequent recession, and the AS gradually returned to the its early corporatist position. Since then, the AS has fought for collective labour contracts going against established workers' rights. The leadership of the group does not care much about the protective measures already found in labour law, and they court the privatization of health and pension plans. The AS has also distanced itself from public services, in order to seek narrow contracts offering private health insurance to their own members. The AS is also attempting to manage private pension funds. This trade union elite has abandoned its welfare state programme of the 1980s, and insulated itself in a social micro-corporatism, defending only industries and sectors employing workers directly connected with its base. Mass strikes have been abandoned. In other words, the union elite has been nurturing the notion that it can save itself by adapting basic elements of the neoliberal model to its narrow interests, and doing away with social and labour rights – that is, dispensing with the state's regulatory role.

The AS has sought to support the administration's 'liberal development' side, represented by the president's chief of staff Dilma Roussef, and finance minister Guido Mantega. In reality, their policies are closely coordinated with those of the large domestic industrial and agrarian bourgeoisie, in a of liberal development project that departs from the undiluted neoliberalism in charge at the central bank and the lower echelons of the ministry of finance.

Conservative populism

It was shown above that neoliberal economic policies prioritize the banking segment of the domestic bourgeoisie and the financial segment of imperialist capital. These retrograde sections of the ruling classes have managed to build a political support class among impoverished and disorganized segments of the working classes, even though these segments are impoverished partly because of the neoliberal model. This paradoxical alliance between the richest and the poorest brings together the two extremes of Brazilian society. I say 'support class' rather than 'allied class' because this group's support for the power bloc is inorganic and diffuse, and it is *fundamentally ideological* – in other words, it lacks organizational structure, a clear political platform, and it is offered without the needs of these supporters being directly met by the state. This complex situation requires careful examination.

Obviously, not all impoverished workers are included into this support class. An important part of this segment is organized, to a greater or lesser degree, against neoliberalism. For example, the Movimento dos Trabalhadores Rurais Sem-Terra (Landless Peasants' Movement, MST), the Movimento dos Trabalhadores Sem-Teto (Homeless Workers' Movement, MTST), and other social movements that can be classified as 'movements of urgency', involving workers who, because of the loss of land, jobs or housing, have had their immediate physical well-being threatened by neoliberalism.[6] These organizations have been increasingly organizing squats and land occupations around the country, alarming large landowners, the bourgeoisie and the press and, thus, pressuring the Lula administration just as they did during Cardoso's years. The Lula administration has remained committed to a self-inflicted primary fiscal surplus target of 4.25 per cent of GDP, which forced it to reduce significantly the appropriations for land reform. Lula has attempted to defuse the situation through the co-option of members of the land reform movement, and through a well-honed discourse about the need to increase technical assistance to settled peasants, in order to split the movement between those who have been settled and those who are still struggling for land.

The segment of the impoverished working classes that act as a support class for the financial bourgeoisie is not, itself, reactionary. It is moved by a legitimate popular revolt against the exclusionary nature of Brazilian capitalism, although this revolt lacks a clear political direction. The complexity of the situation lies precisely in the fact that a legitimate popular revolt has been co-opted by imperialism and the financial bourgeoisie, and redirected towards a reactionary political goal. Resentment at social inequality has been converted into diffuse support for the neoliberal project of implementing a 'minimal state'. In the neoliberal discourse, the only valid target is the state and its intervention in the economy, and public officials are presented as the direct beneficiaries of intervention and, therefore, rightful targets for public anger. Evidently, the real political goal is to promote, through cuts in entitlements and public spending, a shift in fiscal policy benefitting financial capital and opening up new areas for accumulation. It is in order to promote these objectives that politicians linked to financial capital appeal to the impoverished and politically unorganized, by glossing over the neoliberal adjustment policies with a misleading discourse against 'privileges', and arguing that social justice can be achieved through the compensatory policies developed by the World Bank. President Fernando Collor de Melo inaugurated this approach in 1989, when he appealed to the 'shirtless' to rise against 'maharajah' public servants. Cardoso employed the same strategy when he criticized the privileges of civil servants, while applying narrowly focused compensatory social policies.

This new populism, like any populism, is an appeal by the political leadership – particularly from within the state – to the politically unorganized masses, who respond to it because they have entrusted their hopes to the protective action of the state rather than their own political organization. However, unlike the reformist populism of the period pre-1964, this new populism is regressive because it directly increases social inequality and reinforces the nation's economic dependence. Getúlio Vargas, João Goulart, Leonel Brizola, and other reformist populists located their enemies among the 'powerful', the 'sharks', 'foreign capital', 'the oligarchies' and 'the United States', and sought by this to convert the forces associated with imperialism and the bourgeoisie connected with it to support Brazil's industrialization and to expand labour rights. In contrast, the regressive populism of the neoliberal state suggests doing away with the corruption and cronyism of the bureaucratic elite and of members of Congress, in effect accusing one of the segments of the working class – the civil servants – with having the sole objective of promoting domestic and international capital. This populism does not contradict imperialism; quite the contrary, it is guided by the agents of international financial capital.

The Lula administration diverges from this regressive populism only in terms of degree. Given his working-class origins, the president has been able to implement this new populism more effectively than was possible previously, while maintaining the generalized political sympathies of the unorganized sectors of the population. The administration has increased the funds directed to focused and compensatory social programmes, the ephemeral assistance that neoliberalism provides to workers, in contrast with the social rights of the welfare state. The funds available for the social programmes of the Lula administration, especially Bolsa Família (Family Basket), were redirected from the health and education budgets, in order to be compatible with the aggressive fiscal surplus targets set by the Ministry of Finance.[7] Resources earmarked to secure workers' social rights were diverted in order to promote policies made to look like personal gifts from the president. It is ironic to see Lula, PT and CUT as deteriorated versions of Vargas.

A brief overview of Brazil's political history throughout the twentieth century will illustrate the nature of the current conservative (neo)populism. Brazilian social policy, since its origins in the 1930s, has always marginalized large sectors of the working class. It did not, for example, include rural labourers in the original package of social rights and, until the 1960s, Brazil was a country with a majority rural population. In urban areas, rights were linked to formal sector jobs, excluding both the unemployed and informal sector workers, and these rights were ranked and allocated according to the professional status of each group of workers, so that pensions, healthcare and wage levels depended on whether one was a manufacturing or retail sector worker, employed in the public or the private sector, and so on. This restricted and stratified social citizenship was linked at several levels to the clientelism of the Brazilian state. While it is true that in all capitalist social formations the state bureaucracy can serve as a shelter for members of the ruling class, or as a platform for trading political support, in Brazil, with its peripheral capitalism and unfinished bourgeois revolution, these parasitic features of the state are especially pronounced.

The practice of public examinations for careers in the civil service remains incomplete in Brazil. Thus, during the populist period, public-sector jobs could be offered to members of landowning families, especially in the northeast, as one of the ways to secure their political support. During the military dictatorship (1964–85), bourgeois and middle-class sectors enriched themselves with the distribution of posts in state-owned enterprises, federal universities, public administration, and so on. This practice has evolved after the democratic transition, and it now includes most political parties. The working masses did not, and still do not, participate in this distribution of favours. Unsurprisingly, the clientelist state has become the target of public dissatisfaction and, throughout Republican history, there has been an instinctive and diffuse resentment against restricted and stratified citizenship in Brazil. It was this resentment that provided the basis of support for the neoliberal offensive. In other words, neoliberalism co-opted public feelings of injustice, and redirected them towards the goal of a minimalist state.

In theory, the left could have harnessed these diffuse feelings of resentment against the limited and stratified character of social rights in the country, and against the state's clientelism. This could have been done in a progressive manner, aiming for the extension and rebalancing of citizenship, and the democratization of the state, rather than the destruction of the public services. The revolutionary left could have seen this task as a key link between reform and revolution. However, a large part of the left has remained ideologically dependent on populism and developmentalism. Several left organizations remain committed to this model, and some – including PT – are materially dependent on public resources coming from the official trade unions, ministries and cronyist appointments for government posts for their leaders and activists. In other words, some left organizations have benefited from the Brazilian state, which is currently the target of significant public resentment.

The difficulties of the new phase of neoliberal hegemony

The three new elements of the new phase of neoliberal hegemony in Brazil are the new position of the large national bourgeosie in the power bloc, the co-optation of the unionist elite, and the new and conservative populism. In this arrangement, the large bourgeoisie wins.[8]

The new phase of Brazilian neoliberalism has had important consequences for the working classes. The growth of Brazilian capitalism should be increasingly independent of the domestic market. However, what little has been gained economically under Lula has been concentrated on the export sector, while production for domestic consumption has remained relatively stagnant, with adverse consequences for the urban and rural sector workers. This has also had an adverse impact on wages, as these are becoming increasingly important for the competitiveness of Brazilian exports. It also affects negatively the rural workers, as the government cannot advance with the land reform without increasing tensions with the large landowners on whom it depends to obtain access to foreign markets.

Notes

1 The concept of an internal bourgeoisie was developed by Poulantzas (1976) to indicate the segment of the bourgeoisie that holds an intermediary position between the comprador bourgeoisie that is merely an extension of imperialist interests in colonial and dependent countries and the national bourgeoisie which, in some twentieth-century national liberation movements, positioned itself in opposition to imperialism.

2 In his examination of the period 1992–2000, Ricardo Carneiro (2002: 231) states that:

> What can be concluded from the data set is that the structure of Brazilian foreign trade faithfully reflected changes in the structure of production, with exports concentrated in the sectors with lower technological content and the opposite occurring with imports.

3 The conflict between the government and FIESP seems to have abated, partly because the export sectors gained strength in the late 1990s (Bianchi 2004). However, the tensions were not over. In June 2004, when exceptionally rapid growth rates were being celebrated by the administration and the mainstream press, the industrialist Ivoncy Ioschpe, president of the Instituto de Estudos para o Desenvolvimento Industrial (Institute for the Study of Industrial Development, IEDI), criticized government policy in an interview:

> IEDI always said that it was necessary to put two variables into place: the exchange rate and the interest rate. With the dollar nearing R$3.10, the exchange rate is in the correct spot. Interest rates, however, remain totally out of place ... I honestly thought that [Lula] would have been able to implement a centre-left policy and that this would benefit the country. Unfortunately, Lula's actions have been right-wing. This is the most conservative administration since democratization [in 1985].
>
> (*Isto É*, 30 June 2004)

4 The concept of the support class was developed by Poulantzas (1968: 261–6).

5 This is approximately the way in which Antonio Gramsci used the concept of hegemony, to designate the moral and intellectual direction of society by a given historical bloc. However, in the case of neoliberalism, ideological hegemony does not fit neatly with Gramsci's characterization.

6 The periodical *Crítica Marxista* has published illuminating interviews with the leaders of these social movements, for example, the interviews by Hector Benoit with Luís Gonzaga da Silva, the leader of the Movement of Centre Zone Residents (Silva 2000) and with the leadership of the MTST (Benoit 2002). The notion of 'movements of urgency' was coined by René Mouriaux (2002).

7 Pochmann (2005) shows that social expenditures during Lula's first two years in office increased only 1 per cent relative to the last two years of the Cardoso administration, contradicting official reports. Pochmann shows that social spending remained stable despite the increased costs of the compensatory Family Basket programme, precisely because money was redirected from health and education.

8 Between 1989 and 1999, the number of state-owned enterprises among the 40 largest companies in Brazil fell from 14 to seven (Diniz and Boschi 2004: 69).

References

Arcary, V. (2008) 'Peculiaridades da história política do Brasil contemporâneo: notas para um balanço do ciclo de supremacia da CUT e do PT'. *Lutas Sociais* (PUCSP) 19/20: 150–62.

Benoit, H. (2002) 'O assentamento Anita Garibaldi: entrevista com lideranças do Movimento dos Trabalhadores Sem-Teto (MTST)'. *Crítica Marxista* 14: 134–50.

Bianchi, A. (2004) 'O ministério dos industriais: a Federação das Indústrias do Estado de São Paulo na crise das décadas de 1980 e 1990'. PhD diss., University of Campinas.

Boito, A. (1999) *Política neoliberal e sindicalismo no Brasil.* São Paulo: Editora Xamã.

Boito, A. (2002) 'Neoliberalismo e relações de classe no Brasil'. *Idéias* 9 (1): 13–48.

Boito, A. (2003) 'A hegemonia neoliberal no Governo Lula'. *Crítica Marxista* 17: 10–36.

Boito, A. (2006) 'A burguesia no Governo Lula'. *Crítica Marxista* 21: 52–77.

Carneiro, R. (2002) *Desenvolvimento em crise: A economia brasileira no último quarto do século XX.* São Paulo: Editora UNESP.

Diniz, E. and Boschi, R. (2004) *Empresários, interesses e mercado.* Belo Horizonte: Editora da UFMG.

Diniz, E. and Boschi, R. (2008) *A difícil rota do desenvolvimento: empresários e agendas pos-neoliberal.* Belo Horizonte: Editora UFMG.

Mouriaux, R. (2002) 'A esquerda e a reanimação das lutas sociais na Europa'. *Crítica Marxista* 14: 150–71.

Petras, J. (1996) *Ensaios contra a ordem.* São Paulo: Scritta.

Pochmann, M. (2005) 'Gasto social e distribuição de renda no Brasil'. *Jornal da Unicamp,* 22 May.

Poulantzas, N. (1968) *Pouvoir politique et classes sociales.* Paris: François Maspero.

Poulantzas, N. (1976) *La crise des dictatures.* Paris: Seuil.

Saes, D. (2001) *República do capital – capitalismo e processo político no Brasil.* São Paulo: Editora Boitempo.

Sallum Jr., B. (2008) 'La especificidad del gobierno de Lula. Hegemonía liberal, desarrollismo y populismo'. *Nueva Sociedad* 217: 155–71.

Silva, L.G. (2000) 'A luta pela moradia popular'. *Crítica Marxista* 10: 157–73.

15 Is there an acceptable future for workers in capitalism?

The case of Latin America

Alejandro Valle Baeza[1]

In 2003 a Latin launderess in New York worked more than 80 hours per week, earned US$3 per hour, far less than the legal minimum, received no payment for extra hours, had no vacations and no healthcare (González 2003). The migrant population accepts these working conditions because their situation would be even worse in their own countries. Haiti was once self-reliant in rice, a fundamental component of the national diet, but now a large share of the rice consumed in the country needs to be imported. This is one of the consequences of the implementation of neoliberal policies in the country. Rice imports in Haiti resulted in the destruction of local production capacity and generated none of the promised jobs in alternative industries. For some time now, Haiti has been undergoing an economic and social crisis, which is worsened by the rise in the cost of raw materials and food staples:

> The Haitian crisis is so extreme it forces people to eat (non-food) mud cookies (called 'pica') to relieve hunger. It's a desperate Haitian remedy made from dried yellow dirt from the country's central plateau for those who can afford it. It's not free. In Cite Soleil's crowded slums, people use a combination of dirt, salt and vegetable shortening for a typical meal when it's all they can afford.
>
> (Lendman 2008)

The large rises in food prices in the early 2000s have contributed to the deterioration of working conditions in large areas of the world. A humanitarian organisation in Argentina reported that each day children die of hunger in a country whose per capita income once ranked above those of several developed countries, and that had a positive food trade balance exceeding 10 per cent of GDP in 2004–5.[2] In Argentina and Haiti, as in many countries, capitalism is not providing enough jobs for the vast majority of the population to lead a dignified life.

This chapter examines the question: is there an acceptable future for workers in today's capitalism? The answer seems to be *no*, especially in the 'developing' countries (as the official agencies often call them). The answer to this question relates to the following facts:

- Around the world, living conditions were already bad for a large number of workers, and they were deteriorating further even before the start of the crisis in 2007. This is because capitalism in the last 30 years, i.e. neoliberalism, has successfully managed to increase the exploitation of the workers. This has resulted in the absolute impoverishment of a large part of the population, which has been unable to achieve the requirements for decent conditions of reproduction.
- In the underdeveloped countries, especially in Latin America, these shortcomings of capitalism predate neoliberalism. So, even if neoliberalism was to disappear, the problems of many workers would not necessarily be resolved by capitalism.
- Neoliberalism has intensified the destruction of the environment, directly threatening life on the planet.

Everything points to the conclusion that capitalism is exhausted, and human beings should overcome this form of social organisation in order to avoid going backwards. Socialism or barbarism is the dilemma we will have to face in the not-too-distant future.

The situation of labour in the world

Four out of ten workers in the world are poor,[3] half are own-account workers or family workers classified by the International Labour Organisation (ILO) as being in vulnerable employment. The latter category requires some explanation.

The vulnerable employment indicator is the sum of own-account and family workers as a share of total employment. These workers are less likely to have formal work arrangements. If this ratio is sizeable, it may suggest widespread poverty (ILO 2008a: 11, n.5). This data suggests that capitalism keeps nearly half of the workers in the world in a state of poverty and leaves 40 per cent out of its influence, after several centuries of reigning all over the planet. Poverty among workers is not only found in countries such as Haiti, but everywhere in the world where hunger prevails.

On 10 December 2008, the FAO warned that:

Table 15.1 Selected labour market indicators (% of labourforce)

Region	Unemployment	Youth unemployment	Vulnerable employment	Working poor
World	6.0	12.3	49.9	43.5
Latin America and the Caribbean	8.5	17.2	33.2	25.4
Sub-Saharan Africa	8.3	13.7	72.9	85.4
Developed countries	6.4	13.2	9.2	0.8

Source: author's elaboration from ILO (2008).

Another 40 million people have been pushed into hunger this year primarily due to higher food prices.... This brings the overall number of undernourished people in the world to 963 million, compared to 923 million in 2007 and the ongoing financial and economic crisis could tip even more people into hunger and poverty.

(FAO 2008b)

Nearly one-sixth of the world's population suffer from hunger, even though most of them are employed.

There are huge differences between regions. In sub-Saharan Africa nearly nine in ten workers are working poor, while in the so-called developed world, the ratio is less than one in ten. Nevertheless, the situation of the workers in rich countries is not as good as the ILO suggests:

In advanced industrial countries, near-full employment prevailed until the mid-1970s when the first 'oil shock' induced an employment problem. The problem still persists today despite some improvements in the 1990s. The unemployment rate exceeds 5 per cent in 14 of 23 advanced industrial countries. Over 15 per cent of jobs are part-time in 13 countries, and part time employment appears to have substituted for unemployment to a significant extent. In the 1990s, most countries sought to address the employment problem essentially through policies designed to increase labour market flexibility. But these policies had very limited success in reducing unemployment and instead led to growth of low-paid part-time and temporary jobs and even to two-tier labour markets. This is surprising considering that the 1990s was actually a period of rapid economic growth.

(ILO 2008b: 2)

As early as in the mid-1990s it was widely accepted that jobs had tended to become more precarious:

Part-time and half-time employment has increased from 23% in 1933 to 24% in 1995 in the United Kingdom. In the United States and in Japan, the percentage is about 20%. Half or maybe more of the new jobs created in the eighties in France, Germany, Netherlands, Luxembourg and Spain were temporary hiring. Self-employment has also increased: in Portugal, for instance, it went from 12% of the total work force in 1979, to 17% in 1989.

(OECD 1996: 192)

In 2003 a recovery in some aspects of labour market was publicised: the improvement in the employment level in some countries such as Ireland and Spain, the decline in the unemployment rate that, according to orthodox theory, does not result in accelerated inflation (NAIRU) in most of the OECD, and so on. However, falling unemployment in Spain and Ireland had only reduced it to levels similar to those prevailing during the crisis of the 1930s, in both cases, above 20 per cent. Although the OECD considered that progress had been achieved, it also recognised that there were problems in the quality of jobs because the intensity of labour and worker insecurity had increased. How could labour in the world come to be in this situation?

The United States is a good example of labour precarisation in rich countries. The term 'walmartisation' was coined there to refer to labour hired under low wages, poor benefits, and no right to form trade unions.[4]

Figure 15.1 shows how average wages in the United States have been brought to a standstill since 1964. Productivity increased significantly since then, but inequality among employees has increased, resulting in the impoverishment of many working families in the most advanced capitalist country in the world.

Income inequality in the United States in 2000 was as high as in the 1920s, with households in the highest 5 per cent income bracket earning six times more than those in the lowest 20 per cent bracket. In 1970, the ratio was only four times. Research by Paul Krugman (1992)[5] suggests that 70 per cent of the total income increase in the 1980s ended up in the hands of the richest 1 per cent of households. As to the wealth in the United States, in 1995, the top 1 per cent owned 42.2 per cent of the shares, 55.7 per cent of the bonds, 44.2 per cent of the trust funds, 71.4 per cent of all non-corporate companies and 36.9 per cent of non-housing real estate. This unevenness has grown since then (Yates 2004).

One of the main priorities for neoliberalism was to lift the rate of return of capital (the ratio between earnings and total capital), which had declined since the end of the Second World War. For example, in the 1950s the average rate of return in the United States was around 20 per cent, and in the early 1980s it was only 6 per cent. In order to raise the rate of return, neoliberal governments imposed severe wage contraction and cuts in government spending, especially social spending. Before the 1980s it was not easy to reduce wages in the United States, especially nominal wages, but it has become much easier to do this since then. In 1982, in US

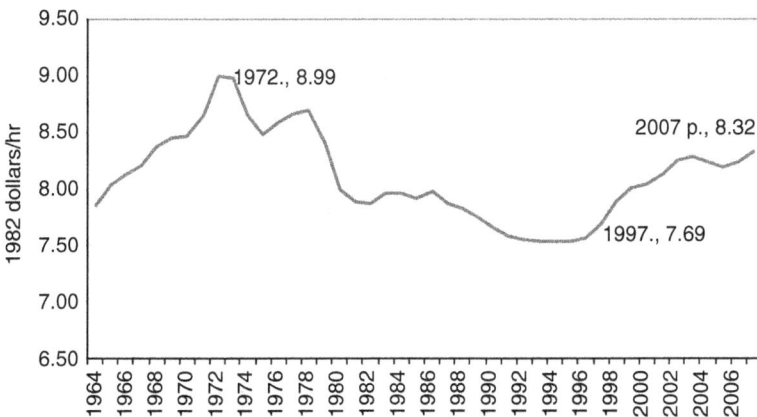

Figure 15.1 Average hourly earnings in the United States (total private) (source: author's elaboration based on the *Economic Report of the President* 2008).

industry as a whole, 36 per cent of the workers agreed to have their wages fixed or reduced during their contracts; this included 43 per cent of manufacturing sector workers and 23 per cent in non-manufacturing industry. In 1987, after a five-year period of growth, 15 per cent of the workers had their contracts renovated without a wage rise (Economic Report of the President 1988: 79). Two emblematic industrial conflicts help to explain why real wages could be cut: the air traffic controllers' strike in the United States in 1981, and the coal miners' strike in Great Britain in 1984–5. The air traffic controllers' strike ended in August 1981 when 11,000 union members were fired and their leaders were imprisoned. The coal miners' strike was defeated, and the entire industry was rapidly closed down with the loss of almost every single coal-mining job in the country. Real wage cuts and higher capitalist earnings have been two of the most remarkable achievements of neoliberalism around the world, as Duménil and Lévy (2004) have conclusively shown.

Neoliberalism in Latin America

Between 1950 and 1980 the labour force grew very rapidly in Latin America. This has often been compared to its growth rate in United States during the period 1870–1910,[6] as shown in Figure 15.2.

It is noticeable that population growth in Latin America was faster than the growth of the labourforce, while the opposite was true in the United States. Obviously, this is because of the exceptionally rapid growth of the migrant labourforce in the United States. It is also noteworthy that a significant share of Latin American jobs were precarious (underemployment or informal employment), or low productivity jobs (Garcia and Tokman 1984: 106). Research by UN–ECLAC shows conclusively that underemployment grew as fast as formal employment between 1950–80 (Couriel 1984). In 1980, 42 per cent of the Latin American labourforce was underemployed, while in 1950 46.1 per cent were underemployed.[7] In the 1970s, 40 per cent of the Latin American population lived in poverty and were considered to be undernourished. There is a clear link between underemployment, undernourishment and poverty.

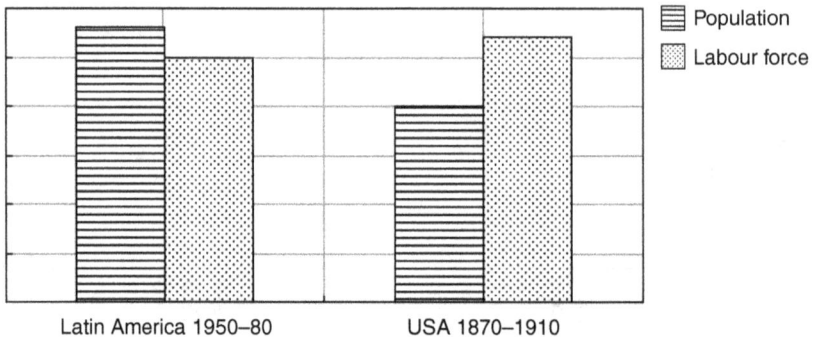

Figure 15.2 Latin America and USA population and labour force growth (source: author's elaboration with data from García and Tokman 1984).

In the 1980s, a time known as the 'lost decade' in Latin America, the region's GDP per capita declined, on average, by 0.9 per cent per year. Inflation skyrocketed: around 1986, three out of every four Latin American countries had annual inflation rates above 30 per cent. Behind these problems there were high interest rates and trade imbalances, along with unpayable foreign debt. Between 1970 and 1979, the Latin American foreign debt increased from US$19 billion to US$166 billion. It continued to grow in the 1980s, reaching US$360 billion in 1984. This explosive growth was due to the abundance of credit, while countries had to go into debt in order to finance their current account deficits and pay interest on their accumulated balances.

Crises occurred when these countries were unable to service their debt, and had to be rescued by International Monetary Fund, which required significant policy changes from the debtors in exchange for its credits (conditionality). Initially most Latin American countries were forced to reduce government spending, which helped to raise the average rate of unemployment in the region to nearly 9 per cent. This labour market shift helps to explain the decline of real wages and the growing share of precarious jobs among the new posts created in the region in the 1980s (Weeks 1999).

Later, especially during the 1990s, a raft of neoliberal policies were implemented across the region: trade and capital account liberalisation, domestic financial deregulation, widespread privatisations and tax cuts for firms and the higher income brackets, supplemented by higher indirect taxes such as VAT.

The neoliberal reforms were called 'structural' and, although they were implemented at different times, in different orders and with different intensity in each case, they were always intended to address the obstacles to growth posed by foreign debt and inflation.[8] For example, it was argued that protection for local industry between 1950–80 favoured the adoption of techniques intensive in capital, which contributed to the persistent unemployment in the region. Consequently, trade liberalisation and the entry of foreign investment would help to create more and better jobs. However, Figure 15.3 shows that the unemployment rate in Latin America rose after the reforms:

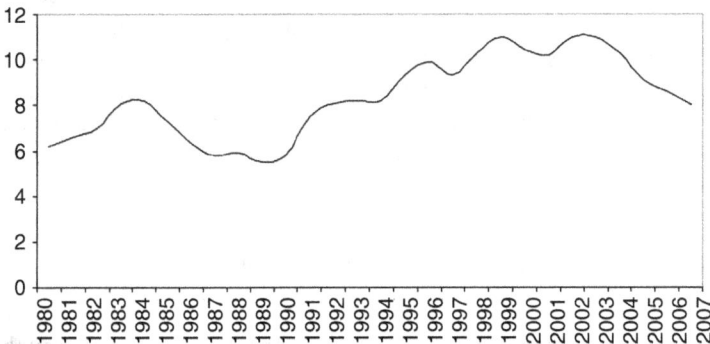

Figure 15.3 The unemployment rate in Latin America (%) (source: author's elaboration with data from CEPAL, Estadísticas e Indicadores Sociales).

The last decade and a half has witnessed profound changes in Latin America's labour market. Growth in gross domestic product (GDP) per capita has been slower than in developed countries, as a result disparity in income levels has deepened, and the labour force has continued to grow at a relatively fast pace. Additionally, the changes brought about by democratisation, economic stabilisation, and globalisation have disrupted the traditional patterns of integration through public and formal employment without producing an alternative channel of social integration through the labour market. And even though unemployment surged to very large numbers in only five countries in the region during this time period, increasing informality and a slow rate of wage growth mean that most jobs being created are 'bad' jobs that are precarious and low-paying.

(Inter-American Development Bank 2007: 85)

The reality is even worse than official reports suggest. For example, according to UN–ECLAC Mexico is one of the countries that have attempted to address poverty most consistently recently. In 2003, urban unemployment in Mexico was 3 per cent, the lowest among the countries in Latin America and the Caribbean. However, 25.3 million workers out of 41.1 million in the country had no benefits such as medical care. This contributes to explain the poor nutritional and health standards of the population. According to Adolfo Chávez, researcher at the National Nutrition Institute, the prevalence of malnutrition in the country has remained unchanged in the last 15 years. In many counties, malnutrition is as severe as in some of the poorest African countries, and it potentially affects 50 million Mexicans across the country, as stated by Norma Bellino, local FAO representative.

If more than half the workers have precarious employment in one of the richest countries in the region, it is not surprising that in poorer countries precarious employment affects an even larger share of the workforce. This suggests that the employment situation in Latin America and other parts of the underdeveloped world cannot be explained as part of a painful but necessary path towards 'development', because it has tended to deteriorate further even as countries become richer. From China to Argentina, and from South Africa to South Korea and India, precarious employment has been encroaching in all regions of the global South. Growing numbers of workers, once organised, are being pushed towards increasingly insecure and precarious jobs, having to struggle to secure minimum standards of subsistence, and without the benefits and security that were once available to them. After more than 20 years of the neoliberal reforms, unemployment and precarious employment are still central problems for the working population.

Explanining employment problems in underdeveloped countries

The first cause of the employment problems outlined above is the type of growth in underdeveloped countries. Just as during the lost decade in Latin America, firms have been hiring fewer workers because they are growing slowly. In the

1980s, many countries in Latin America had to assign a larger share of their output to service their foreign debt, since both interest rates and the amount of debt had increased. Even in countries experiencing rapid growth, such as China and India, precarious employment is not declining as rapidly as should have been expected because of rapid productivity growth in these countries.

Productivity growth is one of the features which make capitalism strong. Usually, firms that manage to produce at lower cost than their rivals earn higher profit rates, grow faster, and tend to prevail on the market. Lower costs usually mean producing with less labour per unit of output. This does not necessarily mean that there will be spare workers because, as productivity rises, more can be produced or a shorter working day may be sufficient to produce the same quantities of goods and services. Capitalism fights the reduction of the working day, and always prefers to produce more per worker.

In 1960, General Motors' (GM) global assets were worth US$8.5 billion dollars. The firm had 595,000 workers, or a capital–labour ratio of US$14,300 per worker. In 2005, GM had only 327,000 workers, and its capital per worker had risen more than 100 times, to US$1,453,000. The firm was producing more, and increasingly complex, automobiles, with much less workers. The computing power of a modern car is similar to that in the lunar module of the Apollo 11. What has happend in the auto industry has also occurred in manufacturing sectors around the world, to the extent that manufacturing employment has decreased in absolute terms despite the growing abundance and sophistication of the goods available for sale.

This type of productivity increase was anticipated by Marx when he stated, in his General Law of Capitalist Accumulation, that capital should grow more rapidly than labour and, in so doing, capital tended to dominate labour. For Marx, capital is due to the surplus extracted from the workers by the capitalists; as it grows faster than the workforce it can restrain them and control wages. *Unemployment is produced by capitalism*, as it achieves productivity increases requiring increasing amounts of capital per worker. In order to control wages and restrain the workers, capital uses not only the unemployed but also precarious labour due to their low wages and poor working conditions. When workers are said to be too demanding, capital can always replace them with its reserve army of spare workers among the unemployed and precarious workers. If the size of the reserve army is sufficient, discipline and wages are controlled by capital; however, if it is too large capitalist expansion is hampered, but there is nothing to force capitalism to absorb all the exploitable workforce. Thus, capitalism raises productivity in such a way that it makes part of the working population unnecessary. Those expelled workers, even if they get to be re-hired, will have been through an instructive experience. They are not necessary for capital, but they cannot live a dignified life without work: capital is vital for them, but not the other way around. Today capitalism is characterised by an enormous amount of spare labour. This is the case all over the world, but in underdeveloped countries it is even more serious because the progress of capitalism has destroyed employment in agriculture without creating industrial employment as fast as it did in the rich countries.

To fully understand the differences in growth in different countries let us assume that there is only one company in the studied branch, and being in an underdeveloped country a considerable amount of its means of production must be imported. This simplification leaves aside rivalry between branches. Because of their need to import means of production, especially machinery, underdeveloped countries must export goods that cost more due to their backward condition. This can only be explained with the Marxist theory of value. This theory holds that capitalist society needs to organise social labour and so it requires counting how much labour is used in production. Capitalism does this calculation through prices that measure how much labour society spends in the production. Such measurements are made in an approximate manner and without letting producers and consumers know. Several functions are accomplished in measuring spent labour. One of great consequence is establishing how much of each product can be consumed: if a product costs ten times more work than another one it can be consumed ten times less. This is an objective fact, so if prices do not mirror cost variations capitalism is not working well.

This point can be illustrated by reference to two countries, Argentina and the United States. Take the price of a 2009 Chevrolet Aveo. In Argentina, this car costs between 48,000 and 60,000 pesos; at the February 2009 exchange rate, this is equivalent to US$13,500–16,900. In the United States, the same car costs between US$12,000–15,400. Their prices are similar (differences may be explained by differences in transportation costs and tax regimes). However, the GDP per worker is very different: it is between three and four times higher in the United States. This implies that average productivity in Argentina is between one-third and one-fourth of average productivity in the United States. A Chevrolet Aveo is much more expensive in labour terms in Argentina than in the United States, despite its similar price in dollars. Similarly, means of production imported by Argentina will cost several times more in labour terms than in the United States, even if they have similar prices. Obviously, it will be more difficult to obtain the necessary means of production to absorb the labourforce in Argentina than in the United States. An underdeveloped country that imports means of production, even if local prices correspond to world prices, will normally pay more for them in labour. This hinders labourforce absorption and productivity growth.

Conclusion

Apologists of the system argue that, thanks to capitalism, 'we are all slowly walking towards utopia', an expression coined by J. Bradford DeLong, an economist at the University of California, Berkeley, who also said that the entire world is slowly but surely advancing towards the lifestyle of the US middle class.[9] This statement contradicts all the evidence available. Capitalism could never fully exploit the available labourforce in Latin America, and perhaps in the entire periphery. A large number of workers were left outside the capitalist sphere as autonomous labour; another significant share is subject to capitalist relations but this cannot be successfully reproduced because they are employed in unprofitable firms. This is almost impossible to change, if we consider what has happened in rapid growth countries such as China, where most new employment remains precarious.

Under neoliberalism, many workers in the so-called developed countries have been falling into precarious employment. Around the world, there is a race to the bottom of labour standards, and every worker has been told to 'reduce your standard of living, renounce your victories, because that is the only way to keep your job'. If what has been happening for years adds to the current world crisis which will surely reduce workers' standards of living, the only possible conclusion is that capitalism does not offer an acceptable future for workers.

Notes

1 Faculty of Economics, Universidad Nacional Autónoma de México.
2 See FAO (2008a: 2).
3 Their earnings are less than two US dollars per day (ILO definition).
4

> Looking at the period between 1992 and 2000, we find that the opening of a single Wal-Mart store in a county lowered average retail wages in that county by between 0.5 and 0.9 percent. In the general merchandise sector, wages fell by 1 percent for each new Wal-Mart. And for grocery store employees, the effect of a single new Wal-Mart was a 1.5 percent reduction in earnings. When Wal-Mart entered a county, the total wage bill declined along with the average wage. Factoring in both the impact on wages and jobs, the total amount of retail earnings in a county fell by 1.5 percent for every new Wal-Mart store. Similar effects appeared at the state level.
>
> (Dube *et al.* 2007: 1).

5 Quoted by Yates (2004).
6 'In general terms Latin America does not seem to move away from the model followed by countries which are now developed' (Garcia and Tokman 1984: 106). It is noteworthy that these comparisons often ignore significant differences between the United States and Latin America. For example, the significant technological innovations in the United States, such as the telephone, the lightbulb, and so on.
7 Data from Couriel (1984: 39), considering rural unemployment as own-account labour and unpaid family workers. Urban unemployment includes these categories but not professional and technicians.
8 It was assumed that reforms would result in 'a greater efficency at a microeconomic level, better use of scale economies, and a moderation of stagnation and progress cycles (stop-go) stemming from scarcity of foreign exchange'. And 'that in eliminating distortions originated by the imports substitution model, more employment would be produced, especially for non qualified workers' (Stallings and Weller 2001: 193).
9 Quoted by Yates (2004: 1).

References

Couriel, A. (1984) 'Pobreza y subempleo en América Latina'. *Revista de la CEPAL* (24), pp. 39–64.
Dube, A., Lester, T.W. and Eidlin, B. (2007) 'A Downward Push: the Impact of Wal-Mart Stores on Retail Wages and Benefits', UC Berkeley Center for Labour Research and Education Research Brief, December.

Duménil, G. and Lévy, D. (2004) *Capital Resurgent. Roots of the Neoliberal Revolution.* Harvard: Harvard University Press.

Economic Report of the President (1988, 2008) Washington, DC: United States Government Printing Office.

FAO (2008a) 'Food Situation in Latin America and the Caribbean', May–June. Online, available at: www.rlc.fao.org/iniciativa/pdf/bolobs1_en.pdf.

FAO (2008b) 'Number of Hungry People Rises to 963 Million'. Online, available at: www.fao.org/news/story/en/item/8836/icode.

García, N. and Tokman, V. (1984) 'Transformación ocupacional y crisis'. *Revista de la CEPAL* (24), pp. 103–15.

González, M.V. (2003) '¿Quién crees que lava la ropa en Nueva York?', *Masiosare* 294, a weekly publication of *La Jornada*, 10 August. Online, available at: www.jornada.unam.mx/2003/08/10/mas-cara.html.

Inter-American Development Bank (2007) *Economic and Social Progress In Latin America Report 2008, Outsiders? The Changing Patterns of Exclusion in Latin America and the Caribbean.* Washington, DC: Inter-American Development Bank. Online, available at: www.iadb.org/res/ipes/2008/footnotes.cfm?language=en.

International Labour Organisation (2008a) *Global Employment Trends.* January. Geneva: ILO.

International Labour Organisation (2008b) *The Global Employment Challenge: Executive Summary.* Geneva: ILO.

Krugman, P. (1992) 'The Rich, the Right, and the Facts'. *The American Prospect* 11 (fall), pp. 19–31.

Lendman, S. (2008) 'Global Food Crisis: Hunger Plagues Haiti and the World'. *Global Research*, 21 April. Online, available at: www.globalresearch.ca/index.php?context=va&aid=8754.

OECD (1996) *Employment Outlook 1996.* Paris: OECD.

Stallings, B. and Weller, J. (2001) 'El empleo en America Latina, base fundamental de la politica social'. *Revista de la CEPAL* (75), pp. 191–210.

Weeks, J. (1999) 'Salarios, empleo y derechos de los trabajadores en América Latina entre 1970 y 1998'. *Revista Internacional del Trabajo* 118 (2), pp. 169–88.

Yates, M. (2004) 'Poverty and Inequality in the Global Economy'. *Monthly Review*, February. Online, available at: www.monthlyreview.org.

16 Progressive Third World Central Banking and the case of Venezuela

Al Campbell and Hasan Cömert

While neoliberalism was broadly adopted by capitalism around the world over the course of the 1980s, it did not clearly articulate its own Central Bank policy until the 1990s. By the 2000s progressives had responded by formulating an alternative approach to Central Bank policy. The government of Venezuela under Hugo Chavez provides an interesting case study of an attempt to implement an anti-neoliberal and progressive Central Bank policy. The second section of this chapter will discuss the nature of neoliberal Central Bank policy and the third section will outline a progressive alternative approach. The fourth section will then look at Central Bank policy in Venezuela following the abandonment of its largely neoliberal Central Bank policy in 2005.

Neoliberal Central Bank policy

Throughout history Central Banks had a dual role: economic development, and stabilization of the currency (in the past referred to as protection of its value). Central Banks were strongly influenced if not controlled by the government, had the goals of financing governments, managing exchange rates and promoting development, including sector-specific development, and used direct methods such as directed credit allocation to promote development. As the neoliberal model of capitalism has come to dominate capitalist ideology and practice over the last 30 years, it has brought with it a fundamentally new model of central banking. This neoliberal Central Bank model is characterized by Central Bank 'independence',[1] inflation suppression (with or without a formal inflation-targeting policy) as its central if not single goal,[2] and the use of short-term interest rates (an indirect and non sector-specific tool) as its dominant policy tool.[3]

Neoliberal Central Bank policy can be thought of in this framework in two different ways. These extensively overlap, but they are not equivalent. On the one hand, neoliberal Central Banks can be considered to have abandoned the goal of development in favour of the goal of monetary stabilization, which they take to mean low and stable inflation. This is the way heterodox critiques often present the present conduct of Central Banks, and they then call for Central Banks to reclaim their abandoned role of developing the economy. On the other hand, neoliberal Central Banks can be considered to have continued their policy of sector-specific development, while shifting their priority to the development of the financial sector.

Since the financial sector considers low and stable inflation its central concern, one could think of these two conceptualizations as equivalent. We would argue rather that the second way of thinking about Central Bank policy is broader than and includes the first. It thereby gives us a frame for thinking about all the neoliberal Central Bank behaviours considered by the first approach (its abandonment of concern with growth, employment, distribution and so on), and in addition the frame also allows us to consider other behaviours. Neoliberal Central Banks not only focus on inflation, they also do at least two other things centrally important to finance capital, which often get much less attention than inflation targeting in heterodox discussions of neoliberal central banking. First, they consistently work for the adoption by the government of laws and interpretations of laws favourable to finance capital. This important behaviour clearly fits better in the frame of 'shifted concern with what to develop' than 'abandoned concern with development'. Second, during crises they intervene massively to absorb potential losses by financial capital with public money, essentially making massive transfers of public money to financial capital. Again, this fits well into a framework that sees the goal of neoliberal Central Banks to promote the development of financial capital by whatever means are available and effective.

One could look at these neoliberal Central Bank behaviours as those of an agent of capital and in particular of financial capital and simply say, 'they have the political power to effect these behaviors, and so as self-interested agents they do'. While that would be consistent with their neoclassical theory, neoliberals in fact often argue that their desired Central Bank policy of financial sector development (or as they like to call it for obvious reasons, 'eliminating financial repression') is 'best for everyone'. Over the last ten years they have produced a number of works that support the claim that an inflation-targeting Central Bank policy is better than alternative monetary policies. A very small sample of such studies, including two by well-known neoclassical authors and a work reflecting the position of the IMF, which has played an important role in pressuring particularly Third World countries to adopt inflation targeting, is Bernanke *et al.* (1999: 275), Mishkin and Schmidt-Hebbel (2001: 11) and Batini *et al.* (2006: 11).

Their argument that inflation targeting is a 'better' policy than alternatives has two steps. First, neoliberals claim that inflation targeting yields what they refer to as 'better substantive outcomes' or 'a very successful new monetary framework' etc. By this they mean primarily, or often entirely, reduced inflation, reduced inflation shocks and reduced inflation expectations. A large part of their empirical work, as for example in the three works just cited, is restricted to testing some form of that claim. The second step consists of arguing that reduced inflation in the very low range they target, reduced inflation shocks and reduced inflation expectations actually improve growth.[4]

With this understood, two types of rejection of their claim that inflation targeting is a better policy than alternatives present themselves. The first type of rejection argues that empirical tests find that inflation targeting in fact does not significantly reduce inflation, inflation shocks or inflation expectations. The second type of rejection argues that lower inflation rates in the minimal range aimed at by inflation targeting, and even in the moderate range,[5] do not show empirical evidence of a higher (and in fact they often lead to a lower) rate of growth.

Although it was not the first paper to make the first type of rejection by documenting the lack of support for the claim that inflation targeting gave better results even by their own inflation-focused definitions, Arestis and Sawyer (2003) carefully reviewed both the theory and empirical work that advocated inflation targeting up to that date. To begin with, they 'identified a number of weaknesses and reservations with [the theoretical foundations of inflation targeting]' (p. 24). Beyond that, their review of the empirical support for inflation targeting led them to reject as unfounded the then much cited claim by Mishkin that countries that adopted inflation targeting reduced inflation below what it would have been without those targets. They concluded, along with the neoclassical work by Ball and Sheridan (2003), that the general 'low inflation' environment in the world that had been in existence for a while at that time was not significantly different for inflation-targeting and noninflation-targeting countries. After four more years of attempts by advocates of inflation targeting to empirically establish that it at least lowered inflation, Epstein (2007: 39) could still safely claim that 'even the impact of these regimes [of formal or informal inflation targeting] on inflation itself is a matter of dispute'. The empirical evidence on the second type of rejection is divided, as it is on most politically controversial issues, but we find very persuasive the position that at least for middle- and low-income countries, moderate inflation countries do as well as, or better than, the minimal inflation countries. Pollin and Zhu (2005), for example, do a careful study of 80 countries over the period 1961–2000 that presents this conclusion. See also the mainstream studies by Bruno (1995) and Bruno and Easterly (1998).

While the inflation-targeting argument that lower inflation increases growth is the main neoliberal proposal for Central Bank policy, a secondary argument is that developing a stock market contributes to the growth of developing countries, and so Central Banks and governments together should promote the development of stock markets. Stock markets are centrally important to financial capital not simply because they create large profits for financial capital, but also for the broader reason that stock markets discipline productive capital to operate in a way beneficial to the (short-term) interests of financial capital.[6] Again, here we see the importance of adopting the broader view of neoliberal Central Bank policy as promoting the development of the financial sector, and not merely as abandoning development in favour of price stability. A careful empirical study by Zhu *et al.* (2002) found this neoliberal Central Bank behaviour of promoting stock markets also showed no significant empirical correlation with improved growth.

International financial capital continues to be successful in convincing an ever growing number of countries to adopt inflation targeting. New Zealand was the first country to adopt this policy in 1990. By November 2000 there were

19 inflation-targeting countries (Mishkin and Schmidt-Hebbel 2001: 1), and in March 2006 there were 23 (seven advanced industrial countries and 16 other countries),[7] with more than 44 indicating that they wanted to move to explicit or implicit inflation targeting (Batini *et al.* 2006: 4, 7).

If one accepts the general progressive position that under capitalism a high level of growth and employment (among other important conditions) are centrally important to the well-being of the majority of society, and one accepts the above evidence that rejects that the neoliberal inflation-targeting policy contributes to this outcome, this immediately poses for consideration the following question: what would constitute a more progressive Central Bank policy? Over the last decade, in response to the increasing hegemony in practice of neoliberal Central Bank policy and its failure in particular to provide an acceptable growth and employment combination, the general frame of a progressive alterative has emerged from the earlier work on the weaknesses of the neoliberal Central Bank policy.

A framework for a progressive Central Bank policy

The goal of a progressive Central Bank policy can be understood both as a rejection of the neoliberal policy, and at the same time in terms of the historical dual goal of Central Banks discussed above. Economic development is the central goal, understood broadly as improved social welfare. The second historical goal of limiting inflation, however, is not abandoned. It enters progressive Central Bank policy now no longer as a goal in itself, but rather in a fundamentally different way as a necessary constraint.

'Real targeting' is a common name for this progressive alternative frame that both indicates its direct focus on social welfare, and its opposition to neoliberal inflation targeting. As suggested by its name, the targets are some variables from the real economy which are important to social welfare. GDP growth and employment are the two leading candidates, but other real variables are possible, such as, for example, investment or distribution (Epstein 2003: 1). We will see that the Venezuelan variant of this progressive Central Bank policy has specified 'social inclusion' as its conceptual target, a real target that involves real sub-targets to specify what it means in concrete policy terms.

There are three important aspects beyond simply having real targets which contribute to making real targeting effective.

First, the targets themselves are country-specific. For example, in the post-2001 sluggish recovery in the United States, the rate of growth was more of a problem than unemployment, which would suggest the former to be the target.[8] On the other hand, two policy packages worked out under this approach for South Africa and Tanzania made unemployment the target, since in these countries this was a more direct problem than the rate of growth.[9] This ability to choose a target most appropriate for a given country constitutes a first aspect of the flexibility of this approach that does not exist in the inflation-targeting approach.

Second, there is no restriction as to the tools that the Central Bank can use to achieve the targets. This is contrary to the inflation-targeting approach that has the interest rate as its dominant tool, and precludes tools that would be harmful to the interests of financial capital. A good example of this type of Central Bank tool is currency conversion and other capital controls. These are often needed to prevent capital flight for the effectiveness of the entire progressive programme, but they would not be acceptable under a neoliberal Central Bank policy. They have been important to the anti-neoliberal orientation of Venezuela. For three good discussions on progressive capital controls, see Grabel (2004a), Epstein *et al.* (2004) and Grabel (2004b). Again, this aspect highlights the greater flexibility of the real targeting approach.

Third, the real target will generally be accompanied by an inflation constraint. This points back to the dual historical objectives of Central Banks discussed above, both real development and monetary stability. If real targeting were pursued without this concern, it could conceivably be carried out in such a way that inflation rose to a level that really was disruptive to the economy. An inflation constraint will prevent that. But the fundamental difference between a minimum inflation target and an inflation constraint must be stressed. As we noted above, the former aims for inflation levels no higher than 3 to 5 per cent, with lower levels always better, and such low inflation levels have not been shown empirically to yield growth better than levels up to around 15 per cent. An inflation constraint would allow social welfare enhancing policies to be actively perused even it they generated inflation, as long as it stayed below some level such as 15 per cent. This would not be possible under inflation targeting.[10]

Hence the strongest claim for the superiority of the real targeting approach over the inflation-targeting approach is exactly that it is more directly linked to social welfare than the assumed (and, as we argued above, empirically unsupported) indirect link of the inflation-targeting approach. To put this another way, one can note that to improve the social welfare the inflation-targeting approach has to indirectly affect some real variables, and since it has to do that anyway, one can ask why it does not simply directly target those variables. In addition, the much greater flexibility of the real targeting approach than the inflation-targeting approach means it is not subject to the sharp charge often directed at the latter, that it constitutes a 'one size fits all' policy.

With this understanding of the general frame of a progressive Central Bank policy as an alternative to the neoliberal recipe of inflation targeting, we now turn to look at the case study of Venezuela.

Venezuela: implementing a progressive Central Bank policy

It is not surprising that the Central Bank of Venezuela, embedded in the Venezuela's Bolivarian Revolution, would have a progressive Central Bank policy. Two things that we do find somewhat surprising, however, are that it did not come to have a progressive anti-neoliberal programme until 2005 (despite the Revolution becoming solidly and consciously anti-neoliberal at least by 2001[11]), and that the progressive anti-neoliberal orientation it developed resembles so strongly the theoretical considerations of a progressive Central Bank policy discussed above.

This section will have three parts. The first part will briefly document that the Central Bank under Chávez before 2005 was consciously, and publically, committed to the standard neoliberal Central Bank agenda. The second part will document the new progressive conceptual framework for its activity that the Central Bank established for itself in 2005. It is not possible to understand why the Central Bank took the particular concrete measures it did after 2005 if one does not understand its goals. The final section will document a number of the most important concrete progressive central banking activities that the Central Bank initiated after 2005 in pursuit of its new goals.

Pre-2005 Central Bank policies

At the end of the first year of the Chávez government, the president of the Central Bank, Antonio Casas González, wrote in his address on the Bank's performance that the Bank had been able to achieve the usual (neoliberal) goals, including in particular an inflation target. He stressed that this had been accomplished despite now being subjected to an expansionary fiscal policy that generated an expanded Treasury deficit as Chávez increased spending, especially on projects to help the poor:

> In 1999, the policies implemented by the Central Bank were framed by the effect of the economic direction taken by the new Administration. In this regard, coordination of monetary and exchange rate policies with fiscal policies has been achieved, which enabled the inflation target to be met. At the same time, financing of the deficit in the Treasury accounts has been facilitated. All this has been done in a stable environment in the foreign exchange market, an increase of international reserves, a reduction of interest rates and a timely servicing of the national debt. On the minus side, the trend of the economy was marked by recession during this period.
>
> (Casas 1999: 19)[12]

Even more interesting for the comparison to the post-2005 nature of the Central Bank was its clear statement of how it conceived of its role in the economy and society.

> [In a new Central Bank Act] we will be able to clarify and spell out the standards that will strengthen the Bank's nature as a fundamentally technical body, separating the sensitive duty of managing the nation's money supply from Venezuela's political concerns.
>
> (Ibid.)

From 2000 to 2004 Diego Luis Castellanos E. was president of the Central Bank, and while like his predecessor he had to adapt to Chávez's fiscal policies,[13] he continued the neoliberal Central Bank orientation. The Central Bank Law of 2001 reinforced the neoliberal orientation of the Bank in two ways. First, it re-emphasized the centrality of an anti-inflation focus to the Bank's activities which had been established with the 1992 Central Bank law, which had been written with IMF assistance: 'The main purpose of the Central Bank of Venezuela is to achieve price stability and preserve the currency value.' Second, it maintained the neoliberal goal of autonomy of the Central Bank, which paradoxically had been established by the progressive new 1999 Constitution under Chávez.

Venezuela's conceptual framework for its post-2005 Central Bank policies

Given the Central Bank autonomy just indicated, Chávez could not remove the existing director in the early 2000s even if he was conducting a Central Bank policy contradictory to Venezuela's overall progressive policy. But by the end of 2004 Castellanos felt so at odds with the general economic orientation of the Chávez government that he chose to resign. Gastón Parra Luzardo became president of the Central Bank of Venezuela in January 2005.[14] It is enough to read the introductory 'General Outlook' section of his first Year-End Address of 2005 to observe the change in the Central Bank policies connected to and represented by his appointment (Parra 2005: 7–12).

Parra posed the central choice between the neoliberal and progressive Central Bank orientations we discussed above as follows: 'Should the Central Bank of Venezuela be only a witness to growth and respond passively to the economy's demands for liquidity? Or should it, on the other hand, become an engine of development?' (ibid.: 7). He answers this in line with the progressive orientation that it must directly address development.

The Central Bank of Venezuela executes multiple policies intended to serve this goal of economic and social development. They include direct support for the economic development of the productive sector, maintaining a low interest rate and direct regulation of bank interest rates, control of international capital flows and the exchange rate, and promotion of economic democracy. In the next section we will discuss concrete results in these areas, but our concern here is to indicate how the Central Bank conceptualizes its relation to these issues. A particular formulation used extensively in Venezuela today in discussions of their progressive social and economic policies is *universal social inclusion*. José Félix Rivas Alvardo, a member of the Board of Directors of the Central Bank, has an extensive discussion of Venezuela's progressive Central Bank policy using this idea, with the above targets as concrete attempts to address this overall concept (Rivas 2006).[15] Here the concern again is to stress the direct targeting of social development and universal social inclusion, contrary to the neoliberal Central Bank approach, that are expressed by the conceptual framework used by the Central Bank of Venezuela for determining its activities.

The inflation constraint that is a part of the real targeting approach has not been forgotten. Parra stresses that a sound and sustainable progressive Central

Bank policy must execute appropriate 'monetary and exchange rate functions', not only at the same time that it carries out its progressive programmes for social and economic development, but as an integral part of those progressive programmes (Parra 2005: 8).

This new orientation established in 2005 has been consistently reasserted since then. It continues to be the framework for the Year-End Addresses of 2006 and 2007 (Parra 2006, 2007), and all current declarations of purpose by the Central Bank.[16]

Concrete results from Venezuela's post-2005 progressive Central Bank policies

There is an inherent difficulty in recording all the positive real economic results attributable to Central Bank policies. For example, two standard real targets are growth and employment. Real GDP growth was 10.3 per cent, 10.3 per cent, 8.4 per cent and 5.6 per cent from 2005 to 2008.[17] Unemployment dropped from 13.3 per cent the year the Central Bank began its progressive polices to 7.8 per cent in 2008 (Weisbrot *et al.* 2009). But as progressive Central Bank policy emphasizes, and Parra argued specifically for the new Central Bank orientation in Venezuela (Parra 2005: 7), Central Bank policy is intended and designed to work together with all other government polices. Hence there is no way of ascribing which 'marginal contribution' to these positive results came from Central Bank policies such as its development activity or the low real interest rate, and which came from the extensive fiscal spending, the high oil prices, government polices to stimulate production and employment through creating cooperatives, and so on.

In this section we will discuss four concrete progressive, anti-neoliberal, sets of policies conducted by the Central Bank of Venezuela since its reorientation in 2005. These four sets of policies include three different types of Central Bank functions. A first type consists of functions still considered Central Bank responsibilities by everyone, although the neoliberals would conduct them completely differently. Controlling the domestic interest rate and influencing the foreign exchange rate are examples of this type. The second consists of functions that used to be commonly exercised by Central Banks, but are now rejected as appropriate Central Bank activities by the dominant neoliberal paradigm. Direct support of economic development and direct control of bank interest rates are examples of this type. The final type consists of a function that has never been seriously undertaken by Central Banks in the past. It is a conscious role by the Central Bank in contributing to an expansion of economic democracy. Such a policy would be appropriate for supporting either a left populist or pro-socialist government orientation.

1   The Optimum Reserve Policy: Creating, and Contributing to the Funding of, the National Development Fund.

   In 2004 prior to the Central Bank reorientation, Chávez had asked the Central Bank to invest US$1 billion from its large reserves into the agricultural sector. This was a request for the Central Bank to directly fund 'strengthening and diversifying the domestic production structure' (Parra 2005: 8). In line with the neoliberal orientation of the Central Bank at that time, it refused. A top priority for Parra from the day he assumed the Central Bank presidency was to create a structure for the Central Bank to directly fund development, working with the National Assembly and the Chávez administration. The Board of Directors of the Central Bank conducted a detailed study of how to do this in accord with article 331 of the Constitution of the Bolivarian Republic of Venezuela[18] and article 5 of the Organic Law of Hydrocarbons.[19] In July the National Assembly used this study to pass the 2005 Partial Reform of the Law of the Central Bank of Venezuela.[20] The most important change included in this 2005 law was the creation of FONDEN (The National Development Fund). FONDEN's purpose was to stop the build-up of 'excess reserves' in accord with an 'optimum reserves policy' developed by the Central Bank, and transfer them to this fund to be used directly for economic development projects.[21] A little less than two years after its formation, the Venezuelan Finance Minister Rodrigo Cabezas reported in May 2007 that FONDEN had received a total of US$27.3 billion from the Central Bank and PDVSA[22] (the state oil company), of which US$20.2 billion had been invested in public projects. He detailed 130 development projects in such areas as infrastructure, energy, defence, housing and health. Cabezas argued that FONDEN had become the main source for the increased investment that had been a necessary part of Venezuela's strong economic performance since the fund's birth (Carlson 2007).[23]

2   Maintaining Low Real Interest Rates, Including in the Face of Inflation Concerns.

The neoliberal inflation-targeting formula calls for a monetary policy that raises interest rates to slow the economy in the face of inflation above 4 or 5 per cent. Even the inflation constraint on a progressive real targeting programme will often cause a move to reduce inflation if it rises above 15 or 20 per cent. The Venezuelan Central Bank has not moved to raise interest rates and has maintained its loose monetary[24] and pro-growth polices even as inflation has climbed above those levels. The nominal inflation rate from 2002 to 2008 has been 31 per cent, 27 per cent, 19 per cent, 14 per cent, 16 per cent, 22 per cent and 32 per cent, respectively.[25] Yet there has been no Central Bank action to drive up the real interest rates on bank lending (we will see next that they in fact have capped the nominal rates), and these rates have in fact been negative under the post 2005 orientation: 1 per cent, −2.3 per cent, −5.7 per cent and −9.1 per cent from 2005 to 2008, respectively.[26] As of the writing of this chapter, the Central Bank has just declared again that its monetary policy will continue to be oriented to assuring sufficient liquidity and credit in the system, with no mention of inflation (BCV 2009).[27]

The first major anti-neoliberal policy from the reoriented Central Bank was its intervention to legally limit lending and deposit rates in the economy, a practice it continues to this day. It established a minimum interest rate that banks could pay savers, and the maximum rate they could charge on loans to both businesses and consumers.[28] The Central Bank has given great importance to this bank interest rate control policy for four real target reasons: it maintains that this will have an immediate effect on people's level of consumption, it maintains it will stimulate production particularly by small producers, it maintains it will increase employment, and it maintains it will reduce inequality[29] (Rivas 2006: 396–9, 412–21; Parra 2005: 8; 2006: 8).

3   Capital Controls.

As indicated above, capital flight can undermine a country's entire progressive programme. This is particularly true for Third World countries, though it was also a central weapon used to destroy Mitterrand's brief 'socialist' experiment in France in 1981. The prevention of a capital outflow haemorrhage by the Central Bank has been one essential contribution to the economic success of Venezuela since the controls were adopted. Weisbrot and Sandoval (2007) concluded that 'the government's currency controls, originally enacted in February 2003 as a means of limiting capital flight from the country, have enabled it to pursue expansionary fiscal and monetary policies while maintaining a fixed exchange rate' (p. 18).

The point being made here is not that these controls do not also have problems connected to them, or even that they are being conducted optimally. Weisbrot *et al.* (2009) argue that the peg to the dollar has not been adjusted appropriately since it was adopted. It is therefore now 50 per cent overvalued in comparison to the dollar, which seriously harms Venezuela's project of diversifying its revenue sources away from oil and into manufactured goods, or services such as tourism. The point being made here is rather that this is another important anti-neoliberal Central Bank policy, in that the expansionary monetary and fiscal policies that have to date successfully contributed to the real targets of improved growth, employment, investment and distribution, could not have been maintained without this policy.

4   Building Economic Democracy.

The centrality of the progressive and anti-neoliberal goal of active popular participation to the vision of socialism promoted in Venezuela implies two goals that should be embraced by all institutions in the country – transparency,[30] and skill-building for participation. Since 2005 the Central Bank has promoted the following programmes that serve these ends. Note these are consciously envisioned as 'stimulating development and supporting qualitative change' (Parra 2005: 8). While these programs are clearly very small contributions to the huge task of building economic democracy, the point here is not a discussion of the path to economic democracy in Venezuela, but rather again the nature of the Central Bank. They are the contributions to building economic democracy currently being consciously pursued by the Central Bank, and as such they are concrete programs that reflect its progressive and anti-neoliberal orientation:

- 'The Central Bank of Venezuela uses diverse means to inform the public concerning economic statistics, its resolutions, and actions and events of a public nature that it considers to be useful for the formation of a documented, critical and participative public opinion' (Rivas 2006: 411). The information system in place before 2005, which was good, has been dramatically improved. The main vehicle for presenting this massive information is the website of the Central Bank: www.bcv.org.ve. This effort which requires the commitment of Central Bank resources includes a continual expansion of the information collected and disseminated (Parra 2007: 10).
- Through its publications and related public seminar series of economics texts and broader socio-economic works, the Central Bank simultaneously addresses two goals. First is its goal of building economic analytical skills in broader circles of the population, a necessary part of economic democracy. The economics texts are introductory in nature, and written by Venezuelans concerning the Venezuelan economic reality. The broader socio-economic series draws more widely on Latin American authors, and is focused on addressing the intersection of Latin America's social, political and economic dimensions, including in particular works with a political-economic focus. The second goal is to combat the neoliberal paradigm that is so powerful throughout the world, including in many economics departments in Venezuelan universities (Parra 2005: 9).
- Related to the last point, the Central Bank has developed and is actively engaged in a programme with teachers, Children Learn Economics with the Central Bank of Venezuela (Parra 2005: 8). Again the two goals are to equip children with the economic tools to enable them to participate actively in economic issues and institutions when they are adults, and to inoculate them against neoliberal economics which are still so widely promoted in Venezuela through newspapers, television and private enterprises.

5   The Southern Bank.

The attempt to create the Southern Bank was not included in this section in the list of four sets of concrete policies reflecting Venezuela's progressive Central Bank orientation, because as of this writing its initial proposed incarnation appears to be dead. At present Ecuador is the major proponent of building a new regional progressive financial architecture, while Venezuela has drawn back slightly (though it supports Ecuador's efforts) to focus on building the ALBA Bank and joint banks with China, Russia and Iran. But the concern here is not the specifics of what international financial structure Venezuela is trying to adopt at this moment. Rather, the point is that the original efforts by Venezuela to create the Southern Bank involved a significant investment of Central Bank human resources (Parra 2006: 9). The attempt to create the Southern Bank deserves a brief mention in this section because despite its fate it reflected the anti-neoliberal orientation of the Central Bank of Venezuela. It was exactly the inability to harmonize this progressive vision with the neoliberal vision, particularly of Brazil, but also of Argentina and Chile, that led to its failure.

Conclusion

A neoliberal model of Central Banking, inflation targeting, has been imposed on much of the world, and continues to be adopted by ever more countries. The social/political/economic reaction against neoliberalism has included the development of a well articulated but flexible alternative, which is referred to by some authors as real targeting. The very different technical aspects of the two approaches are just the surface manifestation of their essential difference: Central Bank policy serving society's social, economic and human development versus serving the development of financial capital. Beginning in 2005 the Central Bank of Venezuela switched from a predominantly neoliberal to a progressive orientation, in line with the Bolivarian Revolution that had been unfolding and deepening there since 1999. Central Bank policy in Venezuela continues to attempt to develop appropriate new progressive policies to this day. It is arguably one of the, if not the, most progressive Central Banks in the world today, and should be carefully studied by all advocates of progressive Central Bank policies. Careful investigation beyond the introductory level of this work is needed of both the effectiveness of what has already been attempted, and what new progressive policies it could develop to support Venezuela's social/political/economic transformation.

Notes

1 This standard term is ideologically misleading and actually means 'independence from the government'. Neoliberal Central Banks are typically not 'independent', but rather are controlled by private finance capital.
2 In theoretically describing the objectives of monetary policy after he had just left the US Federal Reserve (Fed), in his carefully thought-out Robbins Lectures, Alan Blinder wrote: 'Monetary policy makers have certain objectives – such as low inflation, output stability and perhaps external balance' (Blinder 1998: 3). The complete omission of either growth or employment, when employment is even an official objective of the Fed, is revealing as to the real Fed policy.
3 For a short but insightful overview of the history of central banking practice that develops and expands this position, see Epstein (2006).
4 Real economic development is much more than output growth, which neoclassicals almost universally reduce it to. Here, however, we consider only an immanent critique of their claims because they are so weak even on their own terms.
5 Minimal inflation countries would be those near the typical range of inflation targeting, 3 to 5 per cent, while moderate inflation might be in the range above that to around 15 per cent.
6 There is a large literature on this. To mention just three good works: Lazonick and O'Sullivan (1996), Jacoby (2005a and a popularized abbreviated version of that, 2005b), and Duménil and Lévy (2004).

7 From the IMF:

> Under inflation targeting, low inflation is the stated primary goal of monetary policy, and the only one for which a numerical target is announced, although other goals like full employment or low exchange rate volatility may be pursued on a secondary basis. In contrast, other monetary frameworks attempt to influence inflation indirectly by targeting exchange rates or monetary aggregates, or include inflation as only one of a number of policy objectives.
>
> (Batini *et al* 2006: 4)

It is important to note both that the number of official inflation targeters is much lower than the number of countries whose Central Bank makes very low inflation its top priority ('implicit inflation targeters'), and that the IMF and/or national and international financial capital do not consider implicit inflation targeting sufficient and therefore push even these countries to become explicit inflation targeters.

8 Specifically, the recovery was the absolute weakest of the ten post-1949 recoveries as far as growth of GDP, investment, employee compensation and employment (while corporate profits were the second strongest) (Bivens and Irons 2008). Unemployment, however, was kept at relatively healthy levels despite poor employment growth because many workers left the formal employment sector, and so to target unemployment in this case would very much miss the problem.

9 Epstein (2002) (and in more detail, Pollin *et al.* (2006)) and Pollin *et al.* (2007).

10 Epstein (2003: 2) lists four other advantages of real targeting, but they all refer to various ways that under real targeting the Central Bank will be pressured to carry out policies that are socially beneficial which inflation targeting does not promote.

11 Almost all works written on the evolution of the revolutionary process under Chávez note that in the very beginning it was largely anti-neoliberal, and it then went on from there to develop step-by-step the more radical domestic as well as international positions associated with it today. See for example Lander and Navarrete (2007) and Wilpert (2007).

12 A few more details on this typical neoliberal scenario will make clear some of the results Casas referred to in this quote. In 1997 the consumer price index increased by 38.2 per cent, which of course was the central concern of the neoliberal Central Bank policy. So they tightened the growth of the money supply in 1998 and further in 1999 (measured either by the monetary base (79.3 per cent to 23.7 per cent to 21.2 per cent) or M2 (62.5 per cent to 18.6 per cent to 13.8 per cent)). This could have caused interest rates to rise if the economy had kept growing at the same rate. But it induced a recession, with GDP growth dropping from 6.4 per cent to –0.1 per cent to –7.2 per cent. This of course was the cause of the fall in the interest rates in 1999 that Casas referred to. Lending rates at commercial and universal banks first went up with the tightening and then dropped as the economy went into recession, going from 31.7 per cent to 52.1 per cent and then down to 33 per cent. As noted, the Central Bank was successful in its central goal – inflation as measured by the CPI dropped from 38.2 per cent to 31 per cent and then, as targeted for 1999, to 20.1 per cent (Casas 1999: table 'Principal Macroeconomic Indicators', no page number).

13 One rich source of information in English on the Central Bank policies in the different years 1999 to 2007, including the policies during the five years by Diego Luis Castellanos E., is the year-end addresses by the president of the Central Bank. From the opening page of www.bcv.org.ve select 'English Version', and then 'Publications'.

14 The Law of the Central Banking 2001, Article 9, had changed the procedure for selecting a new head of the Central Bank so that he was appointed by the president, subject to confirmation by a majority of the National Assembly.

15 The article includes a discussion of both the usefulness of this concept and its weaknesses. The latter includes both the tremendous elasticity in the use of the concept and the ideological limitations as the concept was developed by its best known proponent,

Amartya Sen. The concern here is not to enter the debate concerning the strengths and weakness of this term, but rather to note how widely this term with all its associated connotations is used in the debates in Venezuela on progressive social policies.

16 Three current reflections in policy statements of this Central Bank framework are the '2008 Annual Agreement on Economic Policies' (BCV 2008a), 'Social Responsibility for Human Development' (BCV 2008b) and 'Social Responsibility' (BCV 2008c).

17 When this was written in February 2009 the final quarter growth for 2008 was not yet available, so 5.6 per cent is the growth to the third quarter from a year before.

18 Available in English at www.misionvenezuela.org/ingles/ConstitutionoftheBolivari-aningles.pdf.

19 For a short but somewhat detailed discussion of the existing Liquid Hydrocarbons and Gas Hydrocarbons laws as of 2007, see CONAPRI (no date).

20 The currently effective Central Bank Law in Venezuela is from 2001, with its modifi-cations in 2002 and 2005. The full law and all its modifications are at www.bcv.org. ve/c3/legislacion.asp.

21 www.bcv.org.ve/blanksite/c4/Conferencias.asp?Codigo=88&Operacion=2&Sec=Fal se gives the speech by the Central Bank president at the creation of FONDEN. Wilpert (2005) gives a good short explanation of the policy in English at the time it was initiated. The law specifically indicated the funds were to be used in projects in the three areas most progressives argue are central for economic development: the real economy, education and health. The law also basically allowed that funds given to FONDEN could be used as reserves if the calculations for the optimum reserves were inadequate due to unexpected circumstances: it specifically allowed them to be used 'for improving the profile and reducing outstanding foreign public debt and attending to special situations' (Parra 2005: 11). To prevent this large-scale govern-ment spending for development from fuelling inflation, the funds could only be spent outside the country, that is, buying foreign inputs for development projects (Wilpert 2005).

22 The National Development Fund was set up to be funded by two sources, the excess reserves and a direct contribution from the state oil company.

23 As this chapter was being finished, Venezuela announced on 9 February 2009, 209 public investment projects funded by FONDEN, and that FONDEN has received US$57.75 billion since 2005 (Pearson 2009).

24 It is worth recalling that despite this refusal to date to induce a standard monetary induced economic slowdown to reduce inflation, the Central Bank has indicated its attention to inflation through a non-restrictive monetary policy means, the mandating that the huge development expenditures by FONDEN could only be spent outside the domestic economy. Without this step inflation would have become a crisis.

25 This is the year-over-year December inflation rate calculated from the monthly General Consumer Price Index Metropolitan Area of Caracas. Data available at www. bcv.org.ve/EnglishVersion/c2/index.asp?secc=statistinf. We need to stress that the point being made here is not that this is good progressive Central Bank policy, since this violates the inflation constraint. Rather, the point of this section of the chapter is the clear rejection of neoliberal Central Bank policy, and this certainly supports that claim. It happens that inflation has dropped in 2008 from a first half year average of 2.4 per cent per month, at which level it was becoming a serious political problem for the Chávez government, to a second half year average of 1.7 per cent per month. That has been due, however, to the economic slowdown in Venezuela and the world and not due to specific Central Bank policies.

26 Nominal lending rates are the yearly average of the weighted average of the data for the six largest commercial and universal banks in Venezuela. Data at www.bcv.org. ve/EnglishVersion/c2/index.asp?secc=statistinf. This was then converted to real values using the inflation data just discussed, which being year over year December data is also the yearly average.

27 This is not to claim the government is not concerned with and discussing inflation, which it is, but rather to stress the very anti-neoliberal position that at 30 per cent inflation their public declarations still stress the need for growth and do not qualify that with inflation considerations.
28 www.bcv.org.ve/Upload/Comunicados/tasasdeinteres010905.pdf gives the 26 April 2005, initial declaration of this policy by the Central Bank.
29 In addition to increased consumption, employment and production by small producers reducing inequality, the Central Bank argues that savings by small savers was discouraged by banks offering them only half the interest rate it offered to large savers. The Central Bank maintains that increased saving by small savers, particularly at increased savings rates, will also contribute to reducing inequality (Rivas 2006: 398).
30 It should be noted that transparency of government institutions is a shared goal of neoliberalism and progressive economists, despite the different reasons for the goal. In the first case it is so that capital owners can be assured that the government serves their interests, while in the second case it is a prerequisite for broad popular participation.

References

Arestis, Philip and Malcolm Sawyer. 2003. 'Inflation Targeting: A Critical Appraisal'. *The Levy Institute*, Working Paper No. 388. Available at: www.levy.org.
Ball, Laurence and Niamh Sheridan. 2003. 'Does Inflation Targeting Matter?'. IMF Working Paper WP/03/129.
Batini, Nicoletta, Peter Breuer, Kalpana Kochhar and Skott Roger. 2006. 'Inflation Targeting and the IMF'. IMF Staff Paper, 16 March.
BCV (Banco Central de Venezuela). 2008a. 'Acuerdo Anual de Políticas Económicas 2008'. Accessed 1 February 2009 at www.bcv.org.ve/c6/AAP2008.pdf.
—— 2008b. 'Responsabilidad Social para el Desarrollo Humano'. Accessed 1 February 2009 at www.bcv.org.ve, then '¿Qué es el Banco Central de Venezuela?', then 'Una Actuación Responsable con el País' and then 'Responsabilidad Social para el Desarrollo Humano'.
—— 2008c. 'Responsabilidad Social'. Accessed 1 February 2009 at www.bcv.org.ve, then '¿Qué es el Banco Central de Venezuela?', then 'Responsabilidad Pública y Social' and then 'Responsabilidad Social'.
—— 2009. 'Orientation of Monetary Policies. First Semester 2009'. Accessed at www.bcv.org.ve/actpm/apm2009s1.asp.
Bernanke, Ben, Thomas Laubach, Adam Posen and Frederic Mishkin. 1999. *Inflation Targeting: Lessons from the International Experience*. Princeton: University of Princeton Press.
Bivens, L. Josh and John Irons. 2008. 'A Feeble Recovery. The Fundamental Economic Weaknesses of the 2001–07 Expansion'. Economic Policy Institute, Briefing Paper #214. Available at www.epi.org.
Blinder, Alan. 1998. *Central Banking in Theory and Practice*. Cambridge: MIT Press.
Bruno, Michael. 1995. 'Does Inflation Really Lower Growth?', *Finance and Development*, September.
Bruno, Michael and William Easterly. 1998. 'Inflation Crisis and Long-Run Growth', *Journal of Monetary Economics*, 41, pp. 3–26.
Carlson, Chris. 2007. 'Venezuela Invests US \$20 Billion in Development Projects'. Accessed on 1 February 2009 at www.venezuelanalysis.com/news/2387.

Casas González, Antonio. 1999. 'Year-End Address of the President of the Central Bank of Venezuela'. Available at www.cbv.org.ve, then select 'English Version' and then 'Publications'.

CONAPRI (Venezuelan Council for Investment Promotion). No date. 'Hydrocarbon Sector'. Accessed on 13 June 2008 at www.conapri.org/english/ArticleDetailIV. asp?ar ticleid=291185&CategoryId2=16036.

Duménil, Gérard and Dominique Lévy. 2004. *Capital Resurgent. Roots of the Neoliberal Revolution.* Cambridge: Harvard University Press.

Epstein, Gerald. 2002. 'Employment-Oriented Central Bank Policy in an Integrated World Economy: A Reform Proposal for South Africa', Political Economy Research Institute Working Paper 39. Available at www.peri.umass.edu.

——— 2003. 'Alternatives to Inflation Targeting Monetary Policy for Stable and Egalitarian Growth: A Brief Research Summary', Political Economy Research Institute Working Paper 109. Available at www.peri.umass.edu.

——— 2006. 'Central Banks as Agents of Economic Development', UNU-WIDER, Research Paper No 2006/54.

——— 2007. 'Central Banks, Inflation Targeting and Employment Creation', International Labour Organization, Economic and Labor Market Papers, 2007/2.

Epstein, Gerald, Ilene Grabel and K.S. Jomo. 2004. 'Capital Management Techniques in Developing Countries. An Assessment of Experiences from the 1990s and Lessons for the Future'. United Nations G-24 Discussion Paper No. 27. New York: United Nations Publications.

Grabel, Ilene. 2004a. 'International Private Capital Flows and Developing Countries'. In *Rethinking Development*, ed. Ha-Joon Chang. London: Anthem Press.

——— 2004b. 'Trip Wires and Speed Bumps: Managing Financial Risks and Reducing the Potential for Financial Crises in Developing Economies'. United Nations G-24 Discussion Paper No. 33. New York: United Nations Publications.

Jacoby, Sanford. 2005a. *The Embedded Corporation: Corporate Governance and Employment Relations in Japan and the United States.* Princeton: Princeton University Press.

——— 2005b. 'Corporate Governance and Society', *Challenge*, 48(4), July/August, 69–87.

Lander, Edgardo and Pablo Navarrete. 2007. 'The Economic Policy of the Latin American Left In Government: Venezuela'. Transnational Institute Briefing 2007/02. Available at www.tni.org under 'Publications' then under 'Briefings'.

Lazonick, William and Mary O'Sullivan. 1996. 'Organization, Finance and Competition', *Industrial and Corporate Change*, 5(1), 1–46.

Mishkin, Frederic and Klaus Schmidt-Hebbel. 2001. 'One Decade of Inflation Targeting in the World: What Do We Know and What Do We Need to Know?', NBER Working Paper 8397.

Parra Luzardo, Gastón. 2005. 'Year-End Address by the President of the Central Bank of Venezuela'. Available at www.cbv.org.ve, then select 'English Version' and then 'Publications'.

——— 2006. 'Year-End Address of the President of the Central Bank of Venezuela'. Available at www.cbv.org.ve, then select 'English Version' and then 'Publications'.

——— 2007. 'Year-End Address by the President of the Central Bank of Venezuela'. Available at www.cbv.org.ve, then select 'English Version' and then 'Publications'.

Pearson, Tamara. 2009. 'Venezuela Announces Public Investment Plan'. Accessed on 10 February 2009 at www.venezuelanalysis.com/news/4192.

Pollin, Robert and Andoung Zhu. 2005. 'Inflation and Economic Growth: A Cross-Country Non-linear Analysis'. Political Economy Research Institute Working Paper 109. Available at www.peri.umass.edu.

Pollin, Robert, Mwangi was Githinji and James Heintz. 2007. 'An Employment-Targeted Economic Program for Kenya'. A UNDP project carried out by the Political Economy Research Institute. Available at www.peri.umass.edu.

Pollin, Robert, Gerald Epsein, James Heintz and Léonce Ndikumana. 2006. *An Employment- Targeted Economic Program for South Africa.* A UNDP project carried out by the Political Economy Research Institute. Available at www.peri.umass.edu.

Rivas Alvardo, José Félix. 2006. 'El BCV y la inclusión social'. In *Inclusión social y distribución del ingreso,* ed. Banco Central de Venezuela. Caracas: Banco Central de Venezuela.

Weisbrot, Mark and Luis Sandoval. 2007. 'The Venezuelan Economy in the Chávez Years'. Online, available at: www.cepr.net/documents/publications/venezuela_2007)97. pdf.

Weisbrot, Mark, Rebecca Ray and Luis Sandoval. 2009. 'The Chávez Administration at 10 Years: The Economy and Social Indicators'. Center for Economic and Policy Research. Available at www.cepr.net.

Wilpert, Gregory. 2005. 'Venezuela's Central Bank Law Reform Allows Limited Government Use of Reserves'. Accessed on 1 February 2009 at www.venezuelanalysis. com/news/1257.

—— 2007. *Changing Venezuela by Taking Power. The History and Policies of the Chávez Government.* London: Verso.

Zhu, Andong, Michael Ash and Robert Pollin. 2002. 'Stock Market Liquidity and Economic Growth: A Critical Appraisal of the Levine/Zervos Model'. Political Economy Research Institute Working Paper 47. Available at www.peri.umass.edu.

17 Transition to neoliberalism and decentralisation policies in Mexico

Aylin Topal

The Mexican Revolution (1910–17) generated a national political force that aimed to diminish the power of local and regional authorities and allies of the dictatorship of Porfirio Díaz (Leal 1986: 22). The goals of the Revolution were articulated in the Constitution of 1917 which set the legal ground for strong state capacity that was concentrated in the federal executive branch and exercised mainly through the presidency. With this institutional structure, the Mexican state has become one of the most centralised states in all of Latin America. However, in the early 1980s, as the country moved to a new period of economic restructuring with neoliberal policies, there have been significant changes in the centralised institutional setting. Decentralisation policies appear to be the key elements of the major changes that the country has experienced since the early 1980s. In this process, top-down control of the corporatist organisations have weakened; regional organisations of the working classes started to emerge; the influence of subnational level (state and municipality) social relations in policy-making processes has increased; local authorities were given fiscal autonomy and authority to initiate socio-economic development programmes; the local governments' own independent assemblies and law-making powers were boosted in order to increase their administrative capacity. These changes have been an important aspect of the transformations of the territorial structure and functioning of the Mexican state.

The main purpose of this chapter is to lay out the material basis that brought decentralisation policies into the political agenda in the early 1980s in Mexico. It aims to explain why decentralisation policies were implemented hand in hand with the neoliberalisation policies in Mexico. To answer this question, the chapter examines the inter- and intra-class relations that made decentralisation part and parcel of the Mexican transition to neoliberalism.

Existing studies show that in most countries of the periphery, decentralisation policies with varying extent and content have been implemented parallel to neoliberalisation (Pickvance and Pretecielle 1991; Tulchin and Selee 2004). This suggests that the correlation between neoliberalisation and decentralisation processes in Mexico may not be a contingently related phenomenon. Therefore, an analysis of the strategies and alliances of the key actors in Mexico may reach beyond producing ideographic explanations and provide working hypotheses that would be tested in other cases in future research.

The main argument of this chapter is that the decentralisation policies in Mexico can best be understood within the context of the hegemony crisis of the post-war economic development. Within this context, the decentralisation policies were shaped as a result of collective pressures and struggles of certain key actors in Mexican politics: dominant factions of capital, the working classes and the International Financial Institutions (IFIs) such as the International Monetary Fund (IMF) and the World Bank (WB). While certain factions of capital asked for a reorganisation of the state which would allow neoliberal market forces to operate at the local level, the working classes stepped up their demand for more participatory and democratic local politics. To respond to these demands, the crisis of hegemony required a restructuring in the representational ties between the classes and the political party in power. On top of these pressures, when the debt crisis hit the country in 1982, the IFIs 'advised' the government 'structural reforms' as a mechanism for reducing state's deficits and cutting public-sector expenditures. These restructuring reforms were filtered through the institutional settings and class relations of the country and took the form of the decentralisation policies.

The chapter is organised in three sections. The first section provides a brief historical overview of the process of the Mexican state formation and consolidation following the Mexican Revolution. The second section examines the crisis of the late 1970s and maps out how class relations were shaped by the regional development policies and centralised interest representation mechanisms of the Import Substitution (IS) strategy. The third section focuses on the influence of the IFIs on the neoliberalisation and decentralisation processes.

The revolution and establishment of a new state

The pre-revolutionary history as well as new forces, alliances and conflicts emerging from the Revolution shaped the state institutions in Mexico (Hamilton 1982: 3). The 35-year reign of Porfirio Díaz (1876–1911), known as *Porfiriato*, resulted in economic and political domination of a small oligarchic clique at the national, regional and local levels.[1] Díaz's regime maintained close relations with the successful merchants and industrialists of the north, and the major land-owners of the south, all of whom had strong links to foreign capital (Hamilton 1982: 45; Katz 1981: 7). The common motivation behind the uprising of dispersed revolutionary forces was to destroy the liberal oligarchical state (Katz 1981; Leal 1986: 22).

The revolution, however, yielded to new forms of domination and subordination. After the defeat of the common enemy, confrontations arose among the revolutionary forces. As the Díaz bourgeoisie was losing its power neither the peasants nor the industrial proletariat were capable of controlling the establishment of the regime. Rural and urban petty-bourgeois leaders of the revolution took the lead in structuring the new state (Leal 1986: 23). These leaders aimed to bring together and discipline the local and regional revolutionary elements. The Constitution of 1917 outlined the essential features of the Mexican state by encompassing all public employees, giving coherence to the different groups of the political bureaucracy and uniting a multiplicity of local, regional and national electoral organisms (Leal 1986: 27). Despite the constitutional framework, local oligarchies and regional *caudillos*, many with their own armies, threatened the hegemony of the centralist coalitions in the 1920s by seeking to build their own political bases among the peasants, workers and the unemployed (Cockroft 1983: 63; Hamilton 1982: 74–9).[2] In order to contain these local and regional powers, the central government gradually took over the jurisdiction of the agrarian reform and the implementation of labour legislation that had previously been performed by the state governors. Centralisation of national political power in the federal government culminated in the establishment of a single government party – the National Revolutionary Party (PNR) – in 1929, which eventually became the Institutional Revolutionary Party (PRI) in 1946 (González Casanova 1970: 33–5).

During the presidency of General Lazaro Cárdenas (1934–40), the dominant coalition sought to legitimise the state's power vis-à-vis the peasantry and the working classes,[3] and organised Mexican politics into a corporatist model which was already to be found in the Constitutions of 1917. Article 27 gave the president of the Republic the authority to act as a neutral mediator between opposing interests in society making him the 'Supreme Arbiter'. This structure 'recognises the existence of the classes of a capitalist society and proposes an institutional method for regulating the class struggle' (Leal 1986: 30). In this way, both workers and peasants are absorbed into and subordinated to large corporatist organisations – in 1936 the Confederation of Mexican Workers (CTM), and in 1938 the National Peasants Confederation (CNC) – that become pillars of the state party (Leal 1986: 31; Hamilton 1982: 142–83).[4] The direct political control on workers and peasants was established through the authoritarian and top-down control of the union bureaucrats, commonly known as '*charros*' (Cockroft 1983: 156).

The relationship between the state and the private sector was regulated through four national business organisations which the Chamber Law defined as the 'consulting organisations'. The National Confederation of Chambers of Commerce (CONCANACO) and the National Confederation of Chambers of Industry (CONCAMIN) were united under the umbrella of National Chamber of Commerce and Industry (CANACOMIN). The National Chamber of Manufacturing Industry (CANACINTRA) was designed as a mixed-activity catch-all chamber for new and emerging manufacturing sectors that lacked chambers of their own (Shadlen 2000: 77).

Although the Mexican Revolution added certain peculiarities, it is important to note that the state institutions were developing in the context of the evolving international economic order. The impact of the world depression of 1929 and the requirements of the post-war world economy shaped the policy framework and the role of the Mexican state. The dominant strategy of capitalist development in the countries that were highly dependent on foreign trade was adherence to a process of rapid industrialisation instituted with the purpose of catching up with the 'developed' countries. This aim forged the idea of a 'mixed economy' which should be guided by the state (Cypher 1990: 11). The guiding role of the state complied with the Import Substitution (IS) strategy which many countries of the periphery adopted after the Second World War. This model called upon the 'state elites' to plan and implement development policies, mostly financed by foreign loans, for the construction of the 'national economy' (Cockroft 1983: 184; Hamilton 1982: 121).

Direct government control over key economic sectors expanded during the Cárdenas administration. Whilst he promised to liberate the people from the exploitation of foreign capital and the oligarchies of Díaz, the promotion of national economic development brought about concentration of capital, the monopolisation of key industrial sectors by foreign capital, and increasing regional disparities.

The crisis of hegemony

The years between 1970 and 1982 are known in Mexico as 'the tragic dozen', identified by intensified social unrest of students, peasants and workers as well as the capitalist classes. In the 1970s, the Mexican economy began to show declining levels of profitability which had serious ramifications for the relations between capital and labour (Soederberg 2001: 65). At the same time, the growing paralysis of the bureaucracy and other institutions of the state reduced the effectiveness of the state's intervention in terms of promoting private capital accumulation (Cypher 1990: 97; Tirado 1987: 491–2). Despite the huge debt, after new discoveries of rich oil reserves in Chiapas and along the Caribbean coast, the United States and other foreign creditors poured US$3 billion worth of new credits into the country between 1976 and 1979 (Cockroft 1983: 260). The availability of foreign loans and the large supply of 'petro-pesos' provided a breathing space for the economy and gave the regime a certain stability. In order to rein in the social discontent, the government allocated new credit funds from revenues brought in by the increasing oil price and foreign borrowings. However, when the oil prices dropped and foreign loans dried up in the early 1980s, major structural reforms were required.

In 1981 and 1982, Mexico witnessed what was then generally considered as the gravest economic crisis in its history. From 1969 to 1982, Mexico's foreign debt climbed from US$3.5 billion to over US$100 billion (Otero 1996: 6). In August 1982, the government declared a moratorium on payments to service its foreign debt. In September 1982, as a last resort, the government announced the nationalisation of the banking system. Due to the increasing debt burden, the crisis was primarily a crisis of balance of payments with implications on rising inflation and aggravating foreign exchange difficulties. However, the combined impact of the debt burden, social unrest and political turbulence led to a crisis of hegemony. Using Gramscian terminology, in the late 1970s 'the ruling class lost its consensus', and 'the great masses became detached from their traditional ideologies, and no longer believed what they used to believe previously'. During this period, Mexico experienced a 'crisis of authority' which was 'precisely [a] crisis of hegemony, or general crisis of the state' (Gramsci 1971: 210). The 'old [was] ... dying and the new [could not] ... be born' (ibid.: 275–6).

At this historical juncture, a new social order had to be born to secure the economic power of the dominant coalitions of the capitalist class and ensure the legitimacy of the state. As Valdés Ugalde notes (1997: 203), the period between September and December of 1982 and the presidency of Miguel de la Madrid (1982–8) marked the opening of a new period that was clearly distinguished from the post-revolutionary period. The transition to neoliberalism involved the withdrawal of public subsidies, privatisation of state-owned enterprises, elimination of tariffs, opening of the capital market and increasing regional integration with North America (Álvarez 1987). The neoliberal restructuring coincided with the implementation of the first decentralisation policies which set the agenda for further decentralisation policies in the 1990s. Together with the launch of the neoliberal economic policies, the de la Madrid government proposed three principal lines of action: decentralisation of the development programmes, decentralisation of the public services, and deconcentration of the federal public administration (SPP 1983: 3). These principles were combined under the strategy of 'Decentralisation of the National Life' which corresponded to a structural change in the fundamental strategy of national development and planning.

In order to lay out the dynamics that brought the processes of decentralisation and neoliberalisation together in the Mexican context, we need to trace the inter- and intra-class relations back to the late 1960s, when the 'hegemony crisis' originated. Certain factions for the Mexican capitalist class, and the US investors as well as the working classes particularly from the south started to show discontent with the post-revolutionary planning and development policies.

Higher productivity and profits generated between 1940 and 1960 (the 'Mexican miracle') resulted in the worsening of regional disparities. In spite of repeated declarations that the construction of 'national economy' with the planning in the centrally guided manner would mitigate and correct imbalances in regional development, capitalist growth and Mexico's integration into world market had widened the disparities among regions (Barkin 1986: 111; Garza 2003: 487–8). IS strategies facilitated the concentration of capital in three major regions in the country: the centre, the west and the north. The central region refers to the Valley of Mexico which includes Mexico City and the contiguous State of Mexico; Guadalajara became the west's main pole of economic and political activity, and Monterrey became that of the north (Valdés Ugalde 1996: 132). More broadly, the country was divided into three regions: industrial zones (Valley of Mexico, Guadalajara and Monterrey); the semi-industrial states (Coahcuila, Chihuahua, Jalisco, Puebla and Veracruz) and the rest of the country (Barkin 1986: 111). While the industrial and semi-industrial states were favoured by the public investments, the agricultural regions of the south were left relatively backward. As a result of the concentration of capital and widening regional disparities, regional and local economies were increasingly found to have their own specific problems which brought centralised state planning under scrutiny (cf. Jessop 2002: 82).

The industrial, commercial and financial groups based in the Valley of Mexico were especially privileged in receiving the IS subsidies, fiscal incentives and credits (Cordero *et al.* 1983: 83; Tirado 1987: 485). The concentration of capital reinforced the concentration of economic activity around Mexico City. In 1930, Mexico City had a 28.5 per cent share of the total manufacturing production of Mexico; in 1940, 32.1 per cent; in 1950, 40 per cent; in 1960, 46.5 per cent; in 1970, 46.8 per cent; and in 1980, 48.0 per cent (Ward 1990: 20). These manufacturing firms – small and medium ones are represented in CANACINTRA, larger firms in CONCAMIN – are referred to as 'the faction of the fourties', since they started to develop with the process of industrialisation protected by the state since that decade (Gaspar and Valdés 1987: 503). These businessmen had close ties with the PRI; it is even possible to find a considerable number of civil servants that had occupied important position in government (Gaspar and Valdés 1987: 504). Some of the more powerful firms were negotiating with the president directly bypassing the 'consultation organization' (Leal 1986: 37).

Although northern capitalists – usually called 'the Monterrey Group' – can be traced back to the pre-revolutionary period, they were also the beneficiaries of the centralised state policies (Gaspar and Valdés 1987: 502). These groups have been ideologically opposed to state intervention and argued that the best way to promote the industrial development of the country was to lure foreign investment and produce for foreign markets, mainly the United States, rather than producing for the internal market (Chand 2001: 20–1).[5] In the early 1960s, these business leaders approached the federal government with concerns about rising unemployment and social unrest in the region.[6] In order to promote the border economy by attracting foreign capital, alleviate unemployment and address the demands of the business groups, the federal government implemented the Border Industrialisation (*Maquiladora*) Programme in 1965 (Gereffi 1996: 85; Schmidt 2000). As a result of the expansion of the assembly export production, both public investments and the private banking sector gave preferential treatment to the north (Appendini *et al.* 1972).

Integration into the world economy through maquiladoras made the northern capitalists less tolerant of central policy-making processes.[7] The interests of these groups were represented in the Mexican Employers Association (COPARMEX) and the corporatist structure left all regional business organisations outside of the dominant power networks (Shadlen 2000; cf. Gaspar and Valdés 1987: 516). Northern business leaders viewed that their influence, as well as their direct representation in policy-making, was becoming weaker compared to the ones in Mexico City (Gaspar and Valdés 1987: 516–17).

In the late 1970s, decentralisation of economic development became one of the strongest demands of the various business associations in northern Mexico.[8] The 'unilateral decision' of bank nationalisation in 1982, which would drastically injure the maquiladora industry, became the tipping point of the discontent about authoritarian central government (Luna 2004). These groups responded to the economic crisis by demanding the restructuring of the state–economy relations towards a more open and liberal economy with more local state involvement. They claimed that usual national macroeconomic policies and standardised industrial and/or regional policies formulated at the centre were inadequate to tap the energies of the dynamic regions.[9] This was, arguably, because the transfer of authority to local governments would divert credit in their favour and increase the economic dynamism of their region.

The position of the northern capitalists became stronger vis-à-vis other factions of capital both politically and economically. Within the context of the economic crisis, alienated by the lack of representation, the northern groups looked for developing their political resources rather than relying on their traditional alliance with the PRI. Since the Revolution, the PNR and its successors had not been able to harness the northern capitalists to its development project. Although the northern capitalists did not overtly challenge the regime, they tended to support the main opposition party, the National Action Party (PAN) since its foundation, in 1939 (Tirado 1987: 487). The PAN defined central state planning in Mexico as socialist, and demanded more autonomy for the northern states and municipalities (Valdés Ugalde 1987: 439). Allegedly, some former PRI supporters among these groups shifted their support to the PAN, which forced the PRI leaders respond to the demands of the northern businessmen (Tirado 1987: 491–5). Economically, the devaluations of the peso and the decline of real wages in the 1970s stimulated tremendous growth in the maquiladora industry. For example, while Mexico's share of US imports was less than 1 per cent in the late 1960s, it became almost 20 per cent in 1976 (Sklair 1989: 12).

Foreign capitalists joined the local capitalists demanding a reorganisation of the institutional infrastructure through which neoliberal market forces would operate in the local markets. The Maquiladora Programme provided the foreign – mostly US – capital with cheap labour and tax exemptions (Sklair 1989). In the 1970s, however, faced with decreasing profits, these companies, in search of more fiscal concessions and easier and more practical bureaucratic procedures, started to challenge the Mexican state by threatening to relocate their business to other countries.[10] Mobile foreign capital in the maquiladora industry demanded less central state regulations in the maquiladora sector, because localised or regionalised development policies would enable them to exploit further the unevenness of natural and social environment and demographic structure of Mexico. To mitigate the economic crisis, the government wanted to encourage foreign investment in border industries. For that reason, the de la Madrid government was careful to grant the demands of foreign capital in order to address the Mexican need for dollars (Hamilton 1986b: 166).

While the concentration of capital created a representation crisis among capitalists, authoritarian decision-making through the corporatist organisations triggered discontent among the students and working classes. The student protests of 1968 constituted a major political earthquake challenging the dominance of the PRI (Álvarez 1987: 17–29). The bloody repression of these student protests on the eve of the 1968 Olympic Games revealed the undemocratic and authoritarian nature of the post-revolutionary order, and ignited further protests. Peasants and workers joined the students in their struggle for a democratic regime (Delarbe 1986: 197). The union leaders attempted to pacify these uprisings and, consequently, lost their remaining credibility among the bottom rungs. In the 1970s, the working classes started to scrutinise the state's neutral arbiter role among social classes as well as the centralised interest representation by state-orchestrated corporatist associations (Carr 1986).

As Carr rightly observes, the economic crisis displaced the centre of the conflict away from the capital–labour relationships at the point of production from the distribution of resources (1986: 222–3). Valdés Ugalde (1987) and Luna (1987) claim that the northern capitalist class was effective in defining the terms of crisis and shaping the demands of the working classes. Once the crisis was defined with reference to distribution, the demands of the working classes could be easily crafted around how to 'deliver the goods' more efficiently. Housing problems, transport problems, the deterioration in urban living conditions and maldistribution of food became the main points of struggle (Carr 1986: 222). The solution to these problems was seen as enhancing participation in local development programmes. Popular discontent in the relatively deprived regions was transformed into local movements with regional identities which, in turn, triggered pressures for participation in development.[11]

Given the failure of their attempts to capture the corporatist organisations, a large number of workers and peasants detached from their organisations and formed alternative unions at the local level (Delarbe 1986). They started to establish their own grassroots organisations which later became the mobilising force of the struggle for democratisation and participation at the local level (Otero 1996: 1).[12] These local organisations were especially effective in the southern states of Puebla, Oaxaca, Chiapas, Morelos, Hidalgo and Guerrero.

Towards the 1970s, widespread poverty in the marginalised regions of the south became politically unsustainable. Responding to the participation and democratisation demands of the working classes was urgent owing to their potential to deepen the crisis by elevating social resistance though incorporating and leading large number of masses. Therefore, the struggle of the working classes for an egalitarian social justice was central in determining the democratisation emphasis of the decentralisation policies.

The international financial institutions

In 1982, when the Mexican governments had already built large foreign debts and could not get new credits anywhere else, stand-by agreements and structural adjustment programmes tailored by the IFIs appeared as the only way out the debt crisis. The IMF and World Bank (WB) became significant actors in shaping the Mexican policy agenda. While the Bretton Woods institutions had previously supported the IS strategies, after the debt crisis the WB became concerned about the grim fiscal problems as the IMF began pushing the Mexican state towards dramatic economic liberalisation and privatisation. The IFIs also 'advised' institutional reforms to remove the administrative and legal barriers to the neo-liberal policies. The WB started to push the Mexican government to improve its administrative and fiscal performance and boost efficiency as a path to achieving economic growth. The government had to find new ways to administer costly service-based programmes, such as healthcare, education, natural resources and parks management (Álvarez 1987: 29–31).

The decentralisation policies were promoted as part of the institutional reforms for weakening central regulation, reducing central government deficits and cutting aggregate public-sector expenditures. In the name of 'bringing service providers closer to the people', the WB pushed for political and adminis-trative decentralisation, thereby leaving the regulatory functions to subnational authorities (Peterson 1997: 4).[13] The Bank provided credits to promote the decentralisation reforms since December 1982. Mexico became one of the WB's principal developing country clients in decentralisation funds, second only to India as a cumulative borrower (Rodríguez 1997: xvii). In addition to the WB, the Ford Foundation and the Interamerican Development Bank have also pro-vided similar decentralisation projects in Mexico since the early 1990s.

Conclusion

Towards the late 1970s and early 1980s, the countries of the periphery were faced with similar problems exacerbated by the economic shocks and the reces-sion in the main capitalist countries, and were forced to adopt crises packages (cf. Gamble 1988: 14–15). These packages can be characterised by economic reforms, involved withdrawing public subsidies concerning development and welfare, privatising state-owned enterprises, eliminating tariffs and opening the capital markets. Tenacity of these reforms and healthy articulation of national economies to the world market were to be restored through state restructuring.

The profound transition in the functioning of capitalism occurred first in the centre, and then was gradually exported to the countries of the periphery through the International Financial Institutions (IFIs). However the transition to neoliber-alism was not an imposition on the periphery countries. In effect, the IFIs could not have such an impact on policy-making processes without domestic defenders of these structural reforms (cf. Chang 2003: 2). Neoliberal structural adjustment programmes were not against the interest of the dominant coalitions in the countries.

The decentralisation policies were advised by the IFIs, yet these policies took their particular shape within the dynamics of class relations. Corporatist interest representation and increasing regional disparities during the post-war era shaped the inter- and intra-class relations which eventually expanded the economic crisis towards a 'hegemony crisis'. Therefore, the decentralisation policies were intended by the 'state elites' as part and parcel of the neoliberal hegemonic project by restoring business confidence and popular consent in the regime with a promise of an alternative form of interest representation and participation.[14]

Notes

1 In 1910, 97 per cent of Mexico's lands was owned by just 830 people or corporations (Wynia 1990: 153) and an estimated 97 per cent of the rural population was landless (Hamilton 1986a: 74).
2 The term *caudillo* means a political-military leader. First caudillos were the generals leading local and regional private armies during the independence and used their military power to achieve economic power in the newly independent regions.
3 The legitimation function was fulfilled for the peasantry through a relatively large land reform which was indeed a land distribution programme focused upon the small holding, with the communal holding, or *ejido*. For the working class the state offered the new labour law that protected the right to unionise and the right to a 'living' wage (Cypher 1990: 11).
4 In 1943, The National Confederation of Popular Organisations (CNOP) was founded to incorporate a 'third section' of the society called the 'popular sector' into the party. The popular sector included teachers, public employees, small farmers and the military.
5 Since the regional economy depends largely on the border with the United States, the northerners saw their interest not in the inward-looking industrialisation policies but in adopting a 'free-market-led' development allowing a greater integration with the world economy. The emphasis on the 'laissez faire liberalism' was brought up by the businessmen from Chihuahua in the interviews.
6 In 1922 and 1942, the US and Mexican governments signed a Contract Workers' Program, known as Bracero. Yet when the Bracero Program was unilaterally terminated by the United States, many workers and peasants employed in the US firms and farms were sent back to Mexico in 1964. This created an estimate loss of 185,000 jobs especially in the north of Mexico. See Baerresen (1971).
7 Antonio Jaime, the President of the CANACO in Ciudad Juárez, argued that 'as a frontier region, the situation of Ciudad Juárez is very special with its very different problems from other cities of the country'. *El Heraldo de Chihuahua*, 7 January 1983. See also Mizrahi (1993: 86) and López Ochoa (1987: 123).
8 Interview with Miguel de la Madrid, Former President of Mexico between 1983 and 1989.
9 Most of these business groups were indeed offspring of the central governments' development policies. However, in the interviews with the leading maquiladora-sector capitalists from Chihuahua, they emphasised that their region was economically self-sufficient and their prosperity was not so much dependent on central governments' protection, concession, contracts, credits or subsidies. For a similar argument, see also, President of the CANACO in Chihuahua, Rodrigo Legarreta Soto 'La Geografía nos ha Favorecido', *El Heraldo de Chihuahua*, 16 December 1982.
10 In an interview with the Chairman of the Board and CEO of an American company investing in the maquiladora sector in Chihuahua, he mentioned that the foreign investors were not content about the centralised administrative and fiscal structure. He claimed that these foreign investors voiced their demands for administrative and fiscal decentralisation in the late 1970s.
11 In 1981, the PRI organised several meetings as part of the election campaign of Miguel de la Madrid. The meetings, which were called *consultas populares*, were held in each state with the invited representatives of the social groups. In 1982, the PRI published the booklets of these meetings. The demand of local democracy and participation was voiced in every meeting by various actors (*Consulta Popular*, 1982).
12 In the 'Federalism and the Decentralisation of the National Life' meeting, held in Mexico City in May 1982, representatives of local labour and peasant organisations claimed that the federal government should delegate most of its political, economic and social functions to state and municipal level governments for better inclusion of local communities in the system. *El Heraldo de Chihuahua*, 31 May 1982.

13 For this purpose, one of the earliest implementations of the decentralisation policies took place in Chile. In 1973, 'to teach the world a lesson in democracy' the Pinochet regime implemented decentralisation reforms accompanied by the structural adjustment programmes (cited in Veltmeyer 2001: 24).
14 This idea was mentioned by Miguel de la Madrid in an interview with the author.

References

Álvarez, A. (1987) *La Crisis Global del Capitalismo en México: 1968/1985*. Mexico City: Ediciones Era.

Appendini, A.K., Murayama, D. and Dominguez, R.M. (1972) 'Desarrollo desigual in México', *Demografía y economía* 6 (1), pp. 1–39.

Baerresen V.D. (1971) *The Border Industrialization Program of Mexico*. Lexington: Lexington Books, D.C. Health and Company.

Barkin, D. (1986) 'Mexico's Albatros: The U.S. Economy', in *Modern Mexico: State, Economy, and Social Conflict*, edited by N. Hamilton and T.F. Harding. Newbury Park, London, New Delhi: Sage Publications.

Carr, B. (1986) 'The Mexican Economic Debacle and the Labor Movement: A New Era or More of the Same?', in *Modern Mexico: State, Economy, and Social Conflict*, edited by N. Hamilton and T.F. Harding. Newbury Park, London, New Delhi: Sage Publications.

Chand, V.K. (2001) *Mexico's Political Awakening*. Notre Dame, Indiana: University of Notre Dame Press.

Chang, H. (2003) 'Rethinking Development Economics: An Introduction', in *Rethinking Development Economics*, edited by H. Chang. London: Anthem Press.

Cockroft, J.D. (1983) *Mexico, Class Formation, Capital Accumulation and the State*. New York: Monthly Review Press.

Consulta Popular (1982) Mexico: PRI.

Cordero, S.H., Santin, R. and Tirado, R. (1983) *El Poder Empresarial en México*. Mexico City: Terra Nova.

Cypher, J.M. (1990) *State and Capital in Mexico: Development Policy Since 1940*. Boulder, San Francisco and Oxford: Westview Press.

Delarbe, R.T. (1986) 'The Mexican Labour Movement', in *Modern Mexico: State, Economy, and Social Conflict*, edited by N. Hamilton and T.F. Harding. Newbury Park, London, New Delhi: Sage Publications.

Gamble, A. (1988) *The Free Economy and the Strong State*. London: Macmillan.

Garza, G. (2003) 'The Dialectics of Urban and Regional Disparities in Mexico', in *Confronting Development: Assessing Mexico's Economic and Social Policy Challenges*, edited by K.J. Middlebrook and E. Zepeda. Stanford: Stanford University Press.

Gaspar, G. and Valdés, L. (1987) 'Las venturas recientes del bloque en el poder' *Estudios Sociológicos* 5 (15), pp. 499–524.

Gereffi, G. (1996) 'Mexico's "Old" and "New" Maquiladora Industries: Contrasting Approached to North American Integration', in *Neo-Liberalism Revisited: Economic Restructuring and Mexico's Political Future*, edited by G. Otero. Oxford: Westview Press.

González Casanova, P. (1970) *Democracy in Mexico*. New York: Oxford University Press.

Gramsci, A. (1971) *Further Selections from the Prison Notebook*. New York: International Publisher.

Hamilton, N. (1982) *The Limits of State Autonomy: Post-Revolutionary Mexico*. Princeton: Princeton University Press.

Hamilton, N. (1986a) 'The Limits of State Autonomy', in *Modern Mexico: State, Economy, and Social Conflict*, edited by N. Hamilton and T.F. Harding. Newbury Park, London, New Delhi: Sage Publications.

Hamilton, N. (1986b) 'State-Class Alliances and Conflicts: Issues and Actors in the Mexican Economic Crisis', in *Modern Mexico: State, Economy, and Social Conflict*, edited by N. Hamilton and T.F. Harding. Newbury Park, London, New Delhi: Sage Publications.

Jessop, B. (2002) *The Future of the Capitalist State*. Cambridge and Oxford: Polity Press.

Katz, F. (1981) *The Secret War in Mexico: Europe, the United States, and the Mexican Revolution*. Chicago and London: The University of Chicago Press.

Leal, J.F. (1986) 'The Mexican State, 1915–1973: A Historical Interpretation', in *Modern Mexico: State, Economy, and Social Conflict*, edited by N. Hamilton and T.F. Harding. Newbury Park, London, New Delhi: Sage Publications.

López Ochoa, M.A. (1987) 'Palabras de despedida', in *Encuentro de presidente municipales: los municipios de la frontera norte III*. Nogales, Sonora: Municipio de Nogales, Sonora.

Luna, M. (1987) 'Hacia un corporativismo liberal? Los empresarios y el corporativismo', *Estudios Sociológicos* 5 (15), pp. 455–77.

Luna, M. (2004) 'Business and Politics in Mexico', in *Dilemmas of Political Change in Mexico*, edited by K. Middlebrook. London: Institute of Latin American Studies University of London, Center for U.S.–Mexican Studies, University of California.

Mizrahi, Y. (1993) 'A New Conservative Opposition in Mexico: The Politics of Entrepreneur in Chihuahua (1983–1992)', unpublished Ph.D. dissertation: University of California at Berkeley.

Otero, G. (1996) 'Neoliberal Reform and Politics in Mexico', in *Neoliberalism Revisited: Economic Restructuring and Mexico's Political Future*, edited by G. Otero. Oxford: Westview Press.

Peterson, G. (1997) *Decentralization in Latin America: Learning through Experience*. Washington, DC: The World Bank.

Pickvance, C. and Pretecielle, E. (eds) (1991) *State Restructuring and Local Power*. London and New York: Pinter.

Rodríguez, V.E. (1997) *Decentralization in Mexico: from Reforma Municipal to Solidaridad to Nuevo Federalismo*. Oxford: Westview.

Schmidt, S. (2000) *In Search of Decision: The Maquiladora Industry in Mexico*. Ciudad Juárez, Chihuahua: Universidad Autónoma de Ciudad Juárez.

Shadlen, K. (2000) 'Neoliberalism, Corporatism, and Small Business Activism in Contemporary Mexico', *Latin American Research Review* 35 (2), pp. 73–106.

Sklair, L. (1989) *Assembling for Development: The Maquiladora Industry in Mexico and the United States*. Massachusetts: Unwin Hyman Inc. Winchester.

Soederberg, S. (2001) 'State, Crisis and Capital Accumulation in Mexico', *Historical Materialism* 9, pp. 61–84.

SPP (1983) *Fortalecimiento Y Desarrollo Municipal*. Mexico City: Secretaria de Programación Presupuesto.

Tirado, R. (1987) 'Los empresarios y la política partidaria', *Estudios Sociológicos* 5 (15), pp. 477–97.

Tulchin, J.S. and Selee, A. (eds) (2004) *Decentralization and Democratic Governance on Latin America*. Washington, DC: Woodrow Wilson Center.

Valdés Ugalde, F. (1987) 'Hacia un Nuevo liderazgo sociopolitico? Ensayo sobre la convocatoria social de los empresarios' *Estudios Sociológicos* 5 (15), pp. 433–54.

Valdés Ugalde, F. (1996) 'The Private Sector and Political Regime Change in Mexico', in *Neoliberalism Revisited: Economic Restructuring and Mexico's Political Future*, edited by G. Otero. Oxford: Westview Press.

Valdés Ugalde, F. (1997) *Autonomía e Legitimidad: Los empresarios, la política y el estado en México.* Mexico City: Siglo Veintiuno.

Veltmeyer, H. (2001) 'The Quest for Another Development', in *Transcending Neoliberalism: Community-Based Development in Latin America*, edited by H. Veltmeyer and A. O'Malley. Bloomfield: Kumarian Press.

Ward, P.M. (1990) *Mexico City: The Production and Reproduction of an Urban Environment.* Boston: G. K. Hall & Co.

Wynia, G.W. (1990) *The Politics of Latin American Development.* Cambridge: Cambridge University Press.

Index

For Product Safety Concerns and Information please contact our EU
representative GPSR@taylorandfrancis.com
Taylor & Francis Verlag GmbH, Kaufingerstraße 24, 80331 München, Germany